TeenCoder™ Series

TeenCoder™: Android Programming

Student Textbook

Second Edition

Copyright 2013

Homeschool Programming, Inc.

TeenCoder™: Android Programming

Second Edition

Copyright © 2013 by Homeschool Programming, Inc.

980 Birmingham Rd, Suite 501-128

Alpharetta, GA 30004

ISBN: **978-0-9830749-8-4**

Terms of Use

This course is copyright protected. Copyright 2013 © Homeschool Programming, Inc. Purchase of this course constitutes your agreement to the Terms of Use. You are not allowed to distribute any part of the course materials by any means to anyone else. You are not allowed to make it available for free (or fee) on any other source of distribution media, including the Internet, by means of posting the file, or a link to the file on newsgroups, forums, blogs or any other location. You may reproduce (print or copy) course materials as needed for your personal use only.

Disclaimer

Homeschool Programming, Inc, and their officers and shareholders, assume no liability for damage to personal computers or loss of data residing on personal computers arising due to the use or misuse of this course material. Always follow instructions provided by the manufacturer of 3rd party programs that may be included or referenced by this course.

Contact Us

You may contact Homeschool Programming, Inc. through the information and links provided on our website: http://www.HomeschoolProgramming.com. We welcome your comments and questions regarding this course or other related programming courses you would like to study!

Other Courses

Homeschool Programming, Inc. currently has two product lines for students: KidCoder™ and TeenCoder™. Our KidCoder™ Series provides easy, step-by-step programming curriculum for 4th through 12th graders. The Visual Basic series teaches introductory programming concepts in a fun, graphical manner. The Web Design series lets students create their own websites in HTML. Our TeenCoder™ Series provides introductory programming curriculum for high-school students. These courses are college-preparatory material designed for the student who may wish to pursue a career in Computer Science or enhance their transcript with a technical elective. Students can learn C#, Java, game programming, and Android application development.

3rd Party Copyrights

This course teaches Java™ as the programming language using the Eclipse™ Integrated Development Environment. Sun, the Sun logo, Sun Microsystems, Java, and all Java-related trademarks are trademarks or registered trademarks of Sun Microsystems, Inc. and Oracle Corporation. Eclipse, Eclipse logos, and related trademarks are properties of the Eclipse Foundation. Android™ is a trademark of Google, Inc.

Instructional Videos

This course may be accompanied by optional Instructional Videos. These Flash-based videos will play directly from a DVD drive on the student's computer. Instructional Videos are supplements to the Student Textbook, covering every chapter and lesson with fun, animated re-enforcement of the main topics.

Instructional Videos are intended for students who enjoy a more audio-visual style of learning. They are not replacements for the Student Textbook, which is still required to complete this course! However by watching the Instructional Videos first, students may begin each textbook chapter and lesson already having some grasp of the material to be read. Where applicable, the videos will also show "screencasts" of a real programmer demonstrating some concept or activity within the software development environment.

This Student Textbook and accompanying material are entirely sufficient to complete the course successfully! Instructional Videos are optional for students who would benefit from the alternate presentation of the material. For more information or to purchase the videos separately, please refer to the product descriptions on our website: http://www.HomeschoolProgramming.com.

Living on the Edge!

The Android OS and Android devices are relatively new, rapidly changing technologies. That means the programming tools may not be as stable or mature as older technologies. Part of the fun and excitement when dealing with cutting-edge innovations is keeping up with the changes and overcoming anything unexpected in the development environment. You might find that certain features don't work exactly the way the Android documentation says they should, or that the software emulator is a bit quirky. We'll guide you through the obstacles we have found and overcome, but you might encounter your own challenges!

Newer versions of the Android Software Development Kit (SDK) and related packages are released over time. **Our course uses a specific version of each component and for best results we highly recommend you use exactly the same component versions.** Detailed installation instructions are available on our website (www.HomeschoolProgramming.com); please follow them carefully to ensure a smooth course experience. If you find any components or 3rd party APIs do not behave as documented, please contact us for updated instructions.

Students are encouraged to explore the online Android reference material and other information at http://developer.android.com/index.html. The tabs across the top such as "SDK", "Dev Guide", and "Reference" contain detailed information about different aspects of the Android development process.

Table of Contents

TeenCoder™: Android Programming

TeenCoder™: Android Programming

Before You Begin

Please read the following topics before you begin the course.

Minimum Hardware and Software Requirements

This is a hands-on programming course! You will be installing the Java Development Kit (JDK), Eclipse (IDE), Android SDK, and Android Development Tools (ADT) on your computer. Your computer must meet the following minimum requirements in order to run the programs:

Computer Hardware

Your computer must meet the following minimum specifications:

	Minimum
CPU	1.6GHz or faster processor
RAM	1024 MB
Display	1024 x 768 or higher resolution
Hard Disk Size	3GB available space
DVD Drive	DVD-ROM drive

Operating Systems

Your computer operating system must match one of the following:

Windows XP (x86) with Service Pack 3 or above (except Starter Edition)
Windows Vista (x86 and x64) with Service Pack 2 or above (except Starter Edition)
Windows 7 (x86 and x64)
Windows 8 or Windows 8 Pro (excluding Windows 8 RT)
Apple Mac OS X (10.6 or above)

You must also have an Internet connection to your computer in order to access online help, download and install software, and complete some of the activities in this course.

Conventions Used in This Text

This course will use certain styles (fonts, borders, etc.) to highlight text of special interest.

```
The source code will be in the 11-point Consolas font, in a single box like this.
```

Variable names will be in **12-point Consolas bold** text, similar to the way they will look in your development environment. For example: **myVariable**.

Function names, properties and keywords will be in **bold face** type, so that they are easily readable.

This picture highlights important concepts within a lesson.

Sidebars may contain additional information, tips, or background material.

This icon indicates a hands-on activity that you will complete on your computer.

What You Will Learn and Do In This Course

TeenCoder™: Android Programming will teach you the fundamentals of writing your own Android programs. You will be writing these programs using the Java programming language. This course is geared for high-school students who have expressed an interest in computer programming or who are looking for college-preparatory material.

You will learn to write *your own* mobile applications and begin to understand the building blocks for Android applications that you may use every day! Starting with the second chapter, you will complete a hands-on programming project at the end of each chapter. These projects will increase in complexity as you learn more about the Android environment.

What You Need to Know Before Starting

You must have completed the *TeenCoder™: Java Programming* course prior to starting this second semester course. The Java and object-oriented concepts taught in the first semester are prerequisites to learning and enjoying this Android programming material. You will need to be comfortable using the Eclipse development environment as taught in the first semester to write, build, run, and debug Java applications.

You are also expected to already know the basics of computer use before beginning this course. You need to know how to use the keyboard and mouse to select and run programs, use application menu systems, and work with the Windows or Mac OS operating system. You should understand how to store and load files on your hard disk, and how to use the Windows Explorer or Mac OS Finder to walk through your file system and directory structures. You should also have some familiarity with using text editors and using web browsers to find helpful information on the Internet.

Software Versions

You will be using the following free software in this course: *Java Development Kit (JDK)*, *Eclipse IDE for Java Developers*, the *Eclipse Android Development Tools (ADT)* plug-in and the *Android Software Developers Kit (SDK)*. Your course contains links to download and install instructions in PDF format on our website, http://www.HomeschoolProgramming.com. 3rd party websites may from time to time change their download process or release newer versions of their software. Our website will contain updated versions of the instructions as needed.

Getting Help

All courses come with a Solution Guide PDF and fully coded solutions for all activities. Simply install the "Solution Files" from your course setup program and you will be able to refer to the solutions as needed from the "Solution Menu". If you are confused about any activity you can see how we solved the problem! You may also contact us through the "Support" area of our website for further assistance.

Course Errata

We welcome your feedback regarding any course details that are unclear or that may need correction. Please contact us using our online "Getting Help" form. You can find a list of course errata for this edition on our website, http://www.HomeschoolProgramming.com.

Support for Multiple Operating Systems

This course was developed for use both on Microsoft Windows and Apple Mac OS X operating systems. The Java platform is compatible with both environments (and others). We will point out in text or by screen shots any differences between the operating systems. Where necessary, we will provide dedicated sets of instructions for handling each operating system. Be sure to follow the instructions that match the operating system you are using!

Directory Naming Conventions

On Windows operating systems, directory paths are traditionally represented with backslashes ("\") between folder names like this: "**TeenCoder\Java Programming**", but forward slashes ("/") work also. Mac OS directories use forward slashes as in "**TeenCoder/Java Programming**". In order to avoid cluttering the textbook with both representations, each time we specify a path, we will simply use one style. Be sure to change that style to match your operating system requirements if needed.

Chapter One: Introduction to Android Devices

Welcome to the *TeenCoder™: Android Programming* course! You are going to learn how to write your own Android™ applications that can run on mobile phones and other hardware. In this first chapter we will take a quick tour of the Android operating system, examine hardware devices that can run Android, and look ahead to the specific topics that will be taught in the course.

Lesson One: Android Operating System

Let's start by reviewing the background of the Android system. The Android operating system is based on a special version of Linux, which is a Unix-type operating system. The original version of Android was the brainchild of a small startup company called Android, Inc. in the early 2000s. This company had some promising ideas but was largely unable to generate any financial success. In 2005, this company was bought by Google, Inc. who hoped to use their software and ideas to enter the mobile computing market. It's safe to say that Google made their vision come true!

Open-Source Software

Android is an excellent example of open-source development. This means that the software is free for anyone to download and use on any capable device. The best part of open-source development is that it's not just the finished program that is available, but the entire body of source code as well. This allows hardware vendors to modify and customize the Android operating system to work with their own special needs and devices.

In fact, this open-source design was instrumental in allowing Android to become as popular as it is today. In the early 2000s, many hardware companies like Motorola and LG Electronics were struggling to come up with software for their devices that could aggressively compete with the popular iPhone™ software from Apple, Inc. The ability to use and customize the Android operating system on their devices allowed these companies to stop trying to create software and return to what they do best: creating hardware.

The open approach to Android also aids software developers who are trying to break into the mobile applications market. Android allows these developers to freely and easily write applications for Android devices. In addition, Android applications are platform-independent, which means you can write one application and it will work on multiple devices (as long as they are running the Android OS). This means that an application written for Android will work the same way on a Samsung Galaxy™ phone as it does on an LG Optimus™ phone.

Android Versions

After Google bought Android, Inc, they worked for several years enhancing their mobile operating system. There were many pre-release versions of Android that were made available for developers starting in 2007. In late 2008, Google finally released the first version of the operating system. This version was only used on one device, but was fairly popular. In early 2009, a second version of the software was released with support for more devices. A series of releases followed, each offering more functionality and support for more devices.

The third official release, version 1.5, started a naming convention that remains through today's Android versions. Apparently, someone at Google has a serious sweet-tooth! Since version 1.5, each release of Android has been given a code name of a sweet treat. It started with "Cupcake" (version 1.5), then followed with "Donut" (1.6), "Éclair" (2.0), "Froyo" (2.2) and "Gingerbread" (2.3).

The most notable early releases were the "Froyo" (or Frozen Yogurt) and "Gingerbread" releases. In addition to becoming more competitive with the functionality of the iPhone OS, these versions occurred around the same time the Android devices were becoming very popular. In late 2010 and early 2011, the "Froyo" version of Android was installed on up to 70% of all Android devices. Later in 2011 the "Gingerbread" version became more popular.

Also in early 2011, Google released version 3.0 (code named "Honeycomb") of the Android OS. This version was created especially for the *tablet devices* that appeared about that time. In fact, all of the 3.x versions of Android were meant only for tablet devices. The versions for mobile phones and tablets were combined in late 2011, when a 4.0 release of Android (code named "Ice Cream Sandwich") was unveiled. This version marked a merging of the operating systems for phone and tablet devices. For reference, here is a list of the important versions of the Android system with the release dates:

Android Version	Release Date	Internal Code Name
1.0	September 2008	Initial release
1.1	February 2009	Update release
1.5	April 2009	Cupcake
1.6	September 2009	Donut
2.0/2.1	October 2009	Éclair
2.2	May 2010	Froyo (Frozen Yogurt)
2.3	December 2010	Gingerbread
3.x	February 2011	Honeycomb
4.0	October 2011	Ice Cream Sandwich
4.1-4.2	November 2012	Jelly Bean
4.3	July 2014	(A Sweeter) Jelly Bean

Android Features

The Android operating system has many features that make it competitive in today's mobile electronics world. The list below shows some of the key features that most Android devices have:

- Network connectivity including GSM, Wi-Fi, WiMAX and Bluetooth
- Messaging – This capability is often the "must-have" on a mobile device
- Web browsing ability, using the WebKit browser and some Chrome capabilities
- Media support for audio, video and image files
- Support for multi-touch, allowing users to "pinch" and fling objects on the screen
- Support for multi-tasking, which allows you to run more than one application at a time
- Flash support – This is a huge difference between Android and Apple devices
- Hardware features like an accelerometer sensor, camera, digital compass, a proximity sensor, and GPS

Google Play

We can't finish our discussion of the Android operating system without mentioning "Google Play" (formerly known as the "Android Market"). Google Play allows users to browse, review and download thousands of different applications for their device. The Google Play application is pre-installed on just about every Android device that is available today.

The best part about Google Play is that it automatically filters the list of applications that is shown to a user, based on the capabilities on their device. If your device does not include a camera, the app will not show you any camera-based applications. If your device is running Android 1.6, the app will not show you any applications that require a later version of the operating system. This filtering service is a great way to avoid frustration from users who download applications that will not work properly on their device.

Lesson Two: Overview of Devices

There are many different types of devices that can run the Android operating system. In this lesson, we will discuss some of the major device types.

Smartphones

The most common hardware platform for the Android system is a *smartphone*. A smartphone is a mobile phone with a graphical operating system that allows you to make phone calls, send text messages, and run many applications like mapping software, web browsers, and games. Some of the more popular device types currently include the Samsung Galaxy™ S series, Google Nexus™ series, Motorola Droid Razr™ and the HTC Evo™ phones, but new hardware is released all the time!

A smartphone device requires a service provider like Verizon or T-Mobile or AT&T to make and receive phone calls and messages. The service provider usually also offers a data connection to the Internet and will cost some amount of money every month.

Tablets

A more recent type of Android device is the *tablet* device. A tablet is around 7 to 10 inches in size (measured diagonally) and so has a much larger, nicer user interface. These devices do not usually offer phone services. Instead, they are used as touch-screen tablet computers with Wi-Fi access to the Internet. You do not usually have a monthly service fee with a tablet device. However, you will need to provide some sort of wireless Internet connection.

E-Readers

If you are an avid bookworm, you are probably aware of the different electronic book reading devices, or "E-Readers" that are currently on the market. These devices offer you the ability to store and read large numbers of books in a device about the size of a single paperback. The Android operating system has found its way into these devices as well! The Barnes and Noble Nook™ and the Kindle Fire™ readers are Android devices. These popular devices will not only let you read full-color books and magazines, but will let you run many Android programs as well. The extra Android application capability has made these devices very popular.

Netbooks

A *netbook* computer is a smaller and more portable version of a laptop computer. These smaller computers do not often have the disk space or speed of the larger laptops, but make up for this in size and convenience. There are currently several netbooks that have chosen the Android operating system over the more traditional slimmed-down Windows or Mac operating systems. Android-based netbooks may offer a cheaper, yet still very capable netbook platrom.

Internet Television

If you haven't been living under a rock recently, you are probably aware that the Internet video streaming is gaining in popularity on traditional television broadcasts. As these two technologies converge, users are requesting more computer-like capabilities in their living room television. The Android system has been used to bridge this gap! By merging a standard television and an Android device, customers get access to Android applications, Flash videos and even messaging and web browsing capabilities.

Currently the most well-known combination of Android on a television is Google TV. This technology will allow you to view normal television in addition to using various websites as if they too were TV channels. Google TV is integrated into some LG televisions as well as set-top boxes from NetGear, Vizio, and Asus.

Lesson Three: The Android Development Environment

So how exactly does a programmer get started writing Android applications? All Android applications are written in Java, and if you are taking this course you should already know how to write Java applications using the JDK and Eclipse. We are going to extend this environment with the Android SDK and the Android Development Tools (ADT) Eclipse Plug-in. You will run your programs in a software emulator that looks like a real hardware device but runs as an application on your Windows or Mac OS computer.

Android SDK

The Android Software Development Kit (SDK) is perhaps the most important component for creating Android applications. The SDK is actually a collection of files and utilities like sample projects, debugging tools, and all the Android-related classes and libraries. In addition, the SDK includes an Android "emulator", which will allow you to test your Android applications right on your computer. No device is necessary!

The Android SDK versions have evolved quite a bit since the first major release in 2009. Each SDK release has a corresponding "API Level". This API Level is an integer value which identifies the specific Android SDK that an application is targeting. Each incremental release of the Android SDK has its own internal API level number. This value will be used in your application to specify the minimum Android version that must be installed on a device in order to run your application. The chart below shows the relationships between the Android SDK Version and the API Levels for the most recent versions of the software.

Android SDK Version	API Level	Android OS Version
2.3.2, 2.3.1, 2.3	9	Gingerbread (2.3)
2.3.3, 2.3.4	10	Gingerbread (2.3)
3.0.x	11	Honeycomb (3.x)
3.1.x	12	Honeycomb (3.x)
3.2	13	Honeycomb (3.x)
4.0, 4.0.1, 4.0.2	14	Ice Cream Sandwich (4.0)
4.0.3, 4.04	15	Ice Cream Sandwich (4.0)
4.1	16	Jelly Bean (4.1.x)
4.2	17	Jelly Bean (4.2.x)
4.3	18	Jelly Bean (4.3.x)

Android Development Tools (ADT) Eclipse Plug-in

Once you have installed the Android SDK, you will need to install a tool that is specially designed for the Eclipse IDE. The Android Development Tools (ADT) is a piece of software that "plugs-in" to the Eclipse software to give you a powerful, integrated environment in which you can easily create and debug Android applications.

The ADT software extends the capabilities of the Eclipse IDE to allow you to quickly set up new Android projects, create application screens, add components and controls, debug your applications, and even create finished Android executable files for publishing to devices or the "Google Play" market.

Developing Android applications in Eclipse with ADT is highly recommended as the fastest way to get started. With the guided project setup, tools integration, custom configuration editors, and debugging tools, ADT gives you an incredible boost in developing Android applications.

Before you can install or use ADT, you must have compatible versions of both the Eclipse IDE and the Android SDK installed. Specifically, you will need certain versions of the SDK "Tools" to run certain versions of the ADT plug-in. These "SDK Tools" are included in the Android SDK download files. The ADT version numbers closely follow the SDK Tool version numbers so you can easily tell which version of ADT goes with which version of the SDK Tools.

The chart below shows the general evolution of the ADT Plug-in versions over the years.

ADT Plug-in Version	Dependencies	General Improvements
0.9.x	SDK Tools r3 – r7	First major release – used from 2009-2010
8.0.x	SDK Tools r8	Version numbers now follow SDK Tools New visual layout editor Faster emulator launching
9.0.x – 10.0.x	SDK Tools r9, r10	Improved visual layout editor Faster re-start of emulator
11.0.x – 14.0.x	SDK Tools r11, r12, r14	Better screen layout control Improved visual layout editor Improved XML editing New Relative Layout option
15.0.x – 18.0.x	SDK Tools r15, r16, r17, r18	General Bug Fix releases
20.0.x – 22.0.x	SDK Tools r20, r21, r22	Improved visual layout editor Improved emulators Improved debugging tools

Google may release newer versions of the Android SDK or Eclipse ADT by the time you are taking this course! For best results, continue to use the specific versions documented in our installation instructions on our website (http://www.HomeschoolProgramming.com).

Running the Emulator

The Android SDK includes an invaluable piece of software called an "Android Virtual Device" (AVD), or an "emulator" for short. The emulator will allow you to "pretend" that your computer is actually an Android device. This is very important because it means you do not need access to a real Android device in order to test your applications!

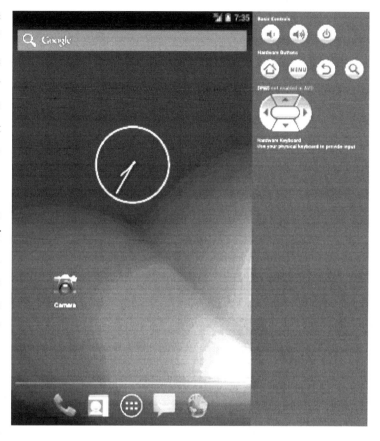

An example emulator screen is shown to the right. The Android emulator mimics most of the hardware and software features of a typical mobile device, with a few limitations. The emulator cannot send or receive actual phone calls, nor can it take pictures or record video or support multi-touch features.

The left side of the emulator screen is a picture of what you would see on your Android device screen. It contains a functional operating system where you can run your own application and other built-in Android programs. The keyboard and navigation keys on the right side of the screen provide a way for you to interact with your application, just as if you were using a real mobile device.

You can configure many different emulators, each of which can emulate a specific type of mobile device or Android OS. For example, you can create one emulator to test Android 2.3 applications and another to test Android 4.2 applications. Or you could create one emulator to test a large-screen device and another to test a small-screen device.

Once your application is running on the emulator, you can simulate just about any Android event. You can use your application to access the network, play audio and video, store and retrieve data, send SMS messages to other emulators, and even simulate incoming phone calls! In addition, you can cause your emulator to create certain device events, like low battery, lost network connectivity, and GPS location updates.

Lesson Four: What You Will Learn In This Course

If you've ever played a game or used an application on a mobile device, you know these programs can be extremely simple or very complicated. In many cases the complicated applications and super-cool games are written by a group of trained programmers, skilled artists and animators that work together for months or years to create their application. However, the mobile market is also a great place for a single programmer to test out their skills with individual ideas and programs.

The Android operating system is a very diverse and full-featured system. There are many different topics and components to learn and master. While it would be impossible to completely cover every aspect of Android programming in one course, we will teach you how to perform the basic operations on a mobile device. Along the way you will create several interesting and useful applications! When you are done with the course you will have a set of tools and concepts you can then apply to your own creative efforts.

Successful completion of our *TeenCoder™: Java Programming* **first-semester course is a pre-requisite to starting this Android Programming course!** You should already understand how to write Java programs and use the Eclipse development environment on your computer. We will build on this knowledge for all of the work you will be doing in this semester. Please ensure you understand all of the material in the pre-requisite course before continuing.

We will cover the following Android topics in this course:

Android Development Tools	• Using the Android Development Tools with Eclipse • Installing the Android Development Kit
XML Documents	• Understanding the importance of XML files in Android • Creating and modifying well-formed XML documents
Activities	• Creating and modifying new Activities (screens) • Switching between Activities with "Intents"
Intents	• Starting new Activities and programs with Intents • Registering your Activities to receive incoming Intents
Basic Screen Design	• Handling different screen sizes and dimensions • Using XML to define your screen layouts
GUI Controls	• Understanding the GUI controls available to Android • Learning how to use controls to retrieve user input
Android File System	• Writing settings to Shared Preferences storage • Reading and writing files to device memory • Reading and writing files to SD cards
Android Debugging	• Finding and solving common coding problems • Viewing the log files to find errors

Image Handling	<ul><li>Displaying images</li><li>Displaying scrolling image sets</li><li>Using launcher icons, backgrounds, and button images</li></ul>
Dialogs	<ul><li>Creating anonymous inner classes</li><li>Using Alert, Date, and Time dialogs</li></ul>
Menus and Notifications	<ul><li>Creating basic menus for your applications</li><li>Creating context menus for specific screen items</li><li>Showing simple messages and notifications</li></ul>
Network Connections	<ul><li>Adding Internet and network support to applications</li><li>Downloading information from the Internet</li><li>Sending SMS Messages</li></ul>
App Widgets	<ul><li>Understanding the purpose of App Widgets</li><li>Creating your own Home Screen App Widget</li></ul>

Within each chapter you will be working on an activity related to the lesson topics. In some cases you will create a larger application over several chapters. The programs that you will create in this course will be fairly simple to start, but you can expand to your heart's content – the sky's the limit! The final project in the last chapter will incorporate many of the topics into a single application that you produce.

We also provide a description of how to publish your Android applications to Google Play (Android Market). Please refer to the documentation links in your Student Menu for details.

Activity: Install Course Software, Android SDK, and ADT Plug-in

The goal of this activity is to enable the Android development environment on your computer. This involves installing the course software, ensuring the JDK and Eclipse are ready to go, and adding the Android SDK and ADT Eclipse plug-in to your environment. Some of these steps you will have already taken in our first-semester *TeenCoder*™: *Java Programming* course. If you have already performed any of these steps then simply skip and go on to the next step. *Note that your computer will need to be connected to the Internet during this activity.*

Installing the Course Files

The first step to this activity is ensuring your course software is installed on your computer. You may have already run the course setup program to install the **Student Files** and/or **Solution Files** before reaching this point. If so, you can skip the first step and move on to installing the JDK.

The course files are installed by a single setup executable that came with your course. The setup program is called "TeenCoder_AndroidProgramming.exe" (for Windows) or "TeenCoder_AndroidProgramming.pkg" (for Mac OS). If you received a printed textbook then the course CD in the back of the book contains this setup program, and the setup program should launch automatically when you place the CD in your Windows or Mac OS computer disc drive. Ensure that you are logged in using an administrator account when you launch the setup program. If the setup does not launch automatically, or if you received your course setup program through some alternate process, simply use Windows Explorer or Mac OS Finder to find your setup program and double-click on it to start the installation.

The setup executable will offer you the choice of installing the Student Files and/or Solution Files. You may install these components on the same computer (if the student should have free access to the solutions) or on different computers (so the teacher can maintain control over the solutions). For a better understanding of the setup process and the files present in the course material, please refer to the "Getting Started Guide" on our website at http://www.HomeschoolProgramming.com.

Go ahead and perform this setup process now. We recommend installing to the default "C:\TeenCoder\Android Programming" directory for Windows or "/TeenCoder/Android Programming" under your Mac OS user's Home directory. We will refer to this default directory structure in the textbook. The setup program will automatically create a "My Projects" directory under the target directory – this is where all of the student projects will go!

Windows Course Menu Shortcuts

On a Windows computer, once installation is complete you will have a new "TeenCoder" group on your Windows Start Menu. Underneath "TeenCoder" is an "Android Programming" folder. Within that folder are one or two menus leading to the Student and Solution files (depending on your setup choices).

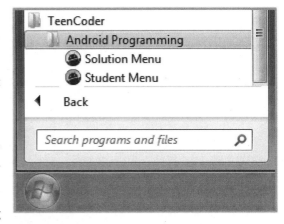

The look and feel of the Windows Start Menu may change between versions of Windows. The Start Menu is not readily available at all in Windows 8! Windows 8 users should refer to our online "Getting Started Guide" for instructions on finding and pinning the the course shortcuts to their applications page for easy access.

Mac OS Course Menu Shortcuts

Once the installation is finished on your Mac OS computer, you will see a "TeenCoder" image in your user's Home folder.

When you double-click on this image, you will see the "Android Programming" folder and the links to the "Android Student Menu" and the "Android Solution Menu" (depending on your choices during setup). Your "My Projects" working directory is located under the "Android Programming" folder.

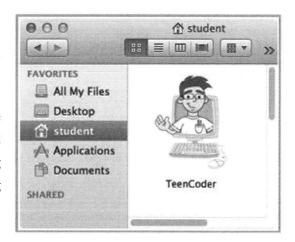

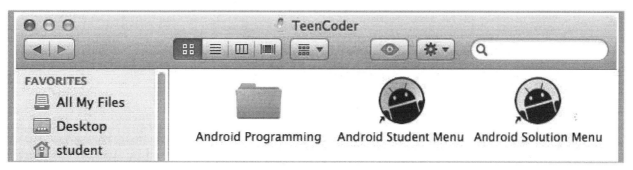

Course File Structure

You can run the Student and Solution Menus for easy, HTML-based access to all of the instructional documents (PDFs), activity solutions, and other material distributed with the course.

You may also simply run Windows Explorer or Mac OS Finder and navigate to your target install directory and launch these files on your

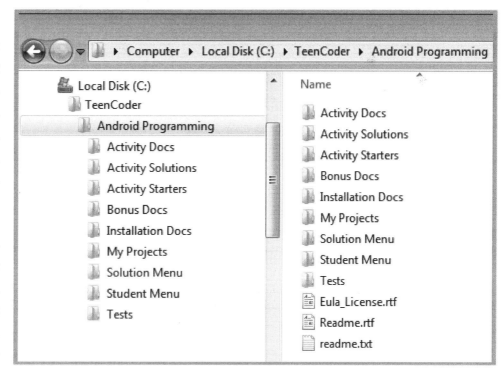

own! Use of the menu shortcuts is optional. The example screen above from Windows Explorer shows the folders and files in your target directory. The Mac OS directory structure is the same.

Most supplemental documents are in PDF format. A ".PDF" file is a common document format that requires the free Adobe Acrobat program to read. Your computer should already have the Acrobat reader installed. If you cannot view the PDF documents, you will need to install Acrobat reader first from http://get.adobe.com/reader/.

Installing the JDK and Eclipse

Your next major job is to install the Java Development Kit (JDK) and Eclipse Kepler IDE on your computer. If you have already installed the JDK and Eclipse (Kepler version), you may skip this step. You will need to be connected to the Internet during the download and installation process. Always ask your teacher before doing any activity online.

Your Student Menu contains a tab called "Software Install Instructions". Click on that tab and you will see a button called "Get Online Documents". Click that button and you will be directed to a page on our website that contains PDF documents with the current download and installation instructions. Find the document titled "Java JDK Install Instructions" (for your operating system) containing complete, step-by-step instructions on downloading and installing the JDK. Please follow the instructions to install the JDK on your computer now. You can also directly access all install documentation from our website, http://www.HomeschoolProgramming.com.

The Working Directory for Projects

Each project you create should be placed in a new sub-folder within your "My Projects" working directory. You may select a different working directory or even create additional working directories on your own; just remember your directory location when you want to save and load your projects.

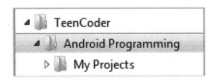

The "My Projects" directory is created automatically in the "TeenCoder/Android Programming" directory. Multiple students may use the same computer for this course by creating different working directories (using Windows Explorer or Mac OS Finder) or installing the course under different user Home folders (Mac OS).

Installing the Android SDK and Android Development Tools

Next you will need to download and install the Android Development Tools for Eclipse and the Android Software Development Kit (SDK). These tools will allow you to quickly and easily create and test Android applications on your computer. Find the "Android Install Instructions" document matching your operating system on our website's TeenCoder Java/Android installation page and follow those instructions now. Once you have successfully installed the course material, JDK, Eclipse Software, Android SDK and ADT then you are ready to start your Android adventure!

Chapter Two: Using Eclipse with Android Tools

You are now ready to start writing Android applications! In this chapter you will learn how to create an Android project, explore the different files that go into the project, and learn how to start the emulator to run your program in a simulated environment. This is a "hands-on" chapter, so start your Eclipse IDE and follow each step as we move through the lessons.

Lesson One: Creating Android Programs in Eclipse

The first thing you need to do is figure out where all of your Android projects will be stored on your hard drive. During the course setup we created a "My Projects" directory for this purpose. If you have not already done so, when you run Eclipse, you should create a new workspace in this directory. Launch the Eclipse IDE now, and if you are not prompted to select a workspace up-front, click on "File", then "Switch Workspace" and then "Other…". You will then see a dialog asking for your workspace directory. Type in or browse to the full path to your "My Projects" directory.

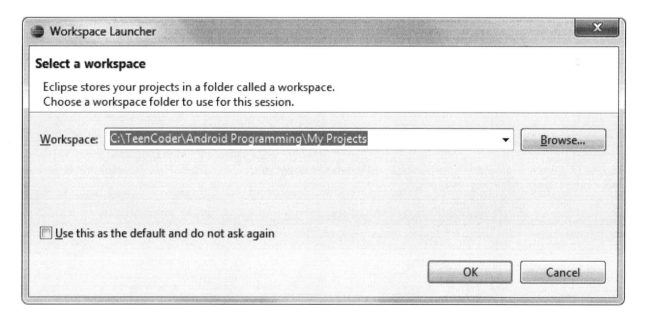

You may store your projects wherever you like, but we recommend choosing your "My Projects" directory as we will refer to this folder as the default location when discussing your activities. The default location on Windows is "C:\TeenCoder\Android Programming\My Projects" and the default location on Mac OS is "/Users/<your name>/TeenCoder/Android Programming/My Projects".

When finished, click on "OK" and Eclipse will restart. Once the software starts up, choose the "Workbench" arrow button from the Welcome screen or select "Window → Open Perspective → Java" and you will see your new workspace. Now you are ready to fill the workspace with your Android projects!

Creating an Android Project

There are two ways to create a new Android project. First, you can use the menu at the top of the screen. Click on "File → New → Android Application Project". Make sure that you avoid "Java Project", since this will just create a plain Java project.

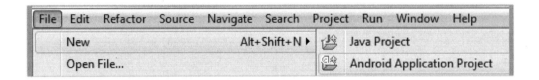

If you are missing the "Android Application Project" selection, you can make it appear by refreshing the Java perspective in Eclipse. To do this, right-click on the Java perspective button in the upper-right corner of Eclipse and choose the "Reset" option. This will make "Android Application Project" appear in the menu.

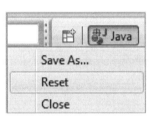

The "New Android Project" screen looks like this:

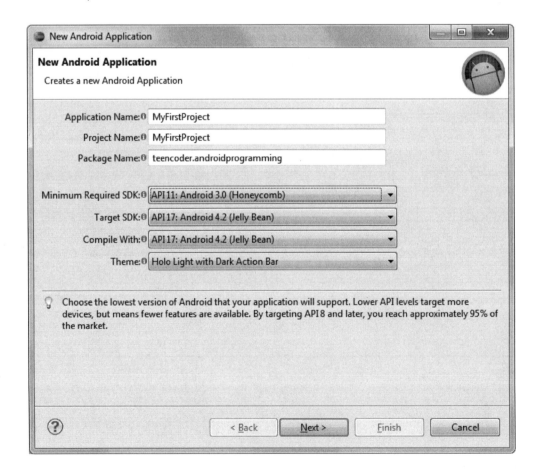

Here, you will need to provide some basic information about your project. We'll use "MyFirstProject" for our first program, so type that text into the "Application Name" field now. You should notice that the "Project Name" field is then automatically populated as the same name as your application. You will also need to select a "Package Name" for your project. Recall in our first semester course we simply chose the default (empty) package. However, all Android applications must have a package name containing at least two words separated by a period. We are going to use "**teencoder.androidprogramming**" for all of our examples.

You can use your own package if you wish, possibly based on your name such as "doe.john". Recall that in Java packages, the most general phrase goes first (such as "teencoder") followed by more specific phrases (such as "androidprogramming"). You must have at least two levels in an Android package name. Enter your chosen Package Name in the field as shown.

The next series of choices will ask you for the Android SDK version that you want to use for your project. The "Minimum Required SDK" setting refers to the lowest version of an Android device that will run your program. **Change the setting to read "API11: Android 3.0 (Honeycomb)"**, because some Android features we will use in this course require Android 3.0 or greater.

The "Target SDK" version is the highest version of Android that your application is known to work with. In this course, we will be targeting "API17: Android 4.2 (Jelly Bean)". Programs developed against 4.2 can also run on later Android versions.

The next choice is the API version that you want to "Compile With". This is typically the version that supports all the functionality that you want to use in your Android application. We will set this to the same value as our "Target SDK" or "API17: Android 4.2 (Jelly Bean)".

The final choice is the "Theme" for your Android application. We'll talk more about themes later in the course. For now, just leave this at the default value and click "Next" to continue.

The next screen will ask for more information about the application we are creating.

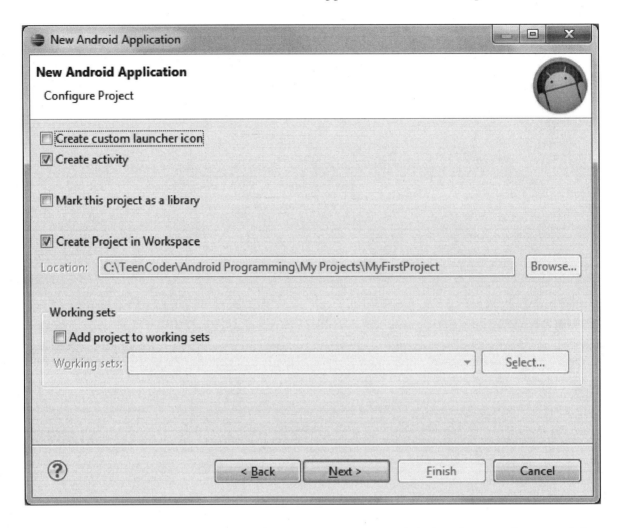

You can uncheck the "Create custom launcher icon" box, leave the default values on the rest of the screen, and click on the "Next" button.

The next screen will require some information about your application's initial activity. An *activity* is an Android screen, and we will just create a "Blank Activity" for this project. Select "Blank Activity" and then click the "Next" button.

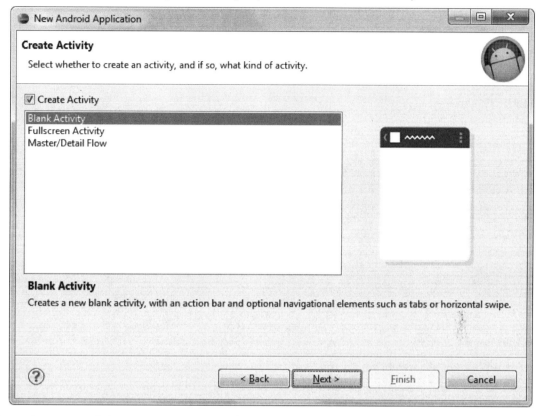

Finally, we will need to give our activity screen a name. We will always call our first screen "Main" and our layout "main" for simplicity. The default names ("MainActivity" and "activity_main") are a bit too wordy for

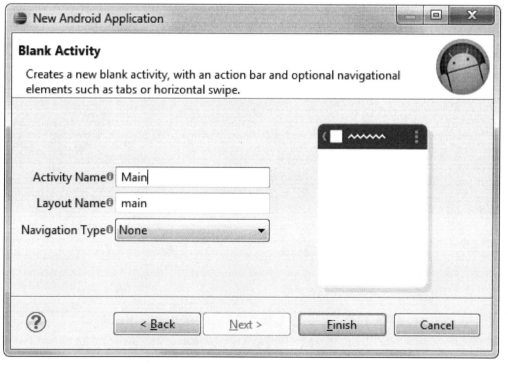

our tastes, so we recommend changing them to "Main" and "main". "Main" in the first line will be a Java class name, so starts with a capital letter. "main" in the second line is a file name, which we start with a lower case.

Now when you click "Finish", Eclipse will create your Android Project!

Lesson Two: Examining Android Project Files

Now that you have created your first Android project, let's take a look at the files that were automatically created. In the Eclipse IDE, find the "Package Explorer" for "MyFirstProject". You can click on the arrows to the left of each folder to expand and see what is underneath.

The first folder is called "src", which contains the source, or code files for your project. Currently, there is only one file, "Main.java". This is the main activity or screen that the wizard created for you. Notice your class was created in your chosen package, which for our example on your computer would be in a directory like "My Projects/MyFirstProject/src/teencoder/androidprogramming".

If you double-click on "Main.java", you will see the default code shown below. The file contains our package name, some imports, the **Main** class, and a couple of methods.

If your curly braces do not line up vertically, then create a "TeenCoder" *Formatter* profile under "Window → Preferences → Java → Code Style → Formatter" as described in the "Configuring Eclipse" document in our online installation isntructions. You can set all of your "Brace Positions" to start on the next line to match our code examples.

```java
package teencoder.androidprogramming;

import android.app.Activity;
import android.os.Bundle;
import android.view.Menu;

public class Main extends Activity
{
    public void onCreate(Bundle savedInstanceState)
    {
        super.onCreate(savedInstanceState);
        setContentView(R.layout.main);
    }
```

```
    public boolean onCreateOptionsMenu(Menu menu)
    {
        getMenuInflater().inflate(R.menu.main, menu);
        return true;
    }
}
```

This is Java code, but it certainly looks different! We'll explore the new features a bit later.

Moving further down in the Package Explorer, the next folder you will notice is the "Android 4.2.2" folder. This contains all of the library files for the 4.2.2 Android SDK. If you are curious about the classes available to you, feel free to drill down into this directory and take a look. We will introduce the major classes as we need them in later chapters.

The "bin" folder contains the executable files for your program. This folder will be empty until you first compile and run your program. At that time, you will see an ".apk" file listed in the folder. This is the Android executable which can be run on the emulator or an actual device.

The "res" directory will contain any resource files that are needed by your program. This includes the user interface objects on your screens, as well as any images, videos or audio that you include. The "layout" directory will hold the layout of your screens (including buttons, textboxes, etc.). You will notice that one layout, called "main.xml" has been created for you. This is the default layout of the **Main** screen. If you double-click on this file, a layout editor will appear where you can add and adjust controls on the screen. We'll talk more about screen layouts in a future lesson.

The "drawable" folders underneath "res" contain the images for your application. There are four different drawable folders, once for high-resolution devices ("-hdpi"), one for low-resolution devices ("-ldpi"), one for medium-resolution devices ("-mdpi") and one for extra-high-resolution devices ("-xhdpi"). It's often a good idea to create different resolution images in each of these categories so that your images appear crisp and clear on any type of Android device.

The "values" directory will hold any data that your program wants to keep outside of the source code itself. You'll notice that there is already a file in this folder called "strings.xml". This file is meant to hold any text such as screen titles, labels, input prompts, etc. that your application may need. Placing these strings outside the code allows you to easily create international versions of your program by swapping in new string files. This means that you can have one string file for English text, one string file for Spanish, one for Chinese, etc. If you follow this approach, making your application available internationally is extremely simple!

There is one notable project file listed under the Package Explorer that is not in a folder: "AndroidManifest.xml". This file will hold important information about your application's screens and interactions. This is a very important file that we will discuss at length in a future lesson!

Lesson Three: Using the Android Virtual Device

Now that we've created our first project and understand the files that were generated, you're probably ready to run your application. But wait! There is one more task to take care of before we can start. We need to figure out how we are going to run the program.

You do not need an Android device in order to complete this course. But how is it possible to test an Android program without any Android hardware? The answer is simple: we use an *emulator* called an "Android Virtual Device". An emulator is a software program that runs on your computer and "pretends" to be some other system, in this case an Android device. This emulator is a fantastic tool for developers. It allows you to "try out" your application without lengthy device downloads or risking potential damage to your precious Android phone!

Configuring an Android Virtual Device (AVD) in Eclipse

In this lesson, we'll take a look at how to set up and run the Android emulator on your computer. The first step is to find the "Android Virtual Device Manager" button on your toolbar. It looks like the highlighted button in the image below:

Once you click on this button, Eclipse will launch the Android Virtual Device Manager screen:

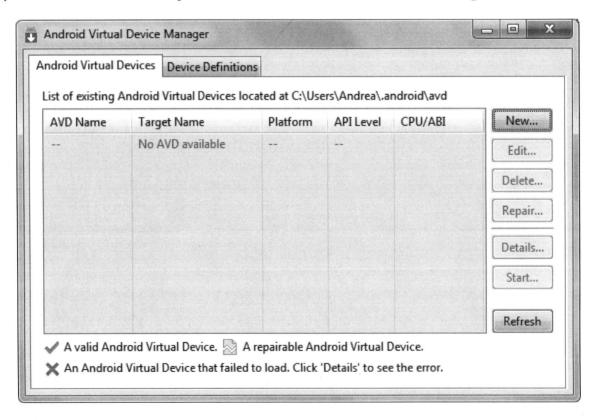

At this point, there aren't any devices configured for us to use. Click on the "New" button on the right side to bring up a dialog that configures a new Android Virtual Device (AVD) as our emulator.

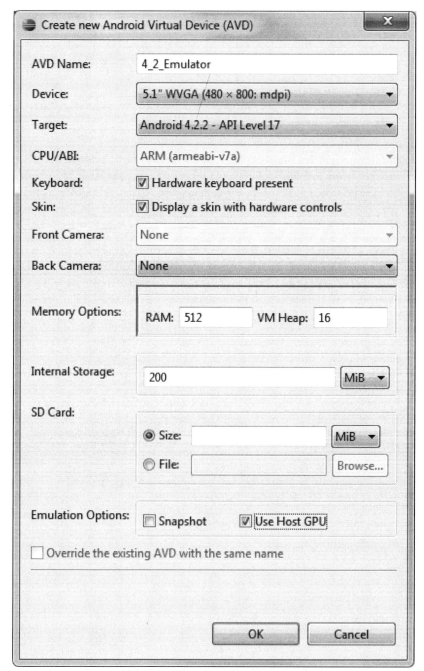

You will need to select a "Name" for the AVD. In the example on the left, we have chosen "4_2_Emulator". You can choose a different name, but we like something descriptive.

The "Device" combo box lets you choose the type of device that will be represented by the emulator. In our case, we will choose a generic device option, "5.1" WVGA (480 x 800; mdpi").

The "Target" combo box lets you select the version of Android OS the emulator will support. In our case, we have selected the 4.2.2 version, which also corresponds to API (or SDK) level 17.

You should leave the "CPU" setting at its default value. In the SD Card section you can actually specify a virtual SD card for your virtual device. This will come in handy later when we are storing data, but for now you can just leave it blank.

The "Emulator Options" section is a very handy feature of the virtual device. The virtual device needs to "boot up" (power on) just like a real Android device. This can often take a long time, sometime minutes! To avoid a virtual reboot each time you start your program, you can check the box labeled "Snapshot". When you launch your program you will then bypass the boot up sequence and jump right back to the last-saved emulator state. If you are making many changes to your application and re-running the emulator often, this can make a big difference in the time it takes to develop your program!

In order to make the Android emulator run faster and be more responsive, you can configure it to take advantage of the hardware acceleration on your desktop computer. If you check the box marked "Use Host GPU" for your AVD, then graphics acceleration is automatically enabled when you run it.

If your emulator occasionally hangs at the "Waiting for Home Screen" state, try unchecking the Snapshot Enabled field. This can clear any unusual errors that may build up in your emulator over time.

When finished, click the "OK" button. You will return to the Android Virtual Device Manager, where you will now see your new device listed.

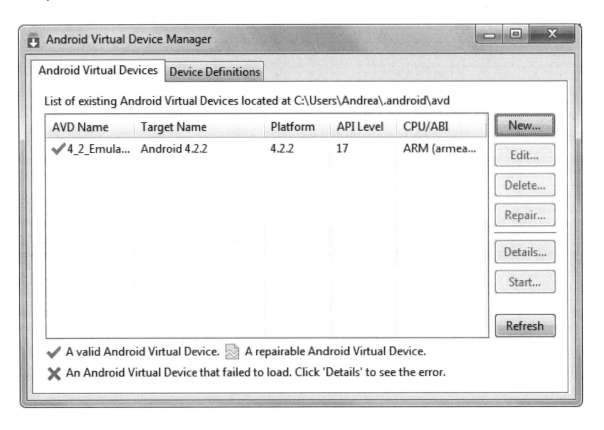

You can now close the AVD Manager window.

Launching Your Project in the Emulator

It's time to run your project on the emulator! Click on the familiar green "Run" button in your Eclipse toolbar.

The first time you run any project, Eclipse will ask you what type of configuration to use. Select "Android Application" and then click on "OK". The emulator will begin automatically.

The first time you run the emulator, it will take some time to load. Be patient! If you click the green "Run" button and the emulator does not start, or if your program does not run in the emulator after it has started, Eclipse may not realize what you are trying to do. Be sure that you have your project name highlighted in the Package Explorer, and also make sure you are looking at a Java source file (*.java) in the main Eclipse window. If you have the Eclipse focus on an XML file, or have not highlighted the project in the Package Explorer, Eclipse may not launch your Android program in the emulator.

Using the AVD Emulator

As your emulator starts it will "boot up" just like a real Android device. You will see a black screen on the left pane that represents what you would normally see on the device's touch screen. You also have a right-pane that gives you access to all of the buttons that you could normally press on the device, plus a convenient keypad. You should see the word "ANDROID" appear on the left a couple of times as the emulator starts.

Finally, when your emulator is started, the virtual screen should look just like a running, "locked" Android device. You may need to "unlock" the virtual device just like a real Android device. Take your mouse and drag the lock image until it displays the "unlock" image as seen in the image on the left.

Once the virtual device is unlocked, your application will run automatically. It may not seem like a spectacular program, but you have created your first fully functional Android application!

To exit your application, you can hit the "Back" button which looks like a curved arrow. The emulator will return to the main Android home screen.

At this point, if you return to Eclipse and re-run your application, it will start in the emulator again. Notice the emulator doesn't have to go through the power-up sequence this time because it was already running. It's a good idea to leave the emulator running to save time. The emulator may occasionally get into a confused state where it doesn't start your program properly. If that happens then just close the emulator out and re-start it through the power-on sequence.

Activity: Hello, Android!

In this project you will practice creating an Android project in the Eclipse software. The end result will be a program much like the one we described in this chapter.

Your project requirements and instructions are found in the "Chapter02_Activity.pdf" document located in your "TeenCoder/Android Programming/Activity Docs" folder. You can access this document through your Student Menu or by directly clicking on it from Windows Explorer (Windows) or Finder (Mac OS).

Complete this project now and ensure your program meets the requirements before continuing!

Chapter Three: XML Resources

In this chapter we need to take a quick detour and examine one of the underlying technologies that Android projects use very heavily: XML. You are going to learn how to read, create, and validate these special text files and examine the XML files in a typical Android project.

Lesson One: XML Overview

In this lesson, we will take a look at a file specification called **XML**. Android projects use this file format for many purposes, so it's important to learn and understand XML before we continue with this course. XML stands for *EXtensible Markup Language*. XML is "extensible" because you can add your own meanings and definitions to the basic markup definition to create advanced markup languages. XML is widely used in business and web applications today.

You may be familiar with another type of markup language – **HTML**. HTML stands for "**H**yper **T**ext **M**arkup **L**anguage" and is used to create web pages. Although HTML and XML look a bit alike, they are actually very different. HTML is used to format the content that you see when you surf the web. XML, in contrast, doesn't actually *do anything* by itself. XML documents are simply used to store information. XML rules are much simpler than HTML but are very demanding! With HTML you can often write "bad" markup and most web browsers will do their best to figure out what you mean. With an XML document it's very important to get every character and tag exactly right, otherwise your whole file is invalid!

XML files are stored as plain text, so they are both human and machine-readable. This means that an XML file can be viewed in most web browsers and text editors like Notepad and TextEdit.

Let's take a look at a simple XML document. The following XML file describes an imaginary arcade game:

```
<?xml version="1.0" encoding="utf-8"?>
<ArcadeGame>
    <Name>Swarm</Name>
    <Player>Peach Kid</Player>
    <CurrentLevel>3</CurrentLevel>
    <HighScore>12930</HighScore>
</ArcadeGame>
```

Without knowing anything about XML, you can glance at this file and have a pretty good idea what is going on. We defined an arcade game called "Swarm" that has a player named "Peach Kid" with a current level of 3 and a high score of "12930". Now let's take a closer look at the XML file *syntax*.

The very first line in an XML file must start with "<?xml" followed by some optional attributes like "version" and "encoding" and finally close with a "?>".

```
<?xml version="1.0" encoding="utf-8"?>
```

This example declares that the XML file uses the 1.0 XML specification and contains characters encoded in the "utf-8" format. You may see variants of these attributes depending on the file. Don't worry about them; you can basically ignore these attributes for our purposes. In our examples we will often leave out the first "<?xml" line when it's obvious we're talking about an XML file.

XML Elements

After the top XML declaration line, the rest of the information in the document is contained in XML *elements*. The top element is referred to as the document "root" element. Each XML document can have only one root element! In our example, the "ArcadeGame" line is the root element:

```
<ArcadeGame>
```

An element begins and ends with a *tag*. Everything between the beginning and ending tags belongs to that element. The starting element tag contains the *name* of the element in a set of angle brackets (< >), as shown above. The ending element tag contains a similar sequence except there is a forward slash before the name. The closing tag for our "ArcadeGame" element is found at the end of the document:

```
</ArcadeGame>
```

All of the information between these two tags is the data for the element. Each element must start with "<*element_name*>" and end with "</*element_name*>". An element may contain other elements or text data.

The first child element under <ArcadeGame> is <Name>. The <Name> element just contains simple text:

```
<Name>Swarm</Name>
```

Here, the name of the element is "Name" and the value is the text "Swarm". The remaining elements in our example XML – <Player>, <CurrentLevel>, and <HighScore> – all contain simple text data as well.

If you are familiar with HTML, you know that HTML elements have specific names and uses, like <br> for a line break and <p> for a new paragraph. XML documents have *no such limitations*. Since XML is used to hold all kinds of data, you can name your elements anything you want. If you can express your data in plain text, it can be held in an XML document.

Multiple Elements

XML can contain multiple elements with the same name. You can also arrange information into a hierarchy or tree with some elements containing other child elements. Let's extend our arcade game example by adding multiple players, each with a unique name and current level.

```
<ArcadeGame>
    <Name>Swarm</Name>
    <Player>
        <Name>Peach Kid</Name>
        <CurrentLevel>3</CurrentLevel>
    </Player>
    <Player>
        <Name>Capt Hook</Name>
        <CurrentLevel>6</CurrentLevel>
    </Player>
    <HighScore>12930</HighScore>
</ArcadeGame>
```

Notice we have built up a hierarchy or tree of information. The <ArcadeGame> element has four direct children: <Name>, <Player>, <Player>, and <HighScore>. Some of these elements simply contain text, while each <Player> element contains other child elements. Each <Name> and <CurrentLevel> in between starting <Player> and ending </Player> tags naturally belong to that <Player> element.

Empty Elements

Sometimes you may want to define an element that contains no value at all. Just having the name in the document may mean something! Or, the element may have only attributes (which we'll describe next). You can define an empty element like this, of course:

```
<IAmEmpty></IAmEmpty>
```

But XML also allows you to combine the starting and ending tags on an empty element like this:

```
<IAmEmpty/>
```

Element Attributes

There are often times when you need to add a little more information to your XML elements, but you don't want to define a full child element. Instead you can use *attributes*. Attributes are extra pieces of information attached to an element within the element's opening tag, like this:

```
<ArcadeGame version="1.45">
```

Here, we have added the attribute "version" with a value of "1.45" to our <ArcadeGame> element. The closing tag for the element is not changed. You can set any number of attribute fields on an element, separating them with spaces. Just use the attribute name, and equals sign, and then single or double quotes to contain the attribute text value. You can also add attributes to otherwise empty elements like this:

```
<IAmEmpty feeling="blue"/>
```

Here we have defined an element called <IAmEmpty> that has no child value or data, but it does have one attribute called "feeling" with a value of "blue". Notice the special empty element ending tag "/>"comes right after the last attribute value.

Now, when should you use an attribute and when should you define a child element? In some cases the answer is obvious, perhaps because the value itself is multi-part and needs to contain other structured information. In that case you'd certainly pick a child element that can hold a text value or other elements. But if you're talking about simple strings, the answer can boil down to your personal preference or the way you like your XML documents to look and feel. Consider this re-written Arcade Game example where we make more use of attributes instead of child elements:

```
<ArcadeGame Name="Swarm">
     <Player Name="Peach Kid" CurrentLevel="3"/>
     <Player Name="Capt Hook" CurrentLevel="6"/>
     <HighScore>12930</HighScore>
</ArcadeGame>
```

This version of the XML takes up less space and can be easier to read. There is no one "right" way to define your own XML document because there are many ways to represent the same data.

However, if you are using someone else's XML definition, then you need to follow their style and match exactly what they expect to see. In your Android project XML files, the Android SDK will expect to see certain elements and attributes that you must fill out exactly the right way.

Lesson Two: XML Rules and Special Characters

In this lesson we are going to teach you some of the rules that must be followed in a correctly formed XML document. We'll also figure out how to embed some special characters into element and attribute values.

XML Rules

When creating an XML document, the goal of the writer is to end up with a *well-formed* document. This means that the XML follows the structure and specifications of the XML language. A well-formed XML document will follow a few simple rules.

First, your document should only contain one root element. In our arcade game example, the root element was <ArcadeGame>. The entire document (other than the "<?xml … ?>" declaration) is contained between the starting and ending tags for the root element.

Second, any child elements must be properly nested in your document. This means that the elements that are opened first must be closed last. For example, the following XML section is well-formed:

```
<Player>
    <Name>Peach Kid</Name>
    <CurrentLevel>3</CurrentLevel>
</Player>
```

But this XML is not well-formed:

```
<Player>
    <Name>Peach Kid</Name>
    <CurrentLevel>3
</Player>
</CurrentLevel>
```

You can see that we opened the <CurrentLevel> element inside of <Player>, but closed it outside the element after the ending </Player> tag. This is not allowed in XML! Because the <Player> element was opened first, it MUST be closed last after all internal child elements are closed.

In addition, you must make sure that all of your elements have both opening and closing tags. You may be able to combine the closing tag with the opening tag if your element has no value, but otherwise ensure that each named element opens with an *<element_name>* tag and gets closed with an *</element_name>* tag.

Element Naming Rules

Just like variables in a Java program, you need to follow some naming rules when creating XML elements and attributes. First, all element and attribute names are case-sensitive. This means that you cannot use an opening tag of "<ArcadeGame>" and a closing tag of "</arcadegame>". This will cause an error whenever a program attempts to read the document. Case-sensitivity also means that the elements <ArcadeGame/> and <arcadegame/> are treated uniquely within the document.

There are some technical restrictions on the characters that you can use to name your elements and attributes. There are also some characters that, while legal, you should avoid because they may cause problems with some software that tries to read your XML. To keep things simple, just use a combination of letters, numbers, underscores, and dashes for your XML element and attribute names. You cannot start a name with a number, and your elements should not contain any spaces. Elements named "<Arcade Game>" or "<1ArcadeGame>" are not allowed.

Namespaces

We just asked you to keep your names simple and avoid unusual characters. However, if you take a quick peek at the "AndroidManifest.xml" file that is part of every Android project, you'll see this request ignored right away with some colons (:) inside some names.

```
<manifest xmlns:android="http://schemas.android.com/apk/res/android"
    package="teencoder.androidprogramming"
    android:versionCode="1"
    android:versionName="1.0" >
```

What's going on here? XML has a *namespace* concept that serves the same general purpose as Java packages. It's possible that more than one person could develop an XML structure that has some of the same element or attribute names as a completely different XML structure created by someone else.

In order to identify that specific elements or attributes are to be interpreted according to one application, you can declare a namespace by using the "xmlns:*prefix*" attribute, where *prefix* is some string that will be used within the file to categorize names. The value of the namespace attribute should be a unique string, and most people will select something based on their company or application Internet domain name as shown above.

The Android namespace in this example is uniquely defined by the string "http://schemas.android.com/apk/res/android" and the prefix used in the XML file to mark names as part of that namespace is "android". When you want to mark an element or attribute name with a namespace, put the prefix first, then a colon ":", and then the remainder of the name. You can see the Android developers did exactly this with the "versionCode" attribute name in the Android Manifest.

```
android:versionCode="1"
```

You will not have to define your own namespaces for this course, but you should understand the syntax when you read it. If you have to add new elements to a file and those elements require a namespace, then make sure you follow the namespace naming pattern already defined within the file.

Special Formatting

You'll notice that the structure of an XML document is defined by a collection of special characters such as the opening and closing brackets, double quotes, and so on. Well, imagine that your element or attribute value itself needs to have one of those special characters embedded inside! Let's say your player name was "<The Boss>". How would you actually embed that value in your XML document? This won't work:

```
<Name><The Boss></Name>
```

While you might be able to figure out what is going on, a computer program reading this XML will get very confused! As soon as the second angle bracket "<" is encountered the program would assume you are trying to start a new element, and "The Boss" is not a valid element name. So what's the solution?

The answer is a special type of formatting called an *entity reference*. Entity references are special combinations of characters, starting with the ampersand (&), that are used to insert these reserved characters.

Below is a table that lists the XML entity references and the special characters they represent:

Entity Reference	Character Represented	Description
&lt;	<	Less than sign
&gt;	>	Greater than sign
&amp;	&	Ampersand
&apos;	'	Apostrophe
&quot;	"	Quotation Mark

Wherever you want to add one of the special characters to your XML data, insert the entity reference instead! Here's the corrected version of our player name "<The Boss>":

```
<Name>&lt;The Boss&gt;</Name>
```

This looks a bit funny to the human eye, but it's now perfectly clear to any software reading your XML document what that data contains. You may wonder why the ampersand (&) itself needs an entity reference. That's because any ampersand character is assumed to start an entity reference, so if you just want to put in an ampersand as part of your value, you'll need to use the entity reference for ampersand instead.

Here is an example that will save the value "Mike & Bob" in the <TeamName> element:

```
<TeamName>Mike &amp; Bob</TeamName>
```

You also need to use entity references for single and double quotes because they are used to define the beginning and ending of attribute values. So anywhere you need one of those characters in your data, use the entity references instead. This example creates the value "My "arcade" game.":

```
<Description>My &quot;arcade&quot; game.</Description>
```

XML Comments

When writing Java code you can add comments by simply using "//" on one line or matching "/*" and "*/" pairs. Comments are very handy descriptions in natural English language without following any syntax rules. You can also add comments to an XML document, but the starting and ending tags are different.

To add a comment in an XML document, start your comment with the characters: "<!--" and end with the characters: "-->". Everything between these two tags is ignored by a program reading the XML.

```
<!-- The following element contains the player name -->
<Name>&lt;The Boss&gt;</Name>
```

You cannot "nest" comments, and in fact two dash characters "--" cannot be used within a comment at all! You can use the special characters <, >, ", ', and & inside comments without using entity references, though.

```
<!-- This is a valid comment: < > ' " & -->
```

XML Whitespace and Indentation

It's easiest for humans to read XML when child elements are indented underneath their parents, like this:

```
<Player>
    <Name>Peach Kid</Name>
    <CurrentLevel>3</CurrentLevel>
</Player>
```

But all the whitespace used for indentation is mostly ignored by any software reading through the XML. So the following document contains essentially the same elements, data, and relationships:

```
<Player><Name>Peach Kid</Name><CurrentLevel>3</CurrentLevel></Player>
```

The "pretty-printed" human-readable format is obviously much easier to read. Just keep in mind that, like Java code, the indentation you see in a document is cosmetic only and can be misleading.

```
<Player>
<Name>Peach Kid</Name>
     <CurrentLevel>3</CurrentLevel>
</Player>
```

At a quick glance you might mistake <CurrentLevel> for a child of <Name>, when actually both <Name> and <CurrentLevel> are direct children of <Player>!

XML Testing

So how do you know that your XML document is well-formed? One of the easiest tests is to try to open it in a web browser window. Most popular web browsers will easily open an XML file and display all of the document content as plain text. They will also decode the entity references and show you the actual values.

Consider the following XML document:

```
<ArcadeGame>
 <Name>&lt;The Boss&gt;</Name>
 <TeamName>Mike &amp; Bob </TeamName>
 <!-- This is a valid comment: < > ' " & -->
 <Description>My &quot;arcade&quot; game.</Description>
</ArcadeGame>
```

If you open this file in Internet Explorer, for example, then you will see the actual data like this:

```
<?xml version="1.0"?>
- <ArcadeGame>
      <Name><The Boss></Name>
         <!-- The following element contains the player <>&'" name -->
      <TeamName>Mike & Bob </TeamName>
         <!-- This is a valid comment: < > ' " & -->
      <Description>My "arcade" game.</Description>
   </ArcadeGame>
```

If your document contains errors, the web browser will likely give you some clues as to the problem. Some browsers may simply stop displaying data when an error is found. Others may be more specific. Let's say you used a closing tag of </teamname> instead of </TeamName>. Firefox will show you the error below:

So, if you are ever wondering if an XML file is well-formed, simply open it in a web browser and see if the file is displayed correctly. If not, you have at least one problem to fix.

We've now covered the basics of XML syntax and formatting. You can find entire books written about this flexible and interesting technology! There are also many online tutorials and XML references you can find in case you run across an example that contains some unfamiliar syntax.

Lesson Three: Android XML

Now that we've talked about XML documents, it's time to take a look at what they have to do with Android programming. Since XML is so flexible, it's the perfect vehicle for handling many different data-driven tasks in Android. Let's examine the major XML documents that make up a typical Android application.

AndroidManifest.xml

One of the most important files in an Android project is "**AndroidManifest.xml**". Every Android project must have this file (with that exact name) in its root directory. The Android Manifest contains many essential pieces of information about your application.

Among other things, the manifest file contains the following data:

- The application's package name, which is required for all the classes in the program
- A list of permissions the program will need in order to interact with the Android device
- The minimum SDK level that the program will support

- The libraries that the program requires
- Information about your program's activities, capabilities, and components. This information lets the Android operating system know exactly what the program is capable of doing on the device.

Here is a simple "AndroidManifest.xml" file that was generated for us while creating the "MyFirstProject" application in the last chapter.

```xml
<?xml version="1.0" encoding="utf-8"?>
<manifest xmlns:android="http://schemas.android.com/apk/res/android"
    package="teencoder.androidprogramming"
    android:versionCode="1"
    android:versionName="1.0" >

    <uses-sdk android:minSdkVersion="11"
            android:targetSdkVersion="17" />


    <application
        android:allowBackup="true"
        android:icon="@drawable/ic_launcher"
        android:label="@string/app_name"
        android:theme="@style/AppTheme">
      <activity
        android:name="teencoder.androidprogramming.Main"
        android:label="@string/app_name" >
        <intent-filter>
            <action android:name="android.intent.action.MAIN" />
            <category android:name="android.intent.category.LAUNCHER" />
        </intent-filter>
      </activity>
    </application>

</manifest>
```

As you can see, there are quite a few unfamiliar elements and attributes here, but you now know how to read the XML structure itself! We'll dive into the contents of this file in detail later on.

Since the manifest is written entirely in XML, it is viewable and editable in any plain text editor, like Notepad or TextEdit. The Eclipse IDE will also give you some powerful GUI editing tools where you can set options in the XML without actually writing the text yourself. We'll talk about Eclipse-based management of the manifest in a later chapter.

Screen Layouts

A *screen layout* controls how each GUI element such as a button or checkbox appears on your Android device. When writing Java Swing programs, you used a similar concept called a *layout manager* to arrange your UI controls. Since each Android device may have a different screen size, and that screen can flip between portrait (vertical) and landscape (horizontal) modes, good screen layout capability is even more important!

All of the screen layouts in Android are written in XML. This is pretty cool! Instead of writing Java code, you just need to fill out an XML file. Each screen that your program will use must have a corresponding XML file. When we created our initial program in the previous chapter, we asked the New Project Wizard to include a "Main" screen. This caused the project to automatically generate a "main.xml" layout file. This file contains all of the layouts, buttons, text boxes, labels, etc. for the screen. Each layout and control is represented as its own XML tags and values. You can find your "main.xml" in the Eclipse project under "res/layout".

When you create additional screens for your application, each screen will need its own XML layout file. You can either create this file from scratch, or use a wizard to automatically generate the file for you. We will talk more about screen layouts in the next chapter.

Android Themes

If you look closely at your "AndroidManifest.xml" file, you'll see an "android:theme" attribute on your <application> element:

```
android:theme="@style/AppTheme">
```

A theme is an overall graphical style that impacts the look and feel of your application. Different themes may present title bars, buttons, text edit fields, and color schemes in different ways. The default theme, for example, shows a small Android icon in your title bar and uses a blue underline for text edit fields.

Some of the Android screen shots in our lesson text will use an alternate theme that is slightly easier to read on a printed page.

```
android:theme="@android:style/Theme.Light" >
```

This theme has a smaller, lighter title bar and the text edit fields are completely highlighted by an orange border. So don't worry if your own applications look a little bit different than our screen shots; we're just using a different theme! If you want, you can change your theme to match in the "AndroidManifest.xml" file.

Menu Layouts

Many Android applications will contain some type of menu. Your program may contain either an "Action Bar", which appears at the top of the screen, or a "Context Menu" which appears whenever the user long-presses something on the screen. In some cases, your Android application will contain both of these menus.

Regardless of the type of menus in your program, you will need to create them using XML. Each menu is represented by its own XML file in your Android project. These menu XML files contain elements representing each menu item's ID, text and icon.

The menu layouts, like the screen layouts, can be created from scratch or can be created with an XML wizard, which will automatically generate the basic menu XML file for you. You will need to know how to add the individual item tags yourself, however! We will talk more about menus in a future chapter.

Resource Files

A *resource* is something used by your program that is not part of the actual code. You can swap resources in and out without actually changing your source code. Pictures and sounds are good examples. Did you know that strings (such as your label contents) can also be resources? By making all text that your program displays on the screen a resource, your program can be converted to different languages very easily!

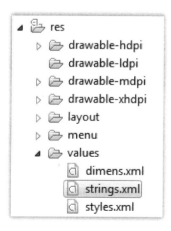

All resources that your application uses will need to be defined in an XML file. The most common of these resource files is the "strings.xml" file. This file can be used to hold any of the text items in your program. Text items can include label text, button text, and even menu descriptions. You can find the default string resource file under your project's "res/values" directory.

If you are creating an application that will be used in the global market, you will definitely want to use the strings resource XML file. For example, if you wanted your program to be used by English-speakers and Chinese-speakers, you could create two "strings.xml" files: One in the "values" folder, and one in the "values-cn" folder. When the program is run on an Android device, it will automatically pull text from the "values" folder for an English device and from the "values-cn" folder for the Chinese device. You don't need to re-write the program!

In addition to strings, Android makes use of XML files for other resources like animations and colors. Animation XML files will define any shapes that you want to draw and any transitions that you want to perform with your shapes. The color XML files will hold the RGB values for any custom colors your application requires to work correctly.

Hopefully, you can now see why it's so important to be able to read, create and understand XML files in Android programming. This file format is heavily used within Android applications and a good working knowledge of XML structure is required in order to create error-free programs. Except for the "AndroidManifest.xml" file, most Android XML filenames tend to use a combination of lower-case letters and possibly some underscores (e.g. "my_layout.xml")..

Activity: Creating your own XML Document

In this project, you will create an XML document that will define a music library. You can create this file in any text editor. When complete, you should be able to view the XML file in any web browser program without errors.

Your project requirements and instructions are found in the "Chapter03_Activity.pdf" document located in your "TeenCoder/Android Programming/Activity Docs" folder. You can access this document through your Student Menu or by directly clicking on it from Windows Explorer (Windows) or Finder (Mac OS).

Complete this project now and ensure your program meets the requirements before continuing!

Chapter Four: Android Activities

When you hear the term "activity", you might think of any general-purpose project or task. When writing Android programs, however, the term *activity* has a very specific meaning that relates to the screens you see within your program. In this chapter we'll introduce Android activities, learn how to create new activities, switch between activates within your program, and pass messages between your activities.

Lesson One: Activity Screens

An Android *activity* is any one task that the user can perform. Typically, this task is wrapped up in a single screen. For example, in an email application, the screen where you can view a list of your emails could be one activity. If you choose one of the emails, you are sent to a second activity where you can view the text of the email. A third screen or activity would allow you to write a new email. Android applications must have at least one activity, and all but most the simplest programs will need more than one activity.

Recall in the last chapter when you created your "MyFirstProject" in Eclipse, the New Android Project wizard had a "Create Activity" checkbox that we enabled and specified "Main" as the activity name. The project then automatically received a new Java class called **Main** that extended the **Activity** class:

```
public class Main extends Activity
```

Each time you want to create a new screen, you'll define a new Java class that extends **Activity** and a new XML layout file to arrange the screen contents. The New Project wizard does both of these things for your first screen.

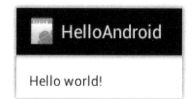

Life on an Android Device

On an Android device, an application can be interrupted at any time by an event with a higher-priority. For example, any application that is running will be interrupted when a phone call arrives. This is necessary behavior, since most devices are phones first and cool gadgets second!

Android activities can be either in the *foreground*, which means running and fully visible on the screen, or in the *background*, which means partially or completely hidden from the user. Activities that are in the background can be killed by the Android system at any time if the device memory resources become too low.

Since an application's activity can be so easily interrupted, we need a well-defined way to start it, stop it, push the activity into the background, and restore it to the foreground. The status of an activity is called its *state*.

There are three main states for an active Android activity.

State	Description
Resumed or **Running**	This means that the activity is running in the foreground on the screen.
Paused	The activity has been sent to the background, but is still partially visible on the screen. This typically occurs if the device has popped up a message box on the screen, perhaps to notify the user of an incoming call.
Stopped	In this case, the activity has been completely covered by another activity and sent to the background. This means the screen is no longer visible to the user at all. Your program is still running in the background, however, and should still keep track of all its data.

The Android operating system will notify your activity (class) whenever it is changing states. It does this by calling one of the **Activity** object methods described below.

Callback Methods

Now that you understand the various states of an activity, let's take a look at the different events that will tell your **Activity** class when its state is being changed. These events come in the form of callback methods which are defined on the **Activity** base class. Your own class, such as **Main**, can override these methods to add special logic just for your application.

onCreate() Method

The **onCreate**() method is called when the activity is first started by the user. In this method, you will want to initialize the user interface for the activity screen.

onStart() Method

The **onStart**() method is called right after the **onCreate**() method and means that your activity is becoming visible to the user. It may also be called when a background activity gets restored to the foreground

onResume() Method

If your activity was in the Paused state, the **onResume**() method will be called when it is returning to the Running state. **onResume**() is also called just after **onStart**() when your activity is becoming visible for the first time.

onPause() Method

This method is called when the system is about to put your application into the Paused state. This means some other activity has moved into the foreground and your activity is now at least partially in the background. At this point the activity can be killed by the Android system at any time, so now is a good time to save any application data so you can restore it next time the activity goes to the foreground.

onStop() Method

When this method is called, your activity is getting moved entirely into the background or Stopped state. At this point, the activity is no longer visible to the user.

onRestart() Method

This method is called when your activity is in the Stopped state and is about to be moved into the Running state again. After **onRestart**() your activity will receive an **onStart**() event. You'd only need to override **onRestart**() if your activity needs to do something special on a restart versus starting the activity for the first time.

onDestroy() Method

The **onDestroy**() callback method is the final callback your activity will receive before it is destroyed, or stopped altogether. This method is either the result of the user finishing with the activity or because it has been destroyed by the Android system from a Stopped state.

Keeping track of all the different callback method and understanding the lifecycle of an activity can be pretty confusing, so let's look at a diagram on the next page that can visually identify states and transitions. After 1000 words it's time for a picture!

The diagram below shows the order in which callbacks occur from the time your **Activity** class is created until the time it is removed. The shaded ovals represent activity states and the arrows represent transitions due to some event.

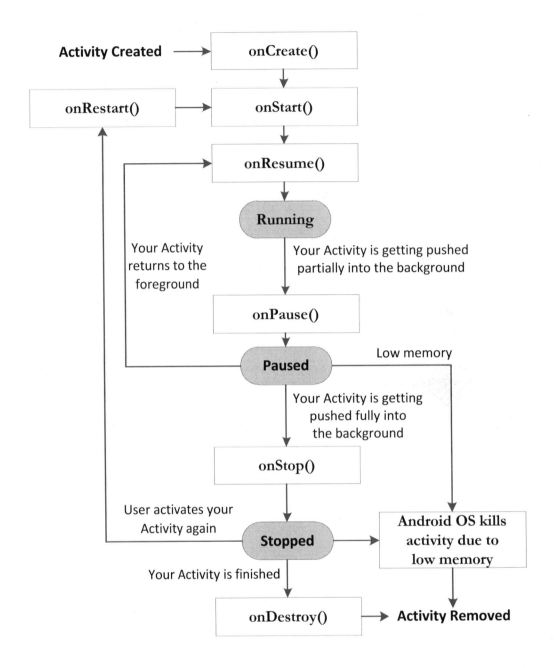

The most important thing to notice in this diagram is that the Android operating system may immediately kill your activity at any time after it becomes Paused or Stopped if there is not enough memory left on the device to handle more important tasks. Therefore, if your activity needs to store any data to load again next time it becomes Running, the **onPause()** method is the place to do it. You might not get another chance!

If your activity is completely removed (either gracefully through **onDestroy()** or killed by the OS), then when re-launching your activity it will go through the entire startup sequence again as a new object.

Lesson Two: Creating Activities

Now that you understand what an activity is and how it interacts with the Android system, let's create a new activity in the Eclipse IDE. An activity requires two new files in your project:

- A .java file that will contain the code for the class derived from the **Activity** base class
- A layout XML file that will hold the visual layout for the activity.

From the New Project Wizard in Eclipse, you can check the "Create Activity" box to create a default activity. In our last chapter we created the **Main** class for the "MyFirstProject" main screen. Let's go look at "Main.java" to see what it contains by default.

This lesson, and many of the lessons throughout the textbook, should be "hands-on".
So pull up your Eclipse IDE and follow along as we cover the important files and topics!

"Main.java" File

After completing the New Project Wizard we ended up with a "Main.java" file in our "src" folder and a "main.xml" file in our "res/layout" folder. Let's examine these two files, starting with "Main.java":

```java
package teencoder.androidprogramming;

import android.os.Bundle;
import android.app.Activity;
import android.view.Menu;

public class Main extends Activity
{
    public void onCreate(Bundle savedInstanceState)
    {
        super.onCreate(savedInstanceState);
        setContentView(R.layout.main);
    }
    public boolean onCreateOptionsMenu(Menu menu)
    {
        getMenuInflater().inflate(R.menu.main, menu);
        return true;
    }
}
```

The first line defines the package name for this class. We will use "teencoder.androidprogramming" as the package name for all example projects, but you can choose another valid package name for your own code.

The next three lines import the necessary Android SDK classes for our activity. Since all application activities inherit from the **android.app.Activity** class, that class is imported for easy reference. Another line imports the **android.os.Bundle** class, which is used to pass information between different activities in your application. We'll discuss this class in more detail in a future lesson. Finally we import the **android.view.Menu** class to handle the action bar, which is a new feature introduced in Android 3.0.

After the imports we find the **Main** class definition. It extends the **Activity** base class from the Android SDK. The New Project Wizard automatically implemented an override for the **onCreate()** event callback.

```
public void onCreate(Bundle savedInstanceState)
{
    super.onCreate(savedInstanceState);
    setContentView(R.layout.main);
}
```

The default **onCreate()** method is very simple. For any callback method you override such as **onCreate()** or **onPause()**, the very first thing you want to do is call the **Activity** base class implementation of that method using the **super** keyword. Make sure to pass in the same parameter you received. This will allow the **Activity** base class to perform any internal processing necessary when callbacks occur.

Calling the base (super) class version of the callback is required for the activity to run correctly. If this line was missing the activity would encounter an error at run-time. Don't forget to call the base class version of all overridden callbacks!

The final line in the **onCreate()** method will tell the **Activity** which screen layout XML to use.

```
setContentView(R.layout.main);
```

Remember that your screen layouts are contained in XML files. In this case the **Main** class has a corresponding "main.xml" in the "layout" folder under the "res" directory. The **setContentView()** method takes one parameter, which selects the layout XML file to use for the activity.

How does **R.layout.main** represent an XML file? The "R" stands for the "res" folder in your project, which contains all of your resources. So "R" is a shorthand way of telling Android that you are going to refer to some resource. The "main.xml" file is in "res/layout/ main.xml", so after the "R" simply add the remaining directory "layout" and filename "main" (without the extension), separated by periods. **R.layout. main** therefore specifies the "main.xml" file in the "layout" directory under the main resources folder.

The second default method, **onCreateOptionsMenu**(), will establish a default menu that will appear when the user hits the menu button.

```
public boolean onCreateOptionsMenu(Menu menu)
{
    getMenuInflater().inflate(R.menu.main, menu);
    return true;
}
```

The **getMenuInflater().inflate**() function call will create a menu based on an XML layout file. In this case **R.menu.main** refers to "res/menu/main.xml" which you can find in the Eclipse Package Explorer. We'll be using action bars instead of menus later on, so you can ignore this function for now.

Settings

The "main.xml" File

Eclipse has a couple of different ways to view and manage your screen layout XML files. You can use a powerful Graphical Layout Editor which hides the XML syntax completely, allowing you to visually add UI widgets and control the screen layout. Or you can view and edit the underlying XML directly. Either way, just double-click on the XML file in the Package Explorer to get started.

Here is an example screen shot of the Graphical Layout editor with "main.xml":

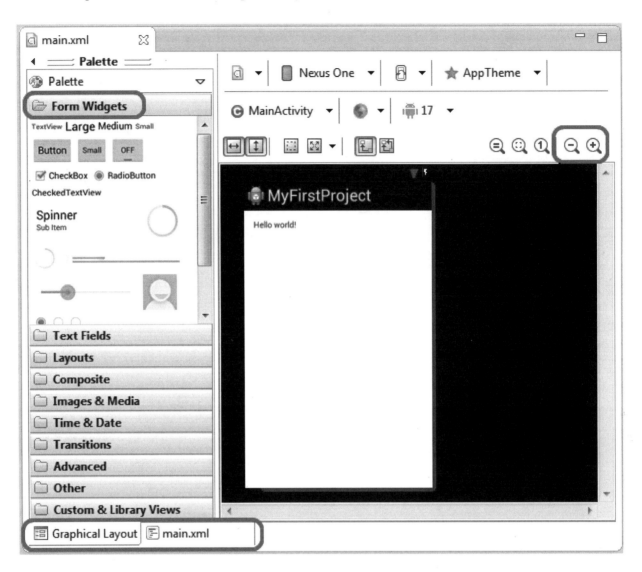

If you are used to building plain Java screens by writing Java code, this is probably very exciting! With this visual Graphical Layout, you can drag and drop controls like buttons and textboxes from the "Palette" of options on the left to the Android screen on the right. This allows you to visually develop your user interface, moving and adjusting controls as you go. On the default **Main** screen, you can see that we have one simple control that displays the message "Hello world!". If you need to expand or shrink the screen view for better visibility, use the two magnifying glass icons on the top-right of this editor.

The Palette on the left contains a number of categories such as "Form Widgets", "Text Fields", and so on. Just click on the category name to see an expanded list of controls under that category. You can add many different controls to your screen. We can't possibly cover them all in one course, but we'll teach you the most common controls and you are encouraged to experiment on your own.

If you take a look at the bottom of the view, you will see two tabs marked "Graphical Layout" and "main.xml". If you click on "main.xml", you will see the actual XML code for the layout.

```
<RelativeLayout xmlns:android="http://schemas.android.com/apk/res/android"
    xmlns:tools="http://schemas.android.com/tools"
    android:layout_width="match_parent"
    android:layout_height="match_parent"
    android:paddingBottom="@dimen/activity_vertical_margin"
    android:paddingLeft="@dimen/activity_horizontal_margin"
    android:paddingRight="@dimen/activity_horizontal_margin"
    android:paddingTop="@dimen/activity_vertical_margin"
    tools:context=".Main" >

    <TextView
        android:layout_width="wrap_content"
        android:layout_height="wrap_content"
        android:text="@string/hello_world" />

</RelativeLayout>
```

We will discuss the details of the XML layout and control elements in the next chapter. But at a glance you can probably tell that we have a "RelativeLayout" that contains a single "TextView" control. You can choose whether to add layouts and controls in the Graphical Layout view or the XML view. If you add controls through the Graphical Layout, the underlying XML file will be automatically updated. Similarly, if you manually add controls to the XML file, the Graphical Layout should update to show the changes.

Adding New Activities

The **Main** class and "main.xml" layout file were automatically created for you by the new project wizard. But how do you add more activities to a project? In order to create a new activity, you need to do three things:

- Create a new Java class that extends **Activity**
- Create a new XML layout file for the activity screen
- Add the new activity to the "AndroidManifest.xml" file

To create a new Java class, select "File → New → Class" from the Eclipse menu. Or you can click the "New Class" button    from the toolbar. The New Java Class dialog should look familiar as you have created new classes before in our first-semester Java Programming class.

You need to change three fields. First, add your package name to the "Package" field.

Next, enter a name for your class. We used "Second" in this example.

Finally, you want to change the "Superclass" to be "android.app.Activity". Your new class should extend the **Activity** class, not the basic Java **Object**.

Click on the "Finish" button when you are done. You now have a new **Second** class in the "Second.java" source file.

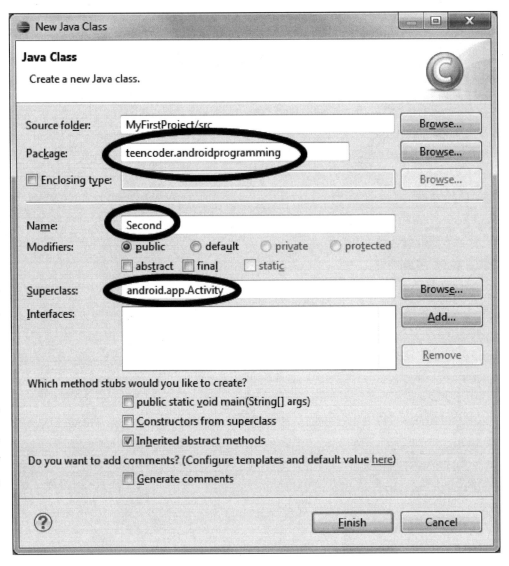

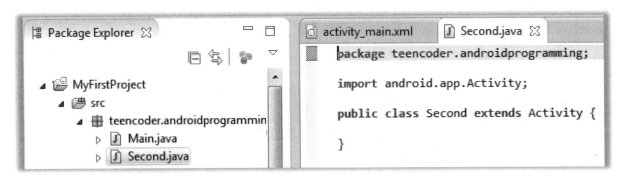

Now we can turn our attention to a new XML layout file for the **Second** activity. To quickly create this file, we can use another wizard, called the "Android XML Wizard". You can launch this wizard from the toolbar with this button , or you can select "File → New → Android XML File" from the Eclipse menu.

The New Android XML File wizard is shown to the right.

We can choose the Resource Type ("Layout"), the project that will hold the new XML file ("MyFirstProject") and then select a name for the file. We would like our layout XML file name to match the activity class, so type in "second" in the File textbox. All Android XML layout filenames must contain *only lowercase letters*.

Finally, we need to choose a root element. There are many kinds of layouts and other elements to choose from. For now, select **LinearLayout** from the list.

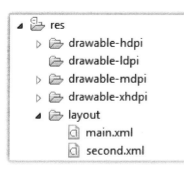

When you click on the "Finish" button, a new "second.xml" file will appear in your "res/layout" folder. You should also see the XML file loaded into the Graphical Layout editor, with tab options to view the underlying XML.

You can see in your "second.xml" file that we now have a **LinearLayout** with nothing inside it!

```xml
<?xml version="1.0" encoding="utf-8"?>
<LinearLayout xmlns:android="http://schemas.android.com/apk/res/android"
    android:layout_width="match_parent"
    android:layout_height="match_parent"
    android:orientation="vertical" >

</LinearLayout>
```

In order to see something useful on the screen when the **Second** activity appears, let's add a **TextView** control with some descriptive text. This should go inside the <LinearLayout> element (right before the closing </LinearLayout> tag is fine). You can type this directly into your XML, or drag a **TextView** object from the Palette to the screen in the Graphical Layout editor.

```
    <TextView
        android:id="@+id/textView1"
        android:layout_width="fill_parent"
        android:layout_height="wrap_content"
        android:text="This is the Second activity!" />
</LinearLayout>
```

Now we need to hop back to our **Second** class and override the **onCreate()** method. This will allow us to load the new "second.xml" layout whenever the **Second** activity is created.

```
package teencoder.androidprogramming;

import android.app.Activity;
import android.os.Bundle;

public class Second extends Activity
{
    public void onCreate(Bundle savedInstanceState)
    {
        super.onCreate(savedInstanceState);
        setContentView(R.layout.second);
    }
}
```

The lines in bold above were added to import the **android.os.Bundle** class, override the **onCreate()** method, call the **Activity** base class **onCreate()** method, and finally set the content view. By using "R.layout.second" as the parameter to **setContentView()** we are selecting the "res/layout/second.xml" resource file.

The final task when creating a new activity is to add it to the "AndroidManifest.xml" file. Just like the layout XML files, the manifest XML can be viewed in different ways. If you double-click on the manifest file from Package Explorer, you will see a graphical editor that lets you modify values without touching the underlying XML directly.

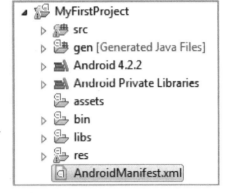

Across the bottom are five tabs that let you drill into different parts of the manifest configuration.

| Manifest | Ⓐ Application | Ⓟ Permissions | Ⓘ Instrumentation | AndroidManifest.xml |

The first four tabs offer a graphical way to change application-specific configurations, like the package name and version number. The final tab, called "AndroidManifest.xml", shows you the XML in a plain text editor.

```xml
<?xml version="1.0" encoding="utf-8"?>
<manifest xmlns:android="http://schemas.android.com/apk/res/android"
    package="teencoder.androidprogramming"
    android:versionCode="1"
    android:versionName="1.0" >


    <uses-sdk
        android:minSdkVersion="11"
        android:targetSdkVersion="17" />


    <application
        android:allowBackup="true"
        android:icon="@drawable/ic_launcher"
        android:label="@string/app_name"
        android:theme="@style/AppTheme" >
        <activity
            android:name="teencoder.androidprogramming.Main"
            android:label="@string/app_name" >
            <intent-filter>
                <action android:name="android.intent.action.MAIN" />
                <category android:name="android.intent.category.LAUNCHER" />
            </intent-filter>
        </activity>
    </application>
</manifest>
```

Within this file, you can see an existing <activity> element for the **Main** activity. Notice that inside the <activity> element is a child element called <intent-filter>. The details inside this element tell the Android system that the **Main** activity should be shown when the application is first launched.

You can add your new **Second** activity to the manifest file either graphically or by directly editing the XML. To do it graphically, select the "Application" tab at the bottom, and then scroll down until you see "Application Nodes".

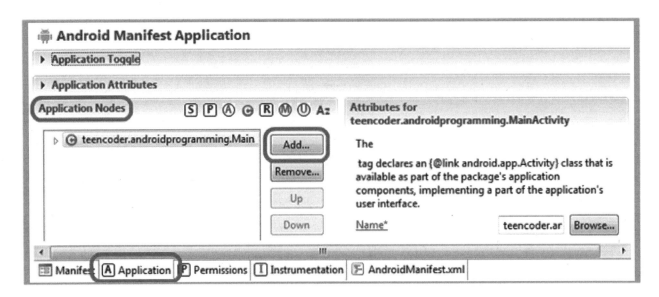

Click the "Add…" button, and ensure "Create a new element at the top level…" is selected.

Then pick "Activity" from the list and click "OK".

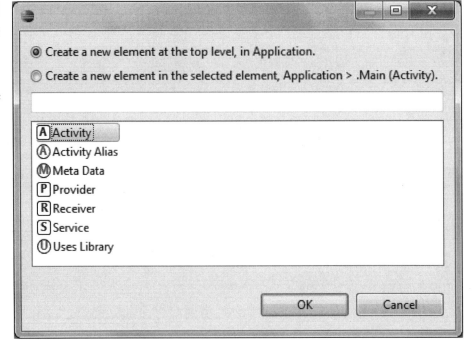

When you return to the main Applications tab you'll see a new entry called "Activity" in the list. Select that node and then on the right "Attributes for Activity" pane, enter ".Second" for the "Name" field. Then save your file. You add the period in front of the class name to tell Android the class is part of the default package you selected for your project.

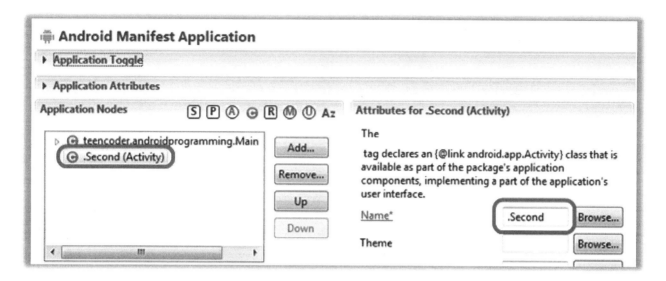

Now if you flip over to your "AndroidManifest.xml" tab to view the raw XML, you'll see a new <activity> element right before the closing </application> tag. Our <activity> tag has just one attribute: "android:name". This just tells the Android the name of the activity class, which is **Second**.

```
    <activity android:name=".Second"></activity>
</application>
```

That was quite a few button clicks in the graphical editor just to add one line of XML! Once you get comfortable with XML files and the Android manifest, it may be faster for you to just add the new <activity> element by hand using the XML editor. But you can continue to use the graphical approach if you like.

That's all the changes that we need to make to add a new activity to our project. But how do we get the new **Second** activity to display from our initial **Main** activity? We'll talk about that in the next lesson!

Lesson Three: Switching Between Activities

Now we have two different activities for our Android project, but how do we switch from one to the other? The first thing we need to do is add a button to our **Main** activity so that we have a way for the user to send a signal to switch to the next screen.

Adding a Button to a Layout

To add a button to the **Main** activity, open the "main.xml" file from your "res/layout" folder.

The Graphical Layout editor will allow you to just drag a button onto our screen. Click the Button graphic under Form Widgets and drag it over to the activity screen on the right, then release the mouse button. Presto! Your new GUI button will snap into place.

Once you add the button to the screen, switch over to the text view for the "main.xml" file. You should see a new <Button> element that looks something like this:

```
<Button
    android:id="@+id/button1"
    android:layout_width="wrap_content"
    android:layout_height="wrap_content"
    android:text="Button" />
```

You can see that Eclipse gave our button an id of "button1" and has set some default width and height properties. We will discuss these properties in detail in our next chapter. For now, we can just leave the default values. The display text on the button is controlled by the "android:text" attribute, so you can add or modify that attribute to say whatever you like!

`android:text="Button" />` Eclipse may show a yellow exclamation point and underline this attribute to warn you the text is hard-coded instead of using a string resource. This type of warning is called "lint" because it is annoying but harmless. You can ignore the warning or disable it completely by switching to the Graphical Layout and clicking on the red box near the top-right corner.

RelativeLayout

Show Lint Warnings for this Layout

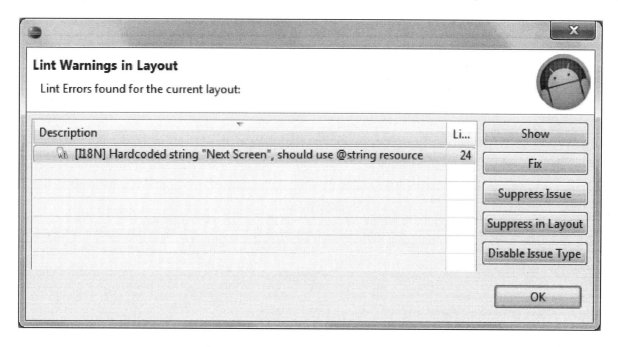

In the Lint Warning dialog, click on the description and then click "Disable Issue Type" and "OK" to make this particular type of warning go away.

Now, let's change the button text to read "Next Screen".

```
android:text="Next Screen" />
```

This will change the text on the button to "Next Screen". Go back to the Graphical Layout and confirm that the button text has changed.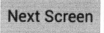

Handling Button Click Events

Buttons in Android work very similar to the way **JButtons** work in a normal Java Swing program. Recall from our first-semester Java course that you need some object to implement a "Listener" interface and then you need to register that object with the button object in order to receive a function callback when the button is clicked.

In the Android world, the interface you need to implement is called **android.view.View.OnClickListener**. Go ahead and add the following three **import** statements to the top of your "Main.java" source file in order to give us easy access to the **OnClickListener** interface and related classes:

```
import android.view.*;
import android.view.View.*;
import android.widget.*;
```

Now you must implement the **OnClickListener** interface on your **Main** class. Add the **implements** keyword followed by the interface name after the "**extends** Activity" text.

```
public class Main extends Activity implements OnClickListener
```

Next, of course, you need to actually implement the **OnClickListener** interface methods. Fortunately there is only one method called **onClick()** as shown below.

```
public void onClick(View v)
{

}
```

The **View** class is the base class for all of your UI widgets, including buttons. If you have more than one button on your activity screen, you'll need to figure out which button generated the event. Unlike Java Swing programming, all of your controls are generated based on the XML layout, so you don't have a great opportunity to save all of your object references at the class level for later comparison.

Fortunately, Android has an easy way to match a **View** to the actual control defined in the screen layout. Every control has a unique id specified in the XML like this:

```
<Button
      android:id="@+id/button1"
```

The name "button1" is translated to an integer that you can access through our familiar "R" (resource) syntax like this: **R.id.button1**. **R.id.button1** is literally a unique integer assigned to this button that you can reference in your code.

Now let's add some logic to our **onClick()** event handler to demonstrate how we can identify the button that generated an event.

```
public void onClick(View v)
{
        int id = v.getId();        // get the ID for the control that was clicked
        if (id == R.id.button1)  // if this ID equals button1's ID
        {
                // button1 was clicked, so handle that event here!
        }
}
```

Of course we only have one button right now, but as you add more controls to your screen you can expand the **if()** logic to check for each unique ID that may have generated the click event.

Starting a New Activity with Intents

So now that we can identify when "button1" caused a click event, how do we change activity screens?

In Android lingo, an *intent* is a message that can be passed between activities. The message may be very simple or may contain lots of data. We'll use an intent to launch our **Second** activity from the **Main** activity.

The **Intent** class is in the **android.content** package, so you'll want to put this **import** in your source file:

```
import android.content.Intent;
```

Now in our **onClick()** method, we can create an **Intent** message from **Main** to **Second** and call the **startActivity()** method with this **Intent**.

```
if (id == R.id.button1) // if button1 was clicked
{
    Intent myIntent = new Intent(Main.this, Second.class);
    startActivity(myIntent);
}
```

The constructor for our **Intent** takes two parameters. The first parameter is a **Context** object. Since **Activity** inherits from **Context**, you can pass in the "**this**" reference to the **Main** object as the **Context**. The second parameter is an identification of the class that we want to target with the message (**Second.class**). When we call **startActivity()** with this new intent, the **Second** activity will be created and started.

We are missing one last step! Recall from your first-semester Java programming course that you need to tell each control where to send its events. To do this in Android we need to obtain the actual object underlying the control and call the **setOnClickListener()** method, passing in "**this**" since the activity class itself has implemented the listener interface.

To get a reference to the button on the **Main** screen, we can use its unique ID again and call the **findViewById()** method. This will return an object reference to the control that we cast to a **Button**.

```
Button myButton = (Button)findViewById(R.id.button1);
```

Then we can call the button's **setOnClickListener()** method, passing "**this**" as the interface for callback:

```
myButton.setOnClickListener(this);
```

71

Where should this code go? It's a one-time setup step that fits nicely into your activity's **onCreate**() method.

```
public void onCreate(Bundle savedInstanceState)
{
    super.onCreate(savedInstanceState);
    setContentView(R.layout.main);

    Button myButton = (Button) findViewById(R.id.button1);
    myButton.setOnClickListener(this);
}
```

That's it! Now you can build and run your program.

When you click on the "Next Screen" button, you will see the **Second** activity screen:

Now, what happened to the first **Main** activity when the **Second** was launched? Thinking back to the state diagram, when the **Main** activity is pushed completely into the background it should receive the **onPause**() event and become Paused. Then because it is completely in the background, **Main** should also receive the **onStop**() event as well and move to the Stopped state. The **Main** activity will then remain in the Stopped state until it is activated again.

To send an exit signal to an activity, hit the back arrow button. The activity that is currently running will then progress through the Paused and Stopped states and be destroyed. The next activity that was in the background will then be restored.

If you hit the back arrow button from your **Second** activity, you will see exactly this sequence! Your **Second** activity will be destroyed and your **Main** activity will be restored to a Running state. If you then hit the back arrow again, your **Main** activity will be destroyed and you will return to the main Android OS screen.

If you need to programmatically close an activity, you can call the **finish**() method from within that activity (when the user clicks a "Save" button, for example). The **finish**() method will close the activity completely just like the back arrow button.

```
finish();          // close the Activity
```

The following diagram shows each event callback and state change in both activities for this simple sequence. The top of the diagram represents the beginning of the application, and then each row shows some callback or user activity in the order they would happen in real-time.

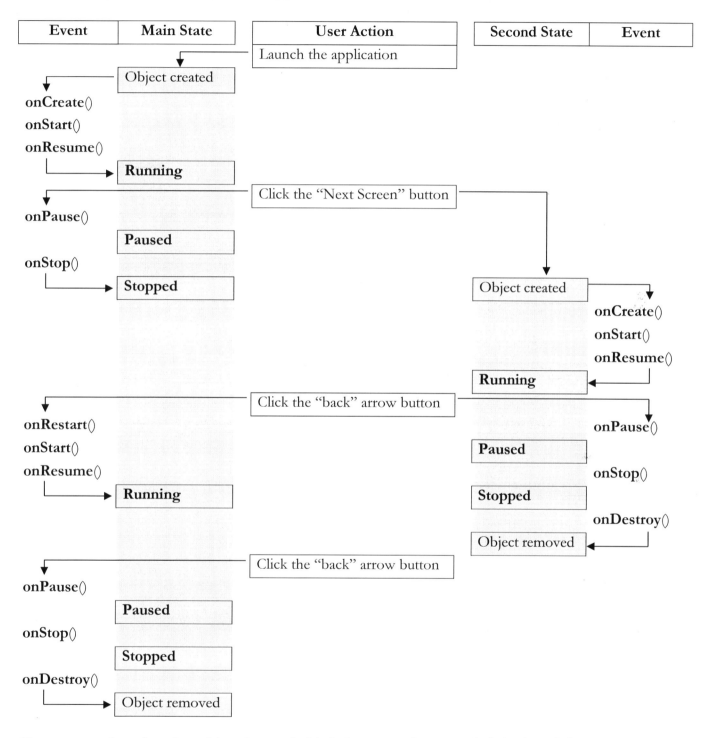

You can see there is quite a bit going on behind the scenes just to switch back and forth between two activities. Understanding the state changes and callback behavior of an activity as it gets moved between foreground and background will allow you to perform special processing at each step if required by your application. In our next lesson, you'll learn how to transfer data between activities in your application.

Lesson Four: Handling Explicit Intents

In our last lesson, we briefly discussed *Intents*. **Intents** are used to send messages between any installed applications on an Android device. An **Intent** can be used to start another activity in your program, start a service or another application outside of your program, or broadcast a message to the Android system. **Intents** can hold information about the action being taken or the application that should receive the Intent. In Android programming, there are two different types of **Intents**: *explicit* and *implicit*.

We'll cover implicit intents later in the course, but explicit intents will be useful to us right away. An *explicit* **Intent** is sent to a particular activity within an Android application. In our last lesson, we used an explicit **Intent** to start the **Second** activity in our program. This is a very common way to use intents.

Adding Data to Intents

In addition to starting activities, an explicit **Intent** can be used to pass information from one activity to another activity. Let's say our **Main** screen has a text box where the user can enter their name. When the user clicks the "Next Screen" button, we want that name to appear on the **Second** activity screen. To do this, we can attach some extra information to the **Intent** used to start the **Second** activity. Look inside our **Main** class and find where we created the **Intent** used to start the **Second** activity.

```
Intent myIntent = new Intent(Main.this, Second.class);
startActivity(myIntent);
```

We can add data to the **myIntent** instance before calling **startActivity()**. The **Intent** object has a method called "**putExtra**(name,value)" that will add a name and a value as a pair. The "name" is a string and the value can be any basic data type such as **int** or **String**, or an array of those data types. The name is just a key which will allow you to retrieve the data later. The value is the actual information you are passing along.

So, let's say we want to pass our user's name to the **Second** activity. We will first add an **EditText** control to the **Main** screen. You can do this dragging and dropping the **EditText** box onto the screen in the Graphical Layout editor. Click on the "Text Fields" category and drag the first "Plain Text" box containing "abc" onto your screen layout.

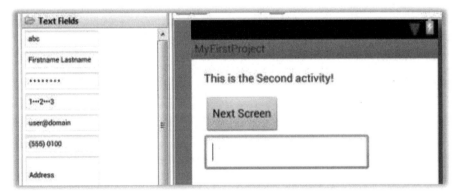

If you look at your "activity_main.xml" file you can see a new <EditText> element has appeared with a unique id of "editText1". We can refer to this **EditText** control from our Java code as "**R.id.editText1**".

Now, when the user clicks the "Next Screen" button, we want to get the value from the text box and attach it to the **Intent** we are creating to launch the **Second** activity. Remember that you can get a reference to any control by calling the **findViewById()** function. Don't forget to cast the result to the actual control type:

```
EditText et = (EditText)findViewById(R.id.editText1);
```

Once we have the **EditText** reference, we can call **getText()** which will return an **Editable** object. **Editable** is just an interface for a fancy kind of **String** that can be changed without making a new copy of the data. To get an actual **String**, we can just call **toString()** right away on the **Editable** interface returned by **getText()**.

```
String nameString = et.getText().toString();
```

Now we create our **Intent** and place the extra data into the **Intent**. We will use the key "name", but you can use any descriptive string that you like for the key.

```
Intent myIntent = new Intent(Main.this, Second.class);
myIntent.putExtra("name", nameString);
```

You're ready to start the **Second** activity using this **Intent** containing some extra information! Let's put all this code together in the **onClick()** method of our **Main** class:

```
public void onClick(View v)
{
        int id = v.getId();
        if (id == R.id.button1) // if button1 was clicked
        {
                // get a reference to the EditText control
                EditText et = (EditText)findViewById(R.id.editText1);

                // get the string value from the EditText control
                String value = et.getText().toString();

                // put the string value from the edit text into the Intent
                Intent myIntent = new Intent(Main.this, Second.class);
                myIntent.putExtra("name",value);

                startActivity(myIntent);
        }
}
```

Reading Data from Intents

Ok, so we have successfully launched our **Second** activity with a data-packed **Intent**. How do we get that data within the **Second** class? First we have to think about *when* to get the data. We know our **Second** activity will receive **onCreate()**, **onStart()**, and **onResume()** callbacks when it is first shown. Since we know our data from **Main** will not change for the entire lifespan of the **Second** activity, it's safe to just grab the data during **onCreate()**. If your application need to get new data while in the Paused or Stopped state, you should reload the data during **onStart()** or **onResume()** instead.

First, at the top of your "Second.java" file, add a couple of **import** statements we'll need:

```
import android.content.Intent;
import android.widget.*;
```

Now, within the **Second onCreate()** method, let's add this code to retrieve our data:

```
public void onCreate(Bundle savedInstanceState)
{
    super.onCreate(savedInstanceState);
    setContentView(R.layout.second);

    // get Intent that launched this activity
    Intent myIntent = getIntent();

    // get Bundle that contains extra data
    Bundle bun = myIntent.getExtras();

    // pull the value from the Bundle using our key
    String value = bun.getString("name");

    // get the TextView control and update the displayed text
    TextView tv = (TextView)findViewById(R.id.textView1);
    tv.setText("Hello " + value);
}
```

First we get a reference to the **Intent** that launched the activity using the **getIntent()** method. Then we get a reference to the **Bundle** of extra information in the **Intent** by calling **getExtras()** on the **Intent**. Finally, we know we stored a **String** in the **Bundle** with the key "name", so we can call **getString()** on the bundle with the key input "name" to retrieve our value!

What do we do with this data once we have it? We have demonstrated how to update the **TextView** control on the **Second** screen and replace the existing text with the value passed from the **Main** screen. If you take a peek at your "second.xml" layout file, you'll see that the existing **TextView** control has a unique ID of "textView1". So we use that value to get a reference to the control using **findViewById()**. Then we place our **String** value into the **TextView** control by calling **setText()**.

Our two activities are now talking to one another. Go ahead and run "MyFirstProject" in the emulator and try it out. In the example below we typed "Allison" into the edit box on the **Main** screen and then clicked the "Next Screen" button. The **Second** activity seems much friendlier this time!

Can you think how you might handle data flowing in the opposite direction? What if the **Second** screen had an **EditText** and you wanted to send the resulting data back to the **Main** activity? In this case you are not creating a new **Intent**. The **Second** activity is simply destroyed and the **Main** activity moves from the Stopped to the Running state. Since you are not creating a new **Intent**, you can't use the same technique to pass information "back" to an existing activity.

Returning Results to Previous Activity

If you know that a child activity like **Second** needs to return data to the parent activity like **Main**, you can use a slightly different technique to launch the **Second** activity from **Main**. This approach will let the parent activity know that the child activity will be creating an **Intent** to send back to the parent when the child activity has ended. Here's how it works:

1. **Main** activity calls **startActivityForResult()** instead of **startActivity()**
2. **Second** activity calls **setResult()** with a new **Intent** containing information
3. **Main** activity receives the result **Intent** when the **Second** activity closes

The **startActivityForResult()** method takes an **Intent** and an integer request code:

```
void startActivityForResult(Intent intent, int requestCode)
```

The **intent** is just a regular explicit **Intent**, possibly with extra information, that will be used to start the target **Activity**. The **requestCode** can be any user-defined value greater than or equal to 0 that will be returned to you when the target activity closes. Let's re-work our earlier example where **Main** launches the **Second** activity, replacing **startActivity()** with **startActivityForResult()**.

```
// put the string value from the edit text into the Intent
Intent myIntent = new Intent(Main.this, Second.class);
myIntent.putExtra("name",value);


// we're expecting to get information back from this Activity!
startActivityForResult(myIntent,0);
```

Now, in the **Second** activity, when we're ready to communicate some information back to the previous activity, we call **setResult()** with a result code and optionally an **Intent** with extra information. In our example the **Second** activity doesn't have any user input fields, so we'll just echo back the same name that was received when the **Second** activity was started. You can call **setResult()** from any convenient place in your code. In this case, since the name is not changing while the **Second** activity is running, we'll set up the response **Intent** right away at the bottom of the **Second onCreate()** function.

```
Intent resultIntent = new Intent();      // create new Intent to hold info
resultIntent.putExtra("name", value);    // store result info in Intent
setResult(RESULT_OK,resultIntent);       // this Intent will be given to Main
```

Finally, how does the **Main** activity receive this response **Intent**? It will need to override an **Activity** method called **onActivityResult()**, which will be called when the **Second** activity closes after calling **setResult()**.

```
protected void onActivityResult(int requestCode, int resultCode, Intent data)
{
    // get returned information from our response Intent
    Bundle bun = data.getExtras();
    String value = bun.getString("name");
    // now do something useful with the value...
}
```

Simply get the **Bundle** from the intent using **getExtras()**, then pull the value using the "name" key with **getString()**. Now you have the value passed back from **Second** and you can do something useful with it!

In summary, to start a new **Activity**, use an explicit **Intent** and call **startActivity()**. To start a new **Activity** and expect a response, call **startActivityForResponse()** instead and ensure that the second activity returns a data **Intent** back using **setResult()**.

Activity: Hello, Again!

In this activity you will add a second screen and some more functionality to your first "HelloAndroid" project. The new version of this program will show three new buttons on the main screen. Each button will provide different information to the second screen in the program. This information will be passed from the main screen to the second screen using explicit **Intents**.

Your activity requirements and instructions are found in the "Chapter04_Activity.pdf" document located in your "TeenCoder/Android Programming/Activity Docs" folder. You can access this document through your Student Menu or by directly clicking on it from Windows Explorer (Windows) or Finder (Mac OS).

Complete this activity now and ensure your program meets the requirements before continuing!

Chapter Five: Screen Layouts and Views

In this chapter you are going to learn how to arrange controls on the Android screen using some of the many available layouts. We'll explore the Graphical Layout editor as well as design screens directly inside your XML layout file. You'll also learn about **Views**, which are the basis for **Buttons**, **TextViews**, and other Android GUI elements.

Lesson One: Android Units of Measure

Before we start talking about the different controls and objects that you can place on an Android screen, let's explore the measurement units that are available. In our first-semester Java programming course you learned about *pixels*, which are simply a 2-dimensional grid of dots that make up the computer screen. In Java Swing GUI programs you could size and place controls on the screen using pixel measurements for width, height, and location. This method works very well on a Mac or PC, because the screen sizes and resolutions on these types of computers are fairly standard. Since those computer screens are so large, slight variations in the look of your applications are not that noticeable.

This is not the case on an Android device! Screen sizes can vary widely from device to device. Your application may run on a device that is only 2 inches wide, or it may run on a tablet that is 10 inches or more in diagonal size. In addition, different devices have different *resolutions* or *screen densities*. This is the measure of how many *pixels per inch* that a screen can display. A low-density screen has fewer pixels per inch and does not have a crisp picture like a high-density screen. These different sizes and screen resolutions make designing an Android application a little bit trickier than a normal computer program.

If we used a width and height of 200 pixels for a simple button, our screen could look very different on devices with different pixel densities. The image to the left shows a low-density device where 200 pixels take

much more room than on the high-density device to the right.

So how do we make our screens look similar across different devices? The answer is something called the *device-independent pixel* or "*dp*" for short. A

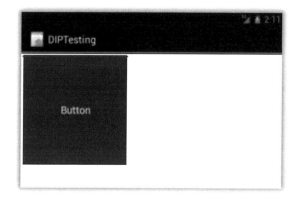

dp is a unit of measurement that is automatically scaled to the size of the display. You can specify "dp" measurements in your layout XML for the "android:layout_width" and "android:layout_height" attributes for the <Button> element. Just append "dp" to the numeric value.

```
<Button
    android:id="@+id/button1"
    android:layout_width="200dp"
    android:layout_height="200dp"
    android:text="Button" />
```

With "dp" sizes the button takes up about the same area on both high-density and low-density devices.

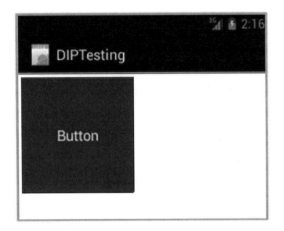 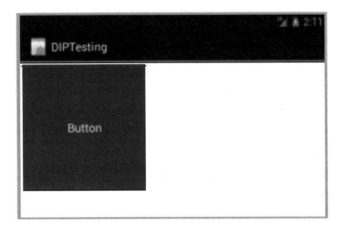

In addition to "dp" units, we can use a few pre-defined sizes for our "layout_width" and "layout_height":

Pre-Defined Size	Description
"fill_parent" or "match_parent"	Make the control fill the width or height of the parent window
"wrap_content"	Only use the space that is needed to properly show the control

If we set our button to use a size of "wrap_content", it would be only wide enough to fully show the text on the button. "wrap_content" is the default width and height for a <Button>. If you review the layout XML for the projects we've already done that contain a <TextView>, you'll see that the default width is "fill_parent" and the default height is "wrap_content". That's why the default **TextView** controls stretch the entire width of the screen and are high enough for one row of text.

There is one more interesting unit of measurement: the *scale-independent pixel* or "sp". This measurement is used for sizing text on the screen. It is possible to set an Android device to show larger or smaller text, depending on the user's needs. If a user wants larger text displayed, you should honor that request in your application. To do this, you would set the font size in "sp" units. Your displayed text would then scale up or down depending on the user's settings. You can use "dp" for your font size also, but "dp" does not take into account any custom text display settings that a user may have configured.

Lesson Two: The Graphical Layout Editor

You've already been briefly introduced to the Graphical Layout editor that will let you design an Android screen by dragging controls onto the display area. Let's take a closer look at some of the features this editor provides. To view the graphical editor, open the "res" folder and then the "layout" folder in your Eclipse Package Explorer. This will display a list of all XML layout files for your application. If you created a **Main** activity initially, you should have a "main.xml" file listed in the layout folder. Double-click on "main.xml", to display the Graphical Layout editor.

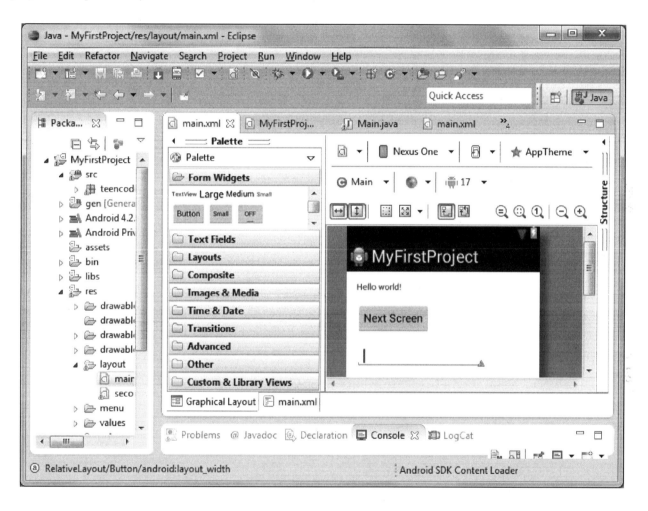

Let's examine this screen section-by-section. At the bottom are two tabs called "Graphical Layout" and "main.xml". You can switch between the Graphical Layout and the XML view by clicking on these tabs. We'll focus on the Graphical Layout tab first.

The first interesting section in the Graphical Layout is the Android "Palette". This contains all of the possible controls that you can place onto your screen. You'll notice the most common controls are at the top of the list in a section called "Form Widgets". The folders below this section contain more specialized controls, grouped by functionality. To add a control from the palette, you would just click and drag the control onto the screen. The placement of the control is determined by the type of layout that the screen is using. We'll discuss layouts in more depth in the next lesson.

Once the control is on the screen, you can configure the control with the Properties tab. If you do not see the Properties window, you can show it by clicking "Window → Show View → Other" from the Eclipse menu. Then expand the "General" folder, choose "Properties" from the list and click "OK".

Your Properties panel may appear at the bottom next to your Problems and Console tab. You can leave it there or drag it to another location on the screen.

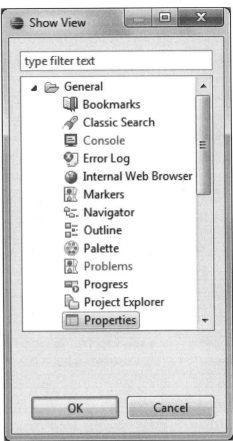

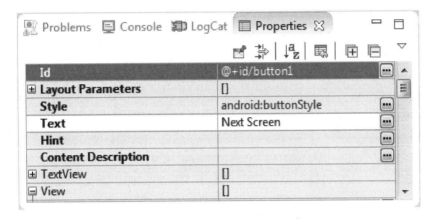

The Properties window will show all of the properties for the current control. Each property has a name and a value. You may need to adjust the column widths or the size of the Properties pane so you can see both the names and the values.

Click on a particular control to see the available properties for that widget. If the Properties window is not displaying the expected data, just click off the control and then back on – this will typically fix the problem. In the Property window you can set the display text, control height, width, ID, etc. As you make changes to the control, the XML is automatically updated.

Near the top of the screen are a series of combo box controls that allow you to change the screen type. You can then preview what your layout will look like on different devices (1), in Portrait (vertical) or Landscape (horizontal) mode (2), and with different device themes (3). In addition, you can easily switch between activity screens (4), languages (5) and SDK versions (6). This is a powerful tool for previewing your application in different ways!

To aid in your screen design, a "Layout Actions" toolbar at the top of the screen will allow you to quickly set some common properties.

The specific icons present on the toolbar will depend on the type of layout your activity uses and the control you have selected in the wizard. Our example above shows the options for a button in a Linear Layout (we will discuss layout types in the next lesson).

The first two icons will allow you to quickly switch between stacking your controls vertically or horizontally. This is only relevant for the Linear Layout model. The next two icons will toggle the control's width and height between "fill_parent" and "wrap_content".

The next icon will allow you to set the control's margins, which adds some empty space around the edges. For instance, if we set a 10dp left and 10dp top margin, then our trusty **Button** object will be moved 10dp down and to the right from the top-left corner of the screen.

Next, you can find the Gravity icon . This is used to align the control in top/down or left/right positions within its assigned space.

The next group of buttons are specific to the Linear Layout: . These buttons will allow you to set and clear the "weight" of the individual controls on the screen. The "weight" of a control determines its importance in the layout. We'll review the Linear Layout details in the next lesson.

The last group of buttons controls the size of the emulator screen in the Graphical Layout editor. These buttons will allow you to quickly resize the design screen to emulate the real size of the screen, make the screen small enough to fit in the layout screen or show it at 100% of its actual size. In addition, you can fine tune the size by using the plus and minus icons.

Of course, as you make changes in the Graphical Layout editor, the underlying XML is updated automatically. You can click on the XML tab to review the changes or make manual changes directly to the XML.

As you can see above, after clicking around in the Graphical Layout editor a little bit, our **Button** has gained a few new properties in the XML layout!

Graphical Layout Pitfalls

The Graphical Layout editor seems to be a great tool; what could possibly go wrong? Unfortunately, there are some snags to consider.

First, the editor itself is a bit buggy. The visual layout may get out of sync with the XML, show controls incorrectly, or fail to display the properties correctly. The editor is frequently patched or updated to new releases as the Eclipse Android developers try to improve the product. So if you ever see some strange mismatch between the XML and the graphical display, trust the XML! A restart of your Eclipse IDE may resolve some problems also.

Second, it may be possible to design very complex screens in your XML layout that cannot be displayed by the Graphical Layout editor. The tool is reasonably complete and handles common operations, but if you start trying to do some advanced layouts then you risk moving beyond what the Graphical Layout can handle.

On occasion you may also see nothing at all in the Graphical Layout! If this happens, ensure that you do not currently have your program running in the emulator. You may need to stop and restart the emulator and Eclipse to get things back on track.

For most of the remaining examples in our course we'll simply show the XML directly. That is easier to view and explain in most cases. You may continue to use the Graphical Layout editor as long as it's doing a good job for you. But if you run into too many issues and it becomes a frustration, simply switch over to the XML view and begin modifying the layouts directly.

Lesson Three: Exploring Common Layouts

Now that we have discussed units of measure and the basics of the screen layout tools, let's talk about some of the layout types. A layout element in XML will have at least four attributes as shown below:

```
<LinearLayout xmlns:android="http://schemas.android.com/apk/res/android"
        android:id="@+id/FrameLayout1"
        android:layout_width="fill_parent"
        android:layout_height="fill_parent" >
</LinearLayout>
```

The attribute "xmlns:android" sets the XML namespace for the layout and is required for the first layout element. Every layout also has a unique ID, a width, and a height. By using "fill_parent" for the width and height we ensure that the layout will use all available screen space.

LinearLayout

A **LinearLayout** is a simple layout that will allow you to add views in either a vertical (column) orientation or a horizontal (row) orientation. Here is the XML code for a **LinearLayout**:

```
<LinearLayout xmlns:android="http://schemas.android.com/apk/res/android"
        android:id="@+id/LinearLayout1"
        android:layout_width="fill_parent"
        android:layout_height="fill_parent"
        android:orientation="vertical" >
</LinearLayout>
```

You can see there is one extra attribute called "android:orientation". The default orientation is "horizontal", so all the controls will be added left-to-right on the screen, as shown below. You can change it to "vertical" so controls are added top-to-bottom instead (see image to the right).

Be careful when setting the widths and heights of individual controls in this layout. If a control's width is "fill_parent" in a horizontal orientation, that one control will expand to cover the entire layout. If a control has a "fill_parent" height in a vertical layout, that control would expand vertically to cover the entire screen.

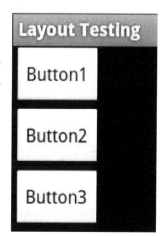

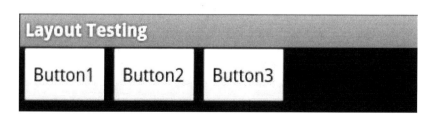

RelativeLayout

The default layout when you create a new Android project is **RelativeLayout**. This layout will allow you to place the controls on the screen relative to one another. This means you can place a control to the left, right, top, or bottom of another control. The first control is laid out relative to the screen itself. The XML element for this layout contains the standard id, layout_width, and layout_height attributes.

```
<RelativeLayout xmlns:android="http://schemas.android.com/apk/res/android"
    android:id="@+id/relativeLayout1"
    android:layout_width="match_parent"
    android:layout_height="wrap_content" >
</RelativeLayout>
```

When adding controls to this layout, you need to specify the location based on the parent layout or another control on the screen. For the first control you'll have to orient based on the parent since there are no other targets. This table shows you some of the attributes you can add to each control for relative positioning.

Layout Attribute	Description
layout_alignParentTop	Places the control at the top of the parent
layout_alignParentBottom	Places the control at the bottom of the parent
layout_alignParentLeft	Places the control at the left edge of the parent
layout_alignParentRight	Places the control at the right edge of the parent
layout_centerHorizontal	Centers the control horizontally within the parent
layout_centerVertical	Centers the control vertically within the parent
layout_above	Places the control above a specific control
layout_below	Places the control below a specific control
layout_toLeftOf	Places the control to the left of a specific control
layout_toRightOf	Places the control to the right of a specific control

Notice that some attributes will locate a child control relative to a parent container such as a layout, while others locate relative to a specific named control. See the Android documentation of the **RelativeLayout.LayoutParams** for a complete list of attributes.

You can use combinations of attributes that make sense (such as "layout_above" and "layout_toLeftOf") but adding attributes that have the opposite effect ("layout_above" and "layout_below") is not a good idea.

It's time for an example! Let's start by putting our first **Button** at the top of the screen, centered horizontally, by setting the "layout_alignParentTop" and "layout_centerHorizontally" attributes to **true**.

```
<Button
    android:id="@+id/button1"
    android:layout_width="wrap_content"
    android:layout_height="wrap_content"
    android:layout_alignParentTop="true"
    android:layout_centerHorizontal="true"
    android:text="Button1" />
```

Next we'll add two more buttons, one "down" and "to the left" of the first button, and the other "down" and to the right of the first button. Notice that we set the relative attribute value equal to the target control's ID.

```
<Button
    android:id="@+id/button2"
    android:layout_width="wrap_content"
    android:layout_height="wrap_content"
    android:layout_toLeftOf="@+id/button1"
    android:layout_below="@+id/button1"
    android:text="Button2" />

<Button
    android:id="@+id/button3"
    android:layout_width="wrap_content"
    android:layout_height="wrap_content"
    android:layout_toRightOf="@+id/button1"
    android:layout_below="@+id/button1"
    android:text="Button3" />
```

What's the result of all this hard work? Take a look!

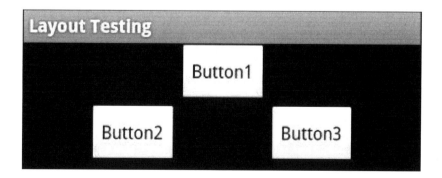

The **RelativeLayout** is more flexible than the **LinearLayout** when placing controls in custom patterns on the screen.

FrameLayout

Another, less common layout is the **FrameLayout**. This layout can only show items in one location! If your **FrameLayout** itself is located in a certain area on the screen, this can be an easy way to display a single control in that exact spot. Here's what this layout looks like in XML:

```
<FrameLayout xmlns:android="http://schemas.android.com/apk/res/android"
        android:id="@+id/FrameLayout1"
        android:layout_width="fill_parent"
        android:layout_height="fill_parent" >
    </FrameLayout>
```

If you add more than one control to this layout, the controls will be placed overlapping one another on the screen. You might be wondering when you would ever want two controls to sit on top of each other. This is useful in cases when you want to overlay an image on top of a button, or when you want to show one of a few possible controls in one place on the screen. Let's say you have three buttons, but only want to show the most relevant button to the user. You can place all three buttons in the same place using the **FrameLayout**, and then make only one button visible at a time in your program.

TableLayout

A **TableLayout** allows you to arrange your controls in rows and columns on the screen. The rows are defined in the XML, and the columns are determined by Android as controls are added to the row. Here is the code to create a **TableLayout** in XML:

```
<TableLayout xmlns:android="http://schemas.android.com/apk/res/android"
        android:id="@+id/TableLayout1"
        android:layout_width="fill_parent"
        android:layout_height="fill_parent">

        <TableRow ...>  <!-- first row of controls (see below) -->
        <TableRow ...>  <!-- second row of controls (see below) -->
    </TableLayout>
```

This XML element starts just like the rest of the layout controls. However, with a **TableLayout**, you will need to create a child <TableRow> for each row to hold your controls. Any controls you want to place in this row will appear in inside a <TableRow> element. You cannot add controls directly to a <TableLayout> element outside of a <TableRow>. Each <TableRow> element itself has an id, layout_width, and layout_height attribute.

Below we have added three buttons to a single row:

```
<TableRow
    android:id="@+id/tableRow1"
    android:layout_width="wrap_content"
    android:layout_height="wrap_content" >

    <Button
        android:id="@+id/button1"
        android:layout_width="wrap_content"
        android:layout_height="wrap_content"
        android:text="Button1" />
    <Button
        android:id="@+id/button2"
        android:layout_width="wrap_content"
        android:layout_height="wrap_content"
        android:text="Button2" />
    <Button
        android:id="@+id/button3"
        android:layout_width="wrap_content"
        android:layout_height="wrap_content"
        android:text="Button3" />
</TableRow>
```

You can have as many table rows as you can fit on the screen in your application. Each additional row has its own <TableRow> element.

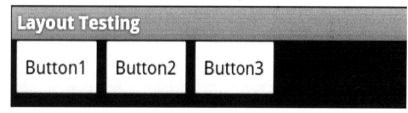

Let's add another row containing a <TextView> and a <Button>:

```
<TableRow
    android:id="@+id/tableRow2"
    android:layout_width="wrap_content"
    android:layout_height="wrap_content" >

    <TextView
        android:id="@+id/textview1"
        android:layout_width="wrap_content"
        android:layout_height="wrap_content"
        android:text="Text Control" />
```

```
    <Button
        android:id="@+id/button3"
        android:layout_width="wrap_content"
        android:layout_height="wrap_content"
        android:text="Button" />
</TableRow>
```

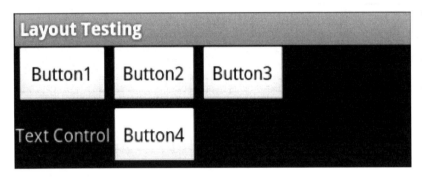

The table's columns will become as large as the largest control in that column. As you add controls to the <TableRow>, Android will place them in columns from left-to-right on the screen.

You can place a control in a specific column with the "layout_column" attribute. The value represents the zero-based column from the left. So this example will place a control in the third column.

```
android:layout_column="2"
```

This attribute will only work if at least one of the table rows contains the required number of columns. If you currently only have 1 or 2 columns and try to specify the third column, the control will not appear at all!

In the example to the right, we used the "layout_column" attribute to place "Button4" in the third column.

You can also make a control span more than one column in the row by adding the "layout_span" attribute containing the number of columns to span.

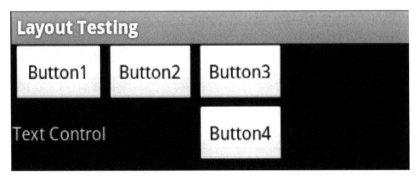

```
android:layout_span="2"
```

This is especially useful when you need to have controls with different widths. In the image to the right, we added the "layout_span" attribute to our <TextView> to span two columns with additional text.

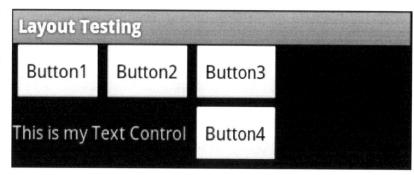

We have only scratched the surface of the different layouts available and the common attributes for each layout. You can use attributes to set the margin around controls and do other types of fine-tuning.

Multiple Layouts

Sharp readers may remember from our first-semester Java course that you could create very detailed, flexible Swing screen arrangements by nesting child **JPanels** inside the parent. Each child panel could have a different type of layout. Android works exactly the same way! For example, if you wanted to have a top area with relative positioning and a bottom area with a table layout, you would first create a top-level **LinearLayout** with vertical orientation. Then add a child **RelativeLayout** and a child **TableLayout** inside. Within each of the child layouts you'd then add the controls for that specific area.

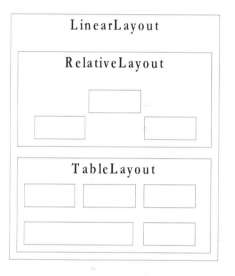

To demonstrate multiple layouts, we have combined our **RelativeLayout** and **TableLayout** examples within a vertical **LinearLayout** as described above. The resulting arrangement would be very difficult to create with a single layout.

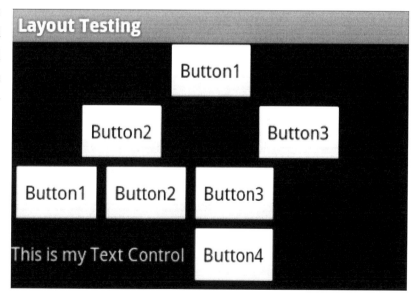

Lesson Four: Views and TextViews

There is one base class at the root of all Android UI widgets: the **View**. In this lesson we'll describe some common properties of all **Views**, and then examine the **TextView** (or label) in more detail.

Views

In Android, every control or widget that appears on the screen is based on an abstract class called a **View**. The **Button** we have been using, for instance, has this class hierarchy:

java.lang.Object ← android.view.View ← android.widget.TextView ← android.widget.Button

That's right; a **Button** is actually a specialized form of **TextView**, which itself inherits directly from **View**.

A **View** is similar to a Java Swing **JComponent** object because it provides common properties and methods for all visible objects, and allows itself to be positioned on the screen by a layout. The **View** can be found in the **android.view** package. If you think about all of the common tasks that a UI widget needs to handle, you won't be surprised to find that the **View** base class handles these chores:

- Getting and setting common properties such as visibility, ID, etc.
- Calculating widget size based on the layout and any child views
- Handling event callbacks for user activity such as clicks or long-clicks
- Handling focus changes, security, and more!

Properties of a particular **View** or control can be set in your layout XML file if you know them in advance. You can also get or set some properties at runtime by getting a reference to the control using **findViewById()** and then calling the corresponding getter or setter method.

Here are some common properties you can set on all **View**-based controls in the XML layout.

XML Attribute	Description
android:id	Sets the unique ID for this View
android:layout_width	"wrap_content" or "fill_parent"
android:layout_height	"wrap_content" or "fill_parent"
android:layout_marginBottom	Sets the bottom margin, in pixels ("10px"), dp ("10dp"), or sp ("10sp")
android:layout_marginLeft	Sets the left margin, in pixels ("10px"), dp ("10dp"), or sp ("10sp")
android:layout_marginRight	Sets the right margin, in pixels ("10px"), dp ("10dp"), or sp ("10sp")
android:layout_marginTop	Sets the top margin, in pixels ("10px"), dp ("10dp"), or sp ("10sp")
android:visibility	See below

The "android:visibility" attribute has three possible values: "visible", "invisible", and "gone". The corresponding values in Java code are **View.VISIBLE**, **View.INVISIBLE**, and **View.GONE**. A control that is "visible" can be seen on the screen normally. An "invisible" control cannot be seen, but still takes up space as if it was still present in the layout. A control marked as "gone" cannot be seen and also does not take up any space when the layout is arranging controls.

The first three attributes ("android:id", "android:layout_width", and "android:layout_height") are required for all **Views** and layouts in the layout XML. You have seen these present on all layout, <TextView> and <Button> examples we've given so far.

There are many other specialized **View** properties which you can find in the online Android reference documentation. Each subclass of **View** such as **TextView** can add its own attributes that make sense for that subclass. In fact, let's take a closer look at the **TextView** now!

TextView

A **TextView** control is the common way to display text on an Android screen. This control is very much like the **JLabel** control in a Java Swing program. You have already seen several examples of a **TextView** in XML:

```
<TextView
    android:id="@+id/textView1"
    android:layout_width="wrap_content"
    android:layout_height="wrap_content"
    android:text="This is my TextView control." />
```

Notice we always set the required id, layout_width, and layout_height properties for the base **View**. The **TextView** defines many additional attributes; the most common are described below.

TextView XML Attribute	Description
android:lines	Sets the number of rows or lines that the **TextView** control will cover
android:maxLength	Sets the maximum number of characters that may be entered in the control
android:text	Sets the actual text contents of the control
android:textColor	Sets the RGB color of the text with optional "alpha" transparency in front. The Alpha, Red, Green, and Blue components are specified in hexadecimal values between 00 and FF. So "#FFFF00" is a yellow color (full Red and Green), while "#800000FF" is a partially transparent blue.
android:textSize	Sets the size in pixels, dp, or sp (sp recommended, e.g. "15sp")
android:textStyle	Styles text as "bold", "italic", or "bold|italic" for both at once.
android:typeface	Sets the font such as "sans", "serif", or "monospace".

The most important attribute, of course, is the "android:text" attribute which contains the actual text to display! For fun we've built an example <TextView> that uses all of these special properties:

```
<TextView
     android:id="@+id/textview1"
     android:layout_width="wrap_content"
     android:layout_height="wrap_content"
     android:lines="2"
     android:maxLength="100"
     android:textColor="#FFFF00"
     android:textSize="30sp"
     android:textStyle="bold|italic"
     android:typeface="serif"
     android:text="This is my really long Text Control" />
```

Here is the result! We have a two-line text view that is yellow in color with bold and italic styles, a "serif" font, and 30 "sp" in size. Notice we used "sp" for text sizing in order to support the user's text size preferences.

Layout Testing

This is my really long Text Control

A "sans" font is your basic, plain lettering style. The "serif" font as shown above is a bit fancier. A "monospace" font is a fixed-width font where every letter or symbol takes up the same width on the screen. This type is best when you are trying to line up columns of text or numbers on the screen.

It's possible to set some combinations of text attributes that confuse the Graphic Layout editor to the point where nothing at all shows up in the graphic preview. If that happens, double-check your XML and try running the program in the emulator to see the actual results. You may not have done anything wrong at all, you just ran into a limitation of the Graphical Layout editor!

When looking at your XML layout, you may notice Eclipse putting some yellow warning icons next to your "android:text" attribute. Eclipse is helpfully trying to point out that you have hard-coded text into a control and therefore the application cannot be easily ported to another language. We'll talk about internationalization more in a later chapter, so you can ignore these warnings or disable them as described in Chapter Four, Lesson Three.

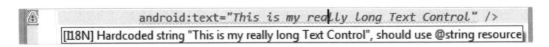

The **TextView** Java object also has many different methods that can be used to set and retrieve properties and information from the control. When accessing controls from an Android program, you will first need to get a reference to the control in your code. We do this by using the **findViewById**() method. If the control "android:id" was set in the XML layout as "@+id/myText" like this:

```
android:id="@+id/myText"
```

…then in your Java code you can reference the id with the syntax "R.id.myText".

```
TextView tv = (TextView)findViewById(R.id.myText);
```

Here, we declare a reference to a **TextView** control and then use the **findViewById**() method to find the **View**. Because we know it's actually a **TextView**, we cast the result to that class type. Now you can call methods on the **TextView** object.

The most common methods to use for a **TextView** are the **getText**() and **setText**() methods, which can be used to get and set the visible text at runtime.

```
tv.setText("I have changed my text!");  // update the display text
String text = tv.getText().toString();  // retrieve the display text
```

Notice that the return value from **getText**() is not a **String**, so we need to call **toString**() to convert it before storing in a **String** variable. There are many other attributes that you can use to customize the look of the **TextView** control. A full listing of all properties can be found in the online Android documentation.

Activity: Simple Whack-A-Mole

In this activity you will use a group of buttons and a label to create a very simple version of the classic Whack-A-Mole game.

Your activity requirements and instructions are found in the "Chapter05_Activity.pdf" document located in your "TeenCoder/Android Programming/Activity Docs" folder. You can access this document through your Student Menu or by directly clicking on it from Windows Explorer (Windows) or Finder (Mac OS).

Complete this activity now and ensure your program meets the requirements before continuing!

Chapter Six: Android User Input Controls

In the last chapter, we laid the groundwork for the basic Android screen. Now you are going to learn about some more common UI controls that let you get different kinds of input from the user. We'll also discuss design approaches for portrait and landscape modes and international support. All of the controls in this chapter belong to the **android.widget** package, so don't forget to import **android.widget.*** at the top of your Java code when using these controls.

Lesson One: Text Input and Option Controls

In this lesson, we are going to explore the **EditText**, **RadioButton**, and **CheckBox** controls. These controls are very similar to their Java Swing equivalents, **JTextField**, **JRadioButton**, and **JCheckBox**, so you should already be familiar with the basic ideas behind each control. Each of the Android controls is a type of **View**, so has at least the familiar three XML attributes for ID, width, and height.

EditText

The **EditText** control will allow the user to enter text into an Android application. The simplest of **EditText** controls can be created in XML like this:

```
<EditText
    android:id="@+id/MyEditText"
    android:layout_width="match_parent"
    android:layout_height="wrap_content"
    android:inputType="text">
</EditText>
```

Notice that we do not have a "text" attribute for this control, since we expect the user to enter the text. The **EditText** will appear as an empty white rectangle on the screen, along with a blue underline, orange rectangle, or other border depending on your theme.

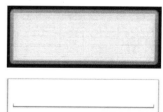

There are many input types for this control as set by the "android:inputType" attribute. The table below shows the most commonly used types and their purposes.

android:inputType	Description
text	Used when entering plain text.
phone	Used when entering a phone number.
number	Used when expecting numeric input.
date	Used when expecting date input.
time	Used when time input is needed.
textPassword	Hides the characters as they are typed with asterisks.
textEmailAddress	Allows the use of @ email addresses.
textMultiLine	Allows for multiple lines of input.

It's important to set the right kind of input type to match the user's expected input. The input type will control the type of keyboard the user will be shown when the control is active on the screen. If you are expecting your user to enter a number, you don't want to show them the letter keyboard. And if you expect them to enter an email address, you want to make sure that the "@" sign is visible on the keyboard. These customizations may seem simple, but when you are entering data on a small device, it helps if the keys you need are on the first keyboard that appears!

You can use the input type to perform some special features such as password-hiding. In this example we have set **android:inputType="textPassword"**, and then Android will hide the characters as the user types them.

When you create a multiple-line **EditText** control with **android:inputType="textMultiLine"**, your control will automatically expand to cover more lines if the user enters more text than can fit in the available width. You can also choose to make the **EditText** control large to start with. For instance you might use a layout height of "fill_parent" to make the control as tall as possible.

```
android:layout_height="fill_parent"
```

With a very tall box, the user's text will be centered vertically by default.

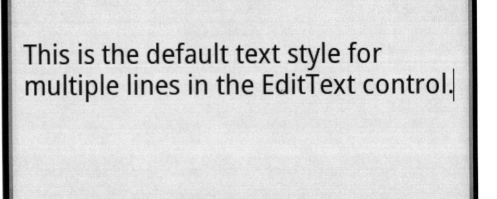

If you'd rather have the user's text start at the top-left of the control, change the control's *gravity* to "top":

```
android:gravity="top"
```

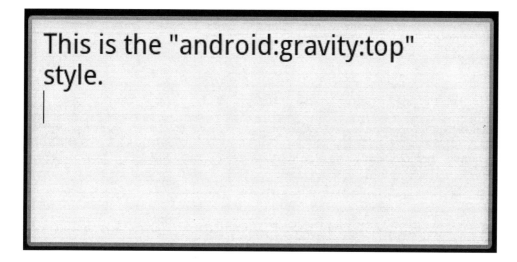

Just like the **TextView** control, the **EditText** control also has many different methods that can be used to set and retrieve properties and information from the control. Once again, we first need to get a reference to the control in our code using the **findViewById()** method:

```
EditText et = (EditText)findViewById(R.id.MyEditText);
```

The most common of the **EditText** methods is the **getText()** method, which can be used to retrieve the text from the control when the user has finished entering data.

```
String myText = et.getText().toString();
```

Just like the **TextView** control, you must use the **toString()** method on the object returned by **getText()** to receive a **String** containing the actual text.

To learn about other attributes and methods that you can use to customize the look of the **EditText** control, please see the online Android documentation. A full listing of all properties and methods can be found at http://developer.android.com/reference/android/widget/EditText.html or by searching online for "Android EditText".

RadioButton

The **RadioButton** control represents one option in a group. This control will display some text and a circle. If the circle has a dot in it, it is selected. If the circle is empty, the radio button is not selected. A **RadioButton** can be created with the following XML code:

```
<RadioButton
    android:id="@+id/rbRed"
    android:layout_width="wrap_content"
    android:layout_height="wrap_content"
    android:text="Red" />
```

You control the text next to the circle with the "android:text" attribute.

RadioButtons are typically found in groups, where only one **RadioButton** can be chosen at any one time. You can define a group of buttons that work together with the <RadioGroup> element in the XML layout.

```
<RadioGroup
    android:id="@+id/rgColors"
    android:layout_width="wrap_content"
    android:layout_height="wrap_content" >

    <RadioButton
        android:id="@+id/rbRed"
        android:layout_width="wrap_content"
        android:layout_height="wrap_content"
        android:text="Red" />

    <RadioButton
        android:id="@+id/rbBlue"
        android:layout_width="wrap_content"
        android:layout_height="wrap_content"
        android:text="Blue" />
</RadioGroup>
```

The image on the right is the result of the <RadioButton> and <RadioGroup> XML layout elements shown above. You can see that the user has selected the "Red" radio button control. If the user were to choose "Blue", the dot would disappear from the "Red" choice and appear in the "Blue" circle.

We don't usually listen for any actions on a **RadioButton** control, although you could get a callback every time an option was changed. Instead, it's convenient to wait for the user to hit some other button and then query the **RadioButton** status in the **onClick()** event handler. To check the status of a **RadioButton**, we can use the **isChecked()** method. This method will return **true** if the control is selected or **false** otherwise.

```
RadioButton rb = (RadioButton)findViewById(R.id.rbRed);
if (rb.isChecked())
{
    // do something when the Red radio button is selected
}
```

We can also programmatically set the current status of the button with the **setChecked()** method, like this:

```
rb.setChecked(true); // select the red radio button
```

When you set one radio button as checked or selected in a group, the rest of the buttons in that group will be automatically de-selected.

CheckBox

The **CheckBox** control will allow the user to select an option. The Android **CheckBox** will display some text and a white square. If the square contains a checkmark, it is selected. If the square is empty, the button is not selected. A **CheckBox** can be created with the following XML code:

```
<CheckBox
    android:id="@+id/cbDog"
    android:layout_width="wrap_content"
    android:layout_height="wrap_content"
    android:text="Dogs" />

<CheckBox
    android:id="@+id/cbCats"
    android:layout_width="wrap_content"
    android:layout_height="wrap_content"
    android:text="Cats" />
```

A **CheckBox** control differs from a **RadioButton** in that it does not have to occur in groups. If there is more than one **CheckBox** present, you can select more than one at a time. This is a great choice if your user will need to select multiple options independently.

The image on the right is the result of the <CheckBox> XML elements listed above. You can see that the user has selected both the "Dogs" and "Cats" options on the screen.

Just like the **RadioButton**, it is not typical to capture the button clicks on a **CheckBox** control itself. Instead, we just query the status of the control once the user has clicked some other button indicating they are done with their selections.

Checking the status of a **CheckBox** control is done with exactly the same methods as the **RadioButton**:

```
CheckBox cb = (CheckBox)findViewById(R.id.cbDog);
if (cb.isChecked())
{
    // do something when the Dog checkbox is selected
}
```

You can programmatically set the current status of the button with the **setChecked()** method:

```
cb.setChecked(true); // select the dogs checkbox
```

Lesson Two: List Controls

You are probably familiar with different "list" controls used by applications on your personal computer. In Android, there are two main list views: the **ListView** and the **Spinner**. We'll discuss the **ListView** now and the **Spinner** in the next lesson.

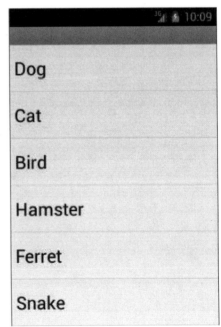

The **ListView** control is used to display a long list of items on the screen. Since the Android screens are typically small and a list box can contain many items, there is actually a special **Activity** class to handle **ListViews**. The **ListActivity** is used to create a screen that holds nothing but a **ListView** control!

The **ListActivity** class already includes all of the layout controls that are needed on the screen. This means that you will not need to create an XML layout file for this activity, but we will need to change the code inside the **onCreate()** method to put data into the list.

To begin, create a new Java class and make sure it extends the **ListActivity** class in the **android.app** package. We'll call our example class **MyPetActivity**. You will, of course, need to override the **onCreate()** method to configure your list.

```
import android.app.ListActivity;


public class MyPetActivity extends ListActivity
{
    public void onCreate(Bundle savedInstanceState)
    {
        super.onCreate(savedInstanceState);
        // list-creation code goes here!
    }
}
```

Since we are not using an XML layout, we do *not* need to call **setContentView()**. Instead you need to write code that will populate the list with the items you want displayed to the user.

Adding Items to a List

The list of items is usually found in a data array. You should remember how to create arrays from our first-semester Java programming course. For this discussion, let's say we have an array of **Strings** like this:

```
String[] pets = {"Dog", "Cat", "Bird", "Hamster", "Ferret", "Snake"};
```

You unfortunately cannot just take an array and directly set the list contents. Instead, you need to use an **android.widget.ArrayAdapter** to place our array into the **ListView** inside the **ListActivity**. There are a number of adapters that can move data from some source into the list, but **ArrayAdapter** is the easiest. We can create an **ArrayAdapter** for our data in the **onCreate()** method like this:

```
ArrayAdapter<String> myAdapter = new ArrayAdapter<String> (this,
                    android.R.layout.simple_list_item_1, pets);
```

This code is a bit complicated, so let's walk through it piece by piece. First, we tell the compiler that we are creating an **ArrayAdapter** for the **String** data type by using the modifier "<String>" after the **ArrayAdapter** class name. We then create a **new ArrayAdapter<String>** and pass in a few important parameters.

The first parameter is a **Context** value for the array. In our case we are using the context "**this**", which is just a reference to the current **Activity**. Next, we pass in a pre-defined list layout called "android.R.layout.simple_list_item_1". The "simple_list_item_1" layout is a popular layout that will display a basic list of plain text items. The final parameter into our **ArrayAdapter** is the array that we will be using to populate our list. In our case, we pass in our **pets** array.

Now we need to tell our **ListActivity** to use the **ArrayAdapter** to populate the list on the screen. We will do this with the **setListAdapter()** method, like this:

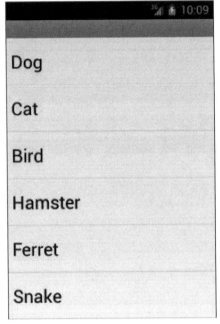

```
setListAdapter(myAdapter);
```

When we start the activity, we see our list of pets appear on the screen!

Retrieving User's Selection from a ListActivity

Once you have displayed the list to the user and they have made their selection, how do you figure out which item was chosen? To determine what item was clicked, you will need to override a method in the **ListActivity** class called **onListItemClick()**. This function will be called when the user selects an item.

```
protected void onListItemClick(ListView l, View v, int position, long id)
```

This method has several parameters which will help you to determine which item was clicked in the list. The first parameter is a **ListView** control, which represents the actual **ListView** control where the click occurred. The second parameter is a **View** class, which represents the individual **View** control that was clicked within the **ListView**. This parameter is only used if you are embedding other **Views** inside of your main **ListView** control. In our simple **ListActivity**, the **View** will be a **TextView** control that contains the text of the item in the list. The third parameter is the zero-based **position** of the view in the list.

The final parameter is an **id** which will give you the row number for the item that was clicked. In our simple **ListActivity**, the **id** and **position** values are the same. If you have a more complicated list with rows and columns, the combination of these two values would allow you to pinpoint the exact item that was clicked.

The parameters that you will use to determine which item was clicked depend on the type of data and the complexity of your **ListActivity** screen. In our simple case, we only really need the **position** value, which will tell us the index value of the item that was selected. We can then use this zero-based index value to pull the corresponding text out of our **pets** array.

```
protected void onListItemClick(ListView l, View v, int position, long id)
{
        String selection = pets[position];
```

Sharp readers will be wondering how this **onListItemClick**() function can access a `pets` array declared locally within the **onCreate**() method. That's a problem! You will need to make sure your data array is declared at the class level outside of any function so it can be accessed by all functions in the class.

Now that you have the user's selection, there are two remaining tasks. First you need to do something useful with the value such as communicate the result back to the parent activity. Then you need to close the **ListActivity** to return to the main screen.

Returning Data and Closing the ListActivity

Remember that a child activity created by a parent with **startActivityForResult**() can communicate data back to the parent with an **Intent**. Let's pull all of our code together into a complete **onListItemClick**() function that will get the selected item, create an **Intent**, and store the value as an extra named "pet" in the **Intent**.

```
protected void onListItemClick(ListView l, View v, int position, long id)
{
    String selection = pets[position];    // get selected value by position

    Intent resultIntent = new Intent();   // create new Intent to hold info
    resultIntent.putExtra("pet", selection);  // store result info in Intent
    setResult(RESULT_OK,resultIntent);     // send Intent back to Main

    finish();  // close the ListActivity
}
```

Once we have successfully called **setResult**() with our data-packed **Intent**, we call **finish**() to gracefully close the **ListActivity** and return control to th`e parent activity.

Don't forget that all of your application's activities should be listed in your "AndroidManifest.xml" file.

```
<activity android:name=".MyPetActivity"></activity>
```

Finally, you're all set! You can run an application and create the **MyPetActivity** from the **Main** activity with **startActivityForResult**(). Your **MyPetActivity** will capture the user's selection in **onListItemClick**() and create an **Intent** to send back to **Main** with the **setResult**() call. **MyPetActivity** then closes itself with **finish**() to move back to the parent activity screen.

Lesson Three: Spinners and Seek Bars

The **ListView** control is great when you want to create a screen that contains nothing but a list of items. But what if you want to display a list in addition to other controls on the screen? For this, you need the more compact **Spinner** control. A **Spinner** is very similar to the **JComboBox** control in a Java Swing application. It will show only one item at a time on the screen. When the user clicks on the item, it will expand out into a full list of items. When the user selects an item, the list shrinks back down to display only that item. To the right we have shown a **Spinner** in between a **TextView** and a **Button** control. The current selection in the **Spinner** is "Dog".

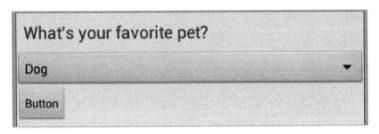

When you click on the **Spinner** control, a pop-up box will display a title and a list of options for you to select. The pop-up box will automatically close after your selection, and your new choice will be shown in the collapsed form.

The **Spinner** does not have its own **Activity** class, so we will need to create the <Spinner> element in the XML layout.

```
<Spinner
        android:id="@+id/MySpinner"
        android:layout_width="match_parent"
        android:layout_height="wrap_content"
        android:prompt="@string/spinner_prompt" />
```

The interesting new optional attribute for the **Spinner** is "android:prompt". This sets the text that will appear at the top of the list when the user expands the **Spinner** into a list of items. This value is special because it must be a string value in the "strings.xml" resource file. The "@string/spinner_prompt" value tells the compiler that we are using a value in the "string.xml" resource called "spinner_prompt". To add this string, find your "strings.xml" file in the "/res/values" directory in your project, and double-click on the file to open in the XML editor. Then add the following line before the ending </resources> tag:

```
<string name="spinner_prompt">Choose your favorite pet</string>
```

Just like the **ListView**, the **Spinner** will use an array of data that we will set using an **ArrayAdapter** class. We will create this adapter just like we did for the **ListView**. Again, the onCreate() method for the **Activity** is a handy place to initialize our **Spinner** data.

```
ArrayAdapter<String> myAdapter = new ArrayAdapter<String> (this,
                android.R.layout.simple_spinner_item, pets);
```

Notice that we used a layout value of "android.R.layout.simple_spinner_item". This is another pre-defined layout that is part of the Android library. This will give you a standard drop-down look for the basic **Spinner**. When the user clicks on the drop-down, a full list of items will appear on the screen.

Now that we have our adapter, we need to get a reference to the **Spinner** control in our code and call **setAdapter**() to add the **ArrayAdapter** data.

```
Spinner spn = (Spinner)findViewById(R.id.MySpinner);
spn.setAdapter(myAdapter);
```

By default our spinner control will appear with the first data item selected. When the user clicks on the control, the full list of items is displayed, headed by the prompt string we added to our string resource XML file.

There are two different looks for the **Spinner** control. The default look displays a full list view when the control is clicked.

You could choose to display a list of radio buttons instead. To do this, call an additional method on the **ArrayAdapter** class called **setDropDownViewResource**(), like this:

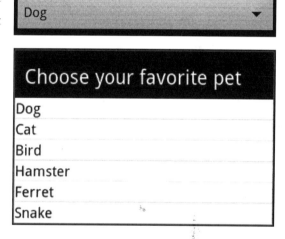

```
myAdapter.setDropDownViewResource(android.R.layout.simple_spinner_dropdown_item);
```

Now the drop-down list will contain radio buttons to show the user's selection!

You'll commonly retrieve the value the user has selected when something else happens on the screen. Perhaps the user has clicked a "Save" button, or closed the activity, or triggered some other event that tells you it's time to grab the current **Spinner** selection.

To get the **Spinner** selection, you first need to get a reference to the **Spinner** control using **findViewById()**. Then get the integer index of the selected position by calling **getSelectedItemPosition()** on the **Spinner** object. Finally, using that index, you can call the **Spinner.getItemAtPosition()** method and then **toString()** on the returned object to get the selected text value.

```
Spinner spn = (Spinner)findViewById(R.id.MySpinner);
int pos = spn.getSelectedItemPosition();
String strSelected = spn.getItemAtPosition(pos).toString();
```

If you want to programmatically set the **Spinner's** current selection you can call the **setSelection()** method and pass in the zero-based index of the item to select.

```
spn.setSelection(3);  // select the 4th item in the list (e.g. Hamster)
```

Seek Bars

The last user input control we'll discuss is the **SeekBar**, which lets the user select a numeric value on a sliding scale. This is a great control for setting numeric preferences. You may want to use this control to let the user pick a game duration, font size, power level, or any other integer value needed by your application.

The look and feel of the **SeekBar** is determined by the overall theme you select in your "AndroidManifest.xml" file. When using the default "@style/AppTheme" we get a thin blue line and circle showing the value selected between 0 and the maximum.

```
android:theme="@style/AppTheme"
```

In this example we've used a **TextView** label with "Duration of Game:" to describe the input and a **SeekBar** control to manage the numeric value.

Switching over to the "@android:style/Theme.Light" theme we use for many examples in this course gives us a solid yellow bar with gray slider.

110

To use a **SeekBar** control, add the following element to your XML layout:

```
<SeekBar
    android:id="@+id/seekBar1"
    android:layout_width="match_parent"
    android:layout_height="wrap_content"
    android:progress="10"
    android:max="30" />
```

The "android:progress" attribute will set the default value for the seek bar slider. The attribute "android:max" defines the range for the bar. The far left side of the bar starts at zero and the "max" value represents the far right side. As the user drags the seek bar control from left to right, the numeric value will increase from 0 up to your max value.

To get and set the current value of the **SeekBar** control, use **findViewById()** to get a reference to the control and then call **getProgress()** or **setProgress()** to get and set the integer value. When the user has finished adjusting the control you can read the value with **getProgress()** to make use of it in your application.

```
SeekBar sb = (SeekBar)findViewById(R.id.seekBar1);
int seekValue = sb.getProgress(); // get the current numeric value
```

Later we'll describe how to save user settings so you can re-load them the next time the activity is started. That way you can use **setProgress()** on startup with the user's previous value instead of resetting the slider to the default value each time.

```
SeekBar sb = (SeekBar)findViewById(R.id.seekBar1);
sb.setProgress(20);                 // set numeric value to 20
```

This has been a whirlwind tour of some common Android UI widgets. We can't cover every possible control in this textbook; in fact, you could write an entire book about Android user interface design. If you want to use a control we don't discuss here, you can refer to the online Android documentation for a list of available controls, methods, and attributes.

Lesson Four: Handling Different Devices and Languages

Now that we've studied some of the many different controls that are available for Android programs, we should take a look at some of the pitfalls of device design.

Targeting Multiple Devices

When you design a screen in Android, you should always keep in mind that this screen could be shown on many types of devices. These devices might differ in screen size, pixel density, or they could even be running different Android versions. As a programmer, you should be aware of these possibilities and you should design your screens appropriately.

One of the most important considerations when you are displaying images is to make sure you add images for several possible device resolutions. This will enable the Android system to choose the best possible image for the user's device. If you only have one image, it could appear fuzzy and distorted as Android attempts to make the image fit different device resolutions.

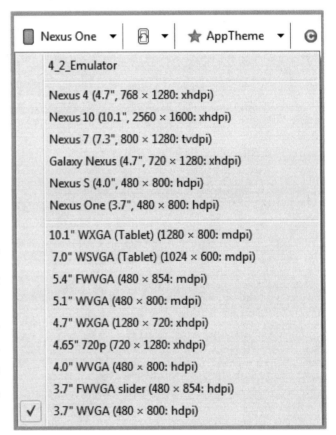

In addition, you should test your application on different screen formats. You can do this in the Eclipse Graphical Layout editor. Click on the "Graphical Layout" tab and take a look at the top of the screen. You should see a drop-down list on the left side of the toolbar that will allow you to quickly switch between different standard device displays. As you switch between these different screen sizes and resolutions, you can view and troubleshoot the appearance of your screen. This will give you some idea if your application will look the same on all devices.

You can also choose different screen "skins" for your emulator. Pull up your Android Virtual Device (AVD) Manager and "Edit" your existing AVD (or you can create a brand new emulator target).

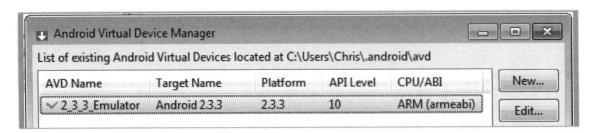

The "Device" section of the target configuration contains a selection of built-in device types. As you select

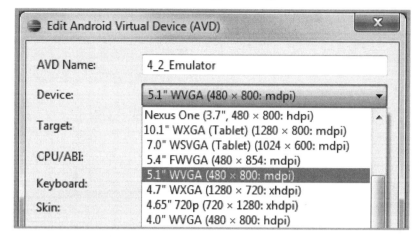

different built-in devices, some of your hardware properties will also change.

Most importantly, some device profiles have a different LCD or pixel density. Once you have chosen a new device, you can run your application in the emulator and experience the different screens first-hand (or as close as you can get without the actual hardware).

Adjusting Views for Landscape

Almost all Android devices will allow the user to change from a portrait view on their device to a landscape view just by turning the device. As you might guess, this can drastically change how your design looks on the screen. A properly designed screen will work well in either portrait or landscape mode.

How can you test this functionality in the emulator? Don't try to turn your monitor! You can emulate device rotation in Windows or Mac OS by hitting the "Control" key and the "F11" key at the same time. To switch

back to portrait mode, hit the same key combination again. The screen shots show portrait mode (left) and landscape mode (right).

The Android system will automatically try to re-arrange all of your screen elements in order to show the screen in landscape mode. Depending on the number and placement of controls on the screen, your design may look fine or may look terrible in landscape mode. So how do you fix a bad landscape screen? You could spend a lot of time re-designing all of your elements so that it looks great in both modes, but that can be a very frustrating and time-consuming process.

A better idea is to create a different layout file for the landscape mode! In fact, this is the accepted method for dealing with portrait and landscape screens in Android. To create a new layout, first create a new directory under the "res" folder called "layout-land".

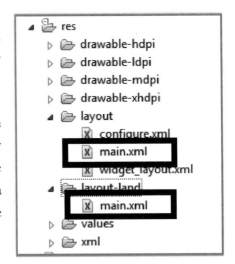

Right-click on the "res" folder and then choose "New → Folder" from the menu. Name your new folder "layout-land". Then you can copy your XML screen layout file(s) from the "layout" directory to the "layout-land" directory. Now you have a starting point for building a dedicated landscape mode layout. Make sure that the name of the layout XML file is the same in both of the layout directories.

To make your new landscape layout look good, you may have to move or re-size controls so that the screen is usable in this format. You can even pick completely different layout arrangements if you like.

When you are finished with your new design, how will you tell Android which layout file to use? You don't have to do anything! Android will know if the user has rotated their device. If they are currently looking at a landscape view of their device, the operating system will automatically look for a landscape layout in the "layout-land" directory. If one exists for the current screen, Android will load this layout automatically.

Creating a separate layout for your screens may seem like a lot of extra work, but it's definitely worth it! Your users will appreciate a seamless and well-designed screen no matter what viewing mode they are using.

Application Internationalization

The Google Play market is a global store. Your application could be downloaded by English-speakers or users in other countries that speak other languages. To reach the most users, your application should keep resources like text and audio in resource files dedicated to each language you want to support. When your application is run, Android will choose the correct resource based on the user's configured location.

The most commonly localized resources are the strings displayed in your application. If you want these strings to appear in different languages for different locations, you will need to use string resources instead of hard-coded strings in your program. These string resources are located in the "strings.xml" file in your project's "res/values" directory. You will need to create a different "strings.xml" file for each country that your application will support. Each new location should have its own "values" directory.

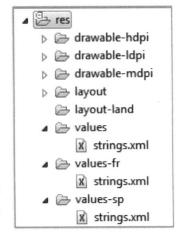

For example, to support French and Spanish languages, you would include a "values-fr" and "values-sp" directory in your project. Each directory would have its own "strings.xml" file containing text for that specific language.

The two-letter abbreviation for each language is part of a well-defined standard called "ISO 639-1". You can also append a region code if desired by adding a dash, the lowercase "r", and then the region code. The region code is also a two-character standard defined by "ISO-3166-1-alpha-2". Consider these examples:

- "fr" – French language, not specific to any region
- "fr-rFR" – French language, specific to France
- "fr-rCA" – French language, specific to Canada

Tables of values for each of these standards can easily be found by searching online for the ISO names.

So what goes into the "strings.xml" file? Each string that you want to include in your program would have its own <string> element, like this:

```
<string name="string_name">string value</string>
```

The name of your string will be used in your program when you need to access that string value. The element value is the actual text in the string. So, if we wanted to display a greeting to the user in three languages, we would start with English in our default "strings.xml".

```
<string name="greeting">Hello!</string>
```

In our French "strings.xml" file, we would keep the same name but change the value to match that language.

```
<string name="greeting">Bonjour!</string>
```

Similarly, the Spanish "strings.xml" would contain the Spanish greeting.

```
<string name="greeting">Hola!</string>
```

Now in an XML layout file, we can refer to this value using the key name instead of hard-coded text:

```
<TextView
        android:layout_width="fill_parent"
        android:layout_height="wrap_content"
        android:text="@string/greeting" />
```

The Android system will use the "greeting" value that matches the language preferences of the user's device. This is an extremely powerful feature that will allow you to write one application and make it available for many different users around the world!

Activity: Whack-A-Mole Options

In this activity, you will add an Option Setting screen to the Whack-A-Mole game.

Your activity requirements and instructions are found in the "Chapter06_Activity.pdf" document located in your "TeenCoder/Android Programming/Activity Docs" folder. You can access this document through your Student Menu or by directly clicking on it from Windows Explorer (Windows) or Finder (Mac OS).

Complete this activity now and ensure your program meets the requirements before continuing!

Chapter Seven: Android File System

So far all of our applications have launched without any way to remember what the user did previously. In this chapter we are going to study several forms of *data persistence*, or ways to save data to the Android device and then load it back again within your application.

Lesson One: Storing Preferences on a Device

There are often times when you want to store data on a more permanent basis outside of your application. We can see this need in our Whack-A-Mole program. In order to pass user changes from our settings screen into the game, we have used **Intents**. This means that every time we start the program, we have to reset our preferences all over again.

To fix this problem, we need to find ways to save data persistently. In this lesson, we'll take a look at the quickest and easiest way to store application data: *shared preferences storage*.

Every application on an Android device is given its own private "shared preferences" area in internal storage. This area can be used to store application settings and preferences, as long as the data is saved as primitive data types, like **String**, **int** and **boolean**. The data itself is stored in key/value pairs and an application can store as many key/value pairs as it needs. This data is saved permanently, even if the application is killed by the system. The Android system will only destroy shared preferences data when the application is uninstalled from the device.

So now that you know what shared preferences are, let's learn how to use them in an Android application!

The SharedPreferences Object

The first step in using an application's shared preferences is to get an instance of the **SharedPreferences** class, which is part of the **android.content** package. You should import the **android.content.*** package at the top of your code when dealing with the Android file system. **SharedPreferences** will be used to handle the saving and loading of data to and from the application's private memory. To get a reference to this class, we will use an **Activity** method called **getSharedPreferences()** like this:

```
SharedPreferences prefs = getSharedPreferences("MyPreferences", MODE_PRIVATE);
```

This method takes two parameters: the first parameter is the name of the preferences file that we are opening or creating. You can name this file anything you want, although a short, descriptive name is best. You can also have more than one shared preferences file associated with your application. This is a great way to separate different groups of application data in storage.

The second parameter is the *mode* that will be used to open the file. There are three main modes that you can use; the default mode is MODE_PRIVATE. This mode will open or create a file that will only be available to your application. No other Android application will be allowed to read or write to your preferences file. If you want to give some access to other applications, you can use the MODE_WORLD_READABLE mode, which will allow other applications to read the file, or MODE_WORLD_WRITEABLE, which will allow other applications to write to your file. If the preferences file that you specify does not exist when you use the **getSharedPreferences()** method, the Android system will create it automatically when you write out your first set of data.

Saving Preference Data

In order to save data into your application's shared preferences, you will need to get a reference to an **Editor**, which is actually defined as part of the **SharedPreferences** object. The **Editor** will help you save the data.

```
SharedPreferences.Editor ed = prefs.edit();
```

Now that you have a reference to an **Editor** for a particular group of shared preferences, you can save your application data. The editor has a series of "put" methods that store a single key/value pair. There is a "put" method for each primitive data type:

```
ed.putBoolean("isMale", true);
ed.putFloat("height", 5.5F);
ed.putInt("age", 16);
ed.putLong("weight", 24);
ed.putString("userName", "Rascal Rabbit");
```

Each of these methods has the same parameters: a **String** value for the key name and a primitive data type value. You can create as many key/value pairs as you wish for your application.

Once you have added all of your data items, you will need to *commit* the changes in order to have them actually written to the shared preferences area.

```
ed.commit();
```

Once you have called **commit()**, your data items have been saved and your information will persist even after the application is ended.

In addition to saving data into the shared preferences area, the **Editor** can be used to remove key/value pairs from storage. To remove a specific key/value pair, just call the **Editor.remove()** method with the key name:

```
ed.remove("KeyName");
```

This method will remove the key/value pair that is identified by the key name. To remove all of the key/value pairs from the file, you can use the **clear()** method:

```
ed.clear();
```

Just like the **put()** methods, these methods do not actually take effect until you call the **commit()** method.

Loading Preference Data

In order to load the saved preference data for your application, you again need to get a reference to the **SharedPreferences** class using the same name as before the preferences group and an access mode:

```
SharedPreferences prefs = getSharedPreferences("MyPreferences", MODE_PRIVATE);
```

Now you can use any one of a series of "get" methods to retrieve your data. You are not using an **Editor** but the **SharedPreferences** itself. Make sure to use the correct method to match the data type that was stored!

```
boolean isMale    = prefs.getBoolean("isMale", true);
float userHeight  = prefs.getFloat("height", 5.5F);
int userAge       = prefs.getInt("age", 16);
long userWeight   = prefs.getLong("weight", 24);
String userName   = prefs.getString("userName", "default value");
```

Notice that we specify not only the string key name, but also another value as the second parameter. This second value will be used as the default if the named key cannot be found. If you think about a typical application, the program will likely make **get()** calls on startup to retrieve any saved data, but it won't know if there is any data present or not. So specifying the default values here is a convenient way to initialize your user settings to known values the first time your application is run and before any data is saved.

 Remember the data type you stored in each of your keys! If you save a value as an int, you cannot retrieve it as a long or String or other data type. An exception will be thrown if you make this mistake.

When to Save, When to Load?

Where in your application code is a good place to load and save persistent data? The answer depends on the callback events your activity will receive, so now is a good time to refresh your memory! We have repeated the main parts of the state flowchart from Chapter Four to study here.

A common application design would use a dedicated activity screen for user settings. So your application will likely be changing between one or more main screens and the user settings screen. As each main application screen is created for the first time or restarted from a Stopped state, it will receive the **onStart()** event. This would be a convenient place to load persistent data needed by the activity. You'll get the most current values each time the activity is started or restarted.

Similarly, from your dedicated settings activity, using **onStart()** will give you a good chance to load the existing settings. When the user has made modifications to their configuration, your setting activity will either be stopped or destroyed. Either way, the **onStop()** method is a good spot to save out your modified settings so all other activities can get access to them when they are restarted.

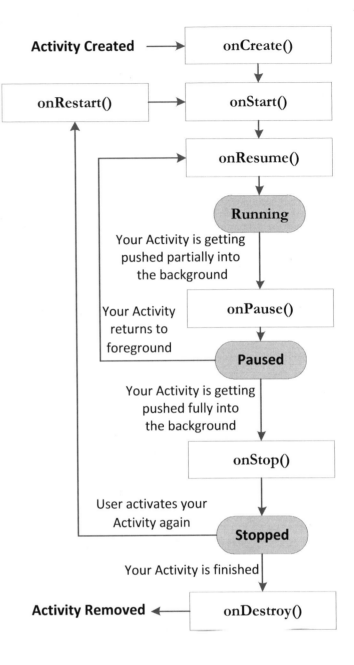

To override the **onStart()** method and load persistent data, you can add the following code to your **Activity**:

```
public void onStart()
{
        super.onStart();
        // load your persistent data here!

}
```

Overriding the **onStop()** method to save your settings is equally easy!

```
public void onStop()
{
        super.onStop();
        // save your persistent data here!
}
```

Of course, your application may have different needs or different activity flows, so you can save and load your settings any place that makes sense. If your settings screen is the first one to start when the program is launched, you might load the settings in **onCreate()** and save the settings when the user clicks a button to move to the next screen. The possibilities are endless!

Activity #1: Whack-A-Mole Options as Preferences

The Whack-A-Mole game that we have been working on for the last few chapters is great, but any settings that you choose are not saved when the user exits the program. This means that they have to re-enter all new values the next time the game is run on the device. To fix this, we will modify the program to save the settings as shared preferences. Then the user settings will be reloaded the next time the game starts!

Your activity requirements and instructions are found in the "Chapter07_Activity1.pdf" document located in your "TeenCoder/Android Programming/Activity Docs" folder. You can access this document through your Student Menu or by directly clicking on it from Windows Explorer (Windows) or Finder (Mac OS).

Complete this activity now and ensure your program meets the requirements before continuing!

Lesson Two: Using Internal File Storage

Sometimes an application needs to save more substantial data than just a collection of primitive key/value pairs. You might need to save large amounts of character data, like notes, or fancy documents, or images, or some other binary data specific to your program. When this is the case, it's often better to store the data as files rather than in the shared preferences area.

The Android system maintains a separate, private directory for each application that is installed on a device. This "internal" storage area is a great place to keep your application's data files. Like the shared preferences area, this private directory will remain until the application is uninstalled. At that time, the Android system will delete the directory and any files that are contained within the directory.

Managing a data file on Android is very much like handling a file in a regular Java application. In fact, you are using the standard Java file objects from the **java.io** package. So make sure you import **java.io.*** at the top of your source code when handling files. You will need to open the file, write or read your data and then close the file again. Every file has a unique name such as "myScores.txt" or "myPicture.png".

Exception Handling with Try/Catch

Many Android features will communicate errors by throwing *exceptions*, so you need to become comfortable handling exceptions at runtime. Let's explore this important concept now! You should be familiar with the concept of runtime exceptions from the first-semester Java programming course. You know that Java will "throw" exceptions for situations such as using a **null** reference or a divide-by-zero attempt. Whenever a line of code throws an exception, normal program flow is interrupted and an **Exception** object is raised up to the first piece of logic that can handle it. The **Exception** object contains detailed information about the error.

In order to catch runtime exceptions, you need to surround "risky" areas of code with a **try** block. Use the **try** keyword followed by a set of curly braces to surround any code that might throw an exception. Then after the final **try** curly brace, add the **catch** keyword, a set of parentheses with the **Exception** object you want to handle, and another block of code in curly braces. Now any **Exception** raised by your risky code can be safely processed in the **catch** block instead of crashing your program!

```
try
{
    // risky code that may raise an exception goes here
}
catch(Exception e)  // give the Exception a variable name "e"
{
    // code to handle the Exception "e" goes here
}
```

Java and Android file methods can throw exceptions that must be caught. This is because file input and output operations frequently fail. You might see a **FileNotFoundException** when trying to open a file that does not exist, for example. So when writing file input and output (I/O) code, you will have to use the **try** and **catch** structures to protect your application. In fact, Java will force you to handle these exceptions with a **try/catch**; it's not optional! Eclipse will tell you exactly what to do if your code is at risk from an unhandled exception.

```
openFileOutput("HighScores.txt", MODE_APPEND);
```
Unhandled exception type FileNotFoundException

1 quick fix available:

Surround with try/catch

Press 'F2' for focus

```java
try
{
    // all file input and output code needs to go into a try block
}
catch (Exception e)
{
    String errorMessage = e.getMessage();
}
```

The **Exception** object has several methods that will give you information about the error. Above we have demonstrated **getMessage()** which returns a simple **String** describing the error. In a real program you might want to display that error message to the user so they have some idea what went wrong.

Writing Data to an Internal File

When creating a new internal file or writing to an existing file, the first step is to *open* the file for output on the device. This can be done using the **openFileOutput()** method:

```java
FileOutputStream fos = openFileOutput("HighScores.txt", MODE_PRIVATE);
```

The **openFileOutput()** method takes two parameters: the first parameter is the name of the file that we are opening. You can name this file anything you want, as long as it does not include path separators like slashes. Internal Android files are all located within the root directory for your application. Your application can store as many files in the internal storage area as it needs.

The second parameter is the mode that will be used to open the file. The main two modes you are likely to use are **MODE_PRIVATE** and **MODE_APPEND**. **MODE_PRIVATE** will create the file if it does not exist and will truncate (erase) any existing file of that same name, leaving you with an empty file to write to. **MODE_APPEND** will open a file that you will add information to, without over-writing the existing data. So if your application has the entire file contents in memory and you need to write the entire data block to the file, use **MODE_PRIVATE** to replace the existing file. If you just have some additional information to add to the end of an existing file, use **MODE_APPEND**.

The **Activity openFileOutput**() method will return a **FileOutputStream** object, which is part of the standard Java Class Library in the **java.io** package. This class handles creating and or opening files for output. The Java classes that refer to reading or writing to a file are called "streaming" classes. This is because they offer a way to "flow" data in pieces between your program and a file. The **FileOutputStream** really only offers the ability to write out individual bytes, or arrays of bytes, using the **write**() method.

```
byte[] myByteArray = {1,2,3};
fos.write(myByteArray);
```

This may or may not be useful to your application. Often it's more convenient to write out human-readable **Strings** instead. To do this, we'll need to wrap the **FileOutputStream** with another class called **OutputStreamWriter**. You can create a new **OutputStreamWriter** by passing the **FileOutputStream** reference into the constructor. Now you can write strings to your file!

```
OutputStreamWriter osw = new OutputStreamWriter(fos);
String strInformation = "High Score:  Joe Blaster, 1024";
osw.write(strInformation);
```

The **write**() method accepts a simple **String** as input and transfers (or streams) this data into your open file.

If you want to write more than one string, each on a separate "line", you can write out a line separator in between each string. Since this value can vary from device to device, it's often a good idea to use the **System** object in Java to retrieve the correct line separator. Here is how to get this property for a device:

```
String strSeparator = System.getProperty("line.separator");
```

Now after each data string where you want a new line to occur, write the separator value.

```
osw.write("line 1");
osw.write(strSeparator);
osw.write("line 2");
osw.write(strSeparator);
```

When you are finished writing data to the file, call the **flush**() method to make sure all of the data has been pushed out into the file. Then finally, you will need to **close**() the stream. All files should be properly closed so they can be opened later by your application or someone else.

```
osw.flush();  // ensure all data is written from the stream to file
osw.close();  // close the file
```

Both the **OutputStreamWriter** and **FileOutputStream** classes have **flush()** and **close()** methods. If you are using just the **FileOutputStream**, call those methods on that object. If you have also created the **OutputStreamWriter**, just call **flush()** and **close()** on the **OutputStreamWriter** only.

Here is a complete example that shows opening a file, writing out some text data, and safely closing the file.

```
try
{
        // open file, overwriting any previous version
        FileOutputStream fos = openFileOutput("HighScores.txt", MODE_PRIVATE);
        // create OutputStreamWriter around FileOutputStream
        OutputStreamWriter osw = new OutputStreamWriter(fos);

        // create some String information and write it to the file
        String strInformation = "High Score:  Joe Blaster, 1024";
        osw.write(strInformation);  // write String to the file

        // flush and close the file through the OutputStreamWriter
        osw.flush();
        osw.close();
}
catch(Exception e)
{
        // handle error...
}
```

Reading Data from an Internal File

Reading an internal file is very similar to writing data. Just like before, our first step is to open the storage file. This time, we will use the **openFileInput()** method to get a class called a **FileInputStream**:

```
FileInputStream fis = openFileInput("HighScores.txt");
```

The **openFileInput()** method takes just one parameter, which is the name of the file you are trying to open. You can use the **FileInputStream** object to read individual bytes or byte arrays from your file.

```
int myByte = fis.read();         // read a single byte between 0-255
byte[] myBytes = new byte[100];  // declare array of 100 bytes
fis.read(myBytes,0,100);         // read up to 100 bytes into myBytes array
```

Again you might prefer to work with **Strings** instead of **bytes**, so you can create an **InputStreamReader** object around the **FileInputStream**, like this:

```
InputStreamReader isr = new InputStreamReader(fis);
```

Unfortunately the **InputStreamReader** doesn't quite give you **String** capability yet…instead it allows you to read individual characters or arrays of characters. Since this is a very tedious process, we will use yet another helper class to make our job easier: the **BufferedReader** class. This class will enable us to read one line of data as a **String** all at once. To create the **BufferedReader**, pass the **InputStreamReader** object into the constructor. Then you can read data from the file in either one character or one-line chunks.

```
BufferedReader buffReader = new BufferedReader(isr);
int myChar  = buffReader.read();         // read one character
String line = buffReader.readLine();    // read one line (to line delimiter)
```

The **readLine()** method will read all the characters up to but not including the line separator characters. If you know you have multiple strings written to your file with line separators in-between, you can simply make calls to **readLine()** to pull out each string in sequence.

```
String line1 = buffReader.readLine();
String line2 = buffReader.readLine();
```

As always, remember to close the file when you are finished with it:

```
buffReader.close();
```

Here is a complete example that opens an existing file and reads out two lines of text:

```
try
{
        // open existing file for reading
        FileInputStream fis = openFileInput("HighScores.txt");

        // create InputStreamReader and BufferedReader
        InputStreamReader isr = new InputStreamReader(fis);
        BufferedReader buffReader = new BufferedReader(isr);

        // read two lines of text
        String line1 = buffReader.readLine();
        String line2 = buffReader.readLine();
```

```
        // close the file when done
        buffReader.close();
}
catch(Exception e)
{
        // handle error...
}
```

Viewing Files on the Emulator

In order to make sure your file is being created and saved properly, you can check the storage area on your Android emulator. To do this, you will first need to switch to the "DDMS" perspective in Eclipse by clicking on DDMS in the upper-right corner of the screen:

 If that button is not yet visible, select "Window → Open Perspective → Other → DDMS" from the Eclipse menu. When your emulator is running, the DDMS screen looks something like this:

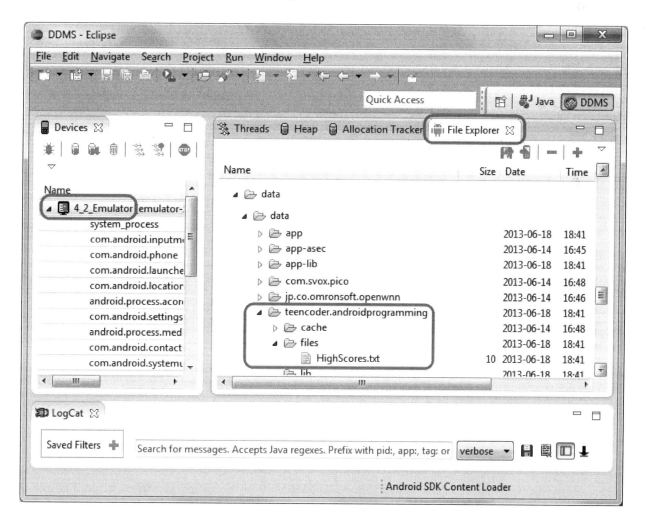

Once you choose your AVD in the "Devices" section, you should be able to see a list of files on the device under the tab "File Explorer". The files for your application are located under the "data/data" directory in its package name, in our case "teencoder.androidprogramming". You'll notice that we can see the "HighScores.txt" file that we created in addition to the "WhackSettings.xml" shared preferences that were created in the last activity.

You cannot view these files directly in the emulator. However, you can transfer the files to your computer and view them from there by "pulling" the file from the emulator. Select the file in File Explorer and then click the ![icon] "Pull a file from the device" button at the top of the File Explorer. Once the file is pulled to your computer, you can view it with any program suitable for that file type.

You can also push files to the emulator with the ![icon] "Push a file onto the device" button. Click on the target directory where the file will go in the emulator, then click the toolbar button to select the file from your host computer that will be transferred to the device.

Activity #2: Whack-A-Mole High Scores

To complete this activity, we will be adding two more screens to our Whack-A-Mole game. The first screen will have "Game Over" information for the user and will contain two buttons: One will allow the user to play the game again. The other button will display the "High Scores" screen.

Your activity requirements and instructions are found in the "Chapter07_Activity2.pdf" document located in your "TeenCoder/Android Programming/Activity Docs" folder. You can access this document through your Student Menu or by directly clicking on it from Windows Explorer (Windows) or Finder (Mac OS).

Complete this activity now and ensure your program meets the requirements before continuing!

Lesson Three: Accessing the SD Card

In addition to internal file storage, most Android devices have some sort of external data storage, typically in the form of Secure Digital or SD cards. This data is often a better place to store data, especially if the data is large or if you want the data to be portable. You can eject an SD card from one device and move it to another.

There are some significant differences between internal files and external SD storage on an Android device. Internal files are always private to the application, unless the application allows access with MODE_WORLD_READABLE or MODE_WORLD_WRITEABLE flags. External storage files, however, do not have any access control and are always readable and writable by any and all applications. Even the user can read, write and delete the files on external storage.

This is an important consideration when deciding whether to save files internally or externally. Any files important to the workings of your application should be stored internally where they can be protected from accidental changes. Files that are not critical to the application can be placed on external storage. The SD card also provides more storage than might be available on the internal file system, so it could be a good idea to manage very large files strictly on the SD card if present. Note that when you uninstall your application, any files that you have saved on external storage will be deleted, just like files in internal storage.

Checking External Storage Status

The first step in using external storage is to see if any external storage is available on the device. There are some devices (tablets mainly) that do not have any support for SD cards. If there is no card, you cannot write to it! The user may have also removed the SD card temporarily or not have an SD card at all.

To check the status of a device's external storage, we will use a method on the **android.os.Environment** class called **getExternalStorageState()**. This method will return a **String** value that will give you more information on available storage. If the string equals one of the two constants shown below, then the SD card is available for read/write or read-only access. Any other state means the SD card can't be used.

```
String state = Environment.getExternalStorageState();
if (state.equals(Environment.MEDIA_MOUNTED))
{
    // we can read and write to the SD card
}
else if (state.equals(Environment.MEDIA_MOUNTED_READ_ONLY))
{
    // we can read from the SD card but not write
}
```

Storage Permissions

We haven't talked about application permissions in detail yet. However, when your program wants to start accessing certain hardware or software features, it needs to register permission to use those things in the "AndroidManifest.xml". When installing the application, the user can view the required permissions and decide if the program will be allowed on their device.

To use the SD Card on the device (or emulator), add the following line to your application's "AndroidManifest.xml" file before the opening <application> tag:

```
<uses-permission android:name= "android.permission.WRITE_EXTERNAL_STORAGE"/>
<application
```

Now your application, when installed, will be authorized to use the SD card.

SD Card on the Emulator

Your default Android Virtual Device does not have a "pretend" SD card for the emulator. If you called **Environment.getExternalStorageState()** on the AVD you've been using so far, you'd get a state that indicated the SD card was not present.

However, you can create a new AVD and give it a virtual SD card. Open the AVD Manager and create a "New" AVD with a different name. Select the same Android 4.2.2 target as before. Then, find the section called "SD Card" and add a Size value such as 10 MiB (10 megabytes). The minimum size is 9 MiB. If you choose a very large value your emulator may become very slow or have problems, so only pick a reasonable value needed for your test data.

 **Do not attempt to edit your existing AVD and change the SD card size form nothing to some value! Your emulator may not react well to this change, causing many problems that can only be resolved by deleting and recreating the AVD. So keep one AVD around with no SD card and one that was created from scratch with a SD card.**

Once you have more than one AVD target, how do you select which emulator your program will use? Normally your program will automatically launch the same emulator each time. But you can select "Run →Run Configurations" from the Eclipse menu to change this behavior.

The "Run Configurations" screen will allow you to pick a target emulator.

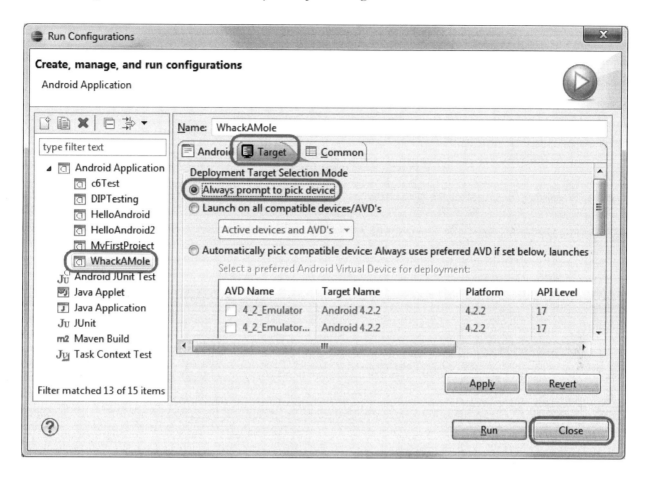

Click on your application (such as our "WhackAMole" example), then click the "Target" tab and switch the

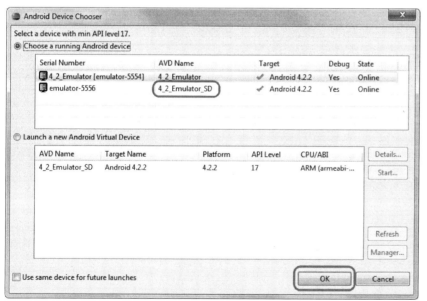

Deployment Mode to "Always prompt to pick device". Then click the "Close" button. Now, each time you "Run" your project from the toolbar, you will get a pop-up asking you to select a running AVD to use (or the new AVD to start).

Select your AVD that has the SD card configured and click OK. Your application will now run on that device!

It's ok to have more than one emulator running at a time on your system, so you don't have to close an existing emulator to start up a new one.

SD Card Directory Structures

The SD Card can store data that is private to your application or data that is intended for sharing with the user and other programs. Your private application files are stored in a directory structure that contains your package name followed by "files" like this:

/mnt/sdcard/Android/data/teencoder.androidprogramming/files

Public or shared files are usually categorized into well-known directories so the Android OS and other applications know where to find them. Examples include:

/mnt/sdcard/Music

/mnt/sdcard/Pictures

The root directory for all files may be "/mnt/sdcard" in the emulator, or just "/sdcard" or other name on a real device. You can use pre-defined constants on the **Environment** object such as **Environment.DIRECTORY_MUSIC** and **Environment.DIRECTORY_PICTURES** that will allow you to query for these directories no matter where the actual root directory is located.

To find the private directory for your application on the SD card, use the **getExternalFilesDir()** method and pass in **null** as a parameter.

```
File privateLocation = getExternalFilesDir(null);
```

This method will return a **java.io.File** object containing the full path your private application file area on the SD card. Similarly, you can call the **Environment.getExternalStoragePublicDirectory()** method and pass in one of the pre-defined directory constants to get the well-known public directories.

```
File musicLocation = Environment.getExternalStoragePublicDirectory(
                                    Environment.DIRECTORY_MUSIC);
```

Finally, you are ready to start writing to the SD card! You have learned how to check and see if the SD card is present, you know how to register for permissions to use the card, how to configure a new AVD with a virtual SD card, and how to obtain the directory locations where private or public files should be written.

Writing to the SD Card

Once you have a **File** object pointing to your target directory (either private or shared), you can begin writing files. Simply registering for the SD card permissions and running your application will cause the Android OS to create your private files directory automatically.

To create a specific file, we use our initial **File** representing the target directory in the constructor of a new **File** object. The second constructor parameter should be the filename you want to create. In this example we get the private application folder and then define a new file called "myfile.txt".

```
File privateLocation = getExternalFilesDir(null);
File myFile = new File(privateLocation, "myfile.txt");
```

The hard part is over! From here you use the same set of Java objects we discussed for the internal Android storage area. We create a **FileOutputStream** object, this time using the target **File** object in the constructor:

```
FileOutputStream fos = new FileOutputStream(myFile);
```

Once you have a **FileOutputStream** you can use the familiar **OutputStreamWriter** to write text to the file. Here is a complete example:

```
try
{
        // get the location for this application's private SD card folder
        File privateLocation = getExternalFilesDir(null);

        // construct a File object representing the target filename
        File myFile = new File(privateLocation, "myfile.txt");

        // build a FileOutputStream and write some text data!
        FileOutputStream fos = new FileOutputStream(myFile);
        OutputStreamWriter osw = new OutputStreamWriter(fos);
        osw.write("my data file contents!");
        osw.flush();
        osw.close();
}
catch(Exception e)
{
        // handle errors...
}
```

You can view and manage your SD card contents in the "DDMS" perspective just like the internal storage area. Click on the "DDMS" button or open the DDMS perspective, click on the "File Explorer" tab, and navigate down the "/mnt/sdcard" directory hierarchy until you reach your new file.

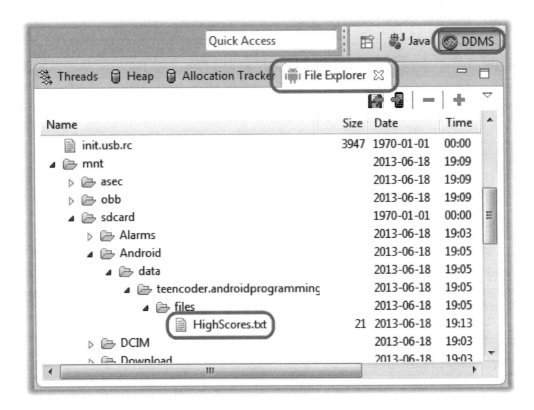

Reading from SD Card

Reading from the SD card is very similar to writing. You need to complete the same basic setup tasks:

- Register for permissions in the "AndroidManifest.xml"
- Get a **File** object representing the target directory
- Build a new **File** object using the target directory and filename
- Surround all file operations with **try/catch** blocks

For example, if we now want to read back the "myfile.txt" we created earlier in the private SD file area for our application, first we call **getExternalFilesDir()** and then create a new **File** object using the filename.

```
File privateLocation = getExternalFilesDir(null);
File myFile = new File(privateLocation, "myfile.txt");
```

Now, instead of creating a **FileOutputStream** for writing, we create a **FileInputStream** for reading.

```
FileInputStream fis = new FileInputStream(myFile);
```

Once you have a **FileInputStream** you can use the **InputStreamReader** and **BufferedReader** to read lines of text. Here is a complete example:

```
try
{
        // get the location for this application's private SD card folder
        File privateLocation = getExternalFilesDir(null);

        // construct a File object representing the target filename
        File myFile = new File(privateLocation, "myfile.txt");

        // create the FileInputStream from the target File
        FileInputStream fis = new FileInputStream(myFile);

        // create InputStreamReader and BufferedReader
        InputStreamReader isr = new InputStreamReader(fis);
        BufferedReader buffReader = new BufferedReader(isr);

        // read two lines of text
        String line1 = buffReader.readLine();
        String line2 = buffReader.readLine();

        // close the file when done
        buffReader.close();
}
catch(Exception e)
{
        // handle errors...
}
```

Using Raw Resources

There is one last way to use and access files in Android: the "raw" resources. Raw resources are files that are added to your project in the "/res/raw" folder. These are files that you want to include in your program, but that you don't necessarily want to store in device memory. This method is typically used for static text like help files, image resources and license agreement text. If you need to include a large amount of text into a screen and you do not want anyone to change this information, a raw file is a great tool.

To add raw files to your project, just go into Windows Explorer or Mac Finder and find the "/res/raw" folder for your project. Create your file and then drop it into this folder.

Raw files are created as resources in your application. The compiler will automatically create an ID for any raw file in the /raw directory. The ID will look something like this: "R.raw.<filename>". The filename will not contain the file extension. For example, if we added a file named "license.txt" to our "/res/raw" directory, it would be given an ID of "R.raw.license" in our program.

To open a raw resource at runtime, you can use a combination of the **getResources()** and **openRawResource()** methods. The first method will get a **Resources** object for the application and the second method can open a specific raw resource file. Here's how the two methods work together:

```
InputStream is = getResources().openRawResource(R.raw.license);
```

As you can see, the return value for this combination is an **InputStream** that contains the information in the file. You can then use the **InputStream** just as you would to read any other file in Java.

Activity #3: Whack-A-Mole SD Scores

In this activity, you will change the Whack-A-Mole game to save and load the user's high scores from the SD card instead of internal memory.

Your activity requirements and instructions are found in the "Chapter07_Activity3.pdf" document located in your "TeenCoder/Android Programming/Activity Docs" folder. You can access this document through your Student Menu or by directly clicking on it from Windows Explorer (Windows) or Finder (Mac OS).

Complete this activity now and ensure your program meets the requirements before continuing!

Chapter Eight: Debugging and DDMS

As you start writing more complex Android applications, you will want access to the same powerful debugging tools available to regular Java programs. In this chapter you will learn how to debug your Android applications in the emulator, how to use the DDMS tool to manage your emulator, and how to log messages to trace your program's activity.

Lesson One: Debugging Android

In our first-semester Java course, you learned how to use the Eclipse *debugger* to examine a Java program at runtime. You should remember how to add breakpoints, step-through a program line-by-line and check variable values. In this lesson, we'll learn how to use these same features on an Android application that is running in the debugger on the emulator.

Making Your Application Debuggable

The first step to debugging an Android application is ensuring the program is marked as "debuggable" in the "AndroidManifest.xml" file. To do this, open your project's "AndroidManifest.xml" file in Eclipse and click on the "Application" tab. You should see the following screen:

▸ *MyProject Manifest ✕   ▭ 🗗

🤖 **Android Manifest Application**

▾ **Application Toggle**

🤖❗ The <u>application</u> tag describes application-level components contained in the package, as well as general application attributes.
☑ Define an <application> tag in the AndroidManifest.xml

▾ **Application Attributes**
Defines the attributes specific to the application.

<u>Name</u>		Browse...	Debuggable	true ▾
Theme		Browse...	Vm safe mode	▾
Label	@string/app_name	Browse...	Manage space activity	Browse...
Icon	@drawable/ic_launcher	Browse...	Allow clear user data	▾
Description		Browse...	Test only	▾
Permission	▾		Backup agent	Browse...

◂   ▥   ▸

⊞ Manifest Ⓐ Application Ⓟ Permissions Ⓘ Instrumentation 🗐 AndroidManifest.xml

---

Find the dropdown list control named "Debuggable" – it may be in the left or right-hand column depending on your screen. By default this box will be blank. Change the value to "true" and save your changes.

According to the online Android documentation, a program cannot be debugged unless this setting is "true". Experimentally we have found that Eclipse will allow you to debug an application regardless of this setting. However it's good practice to enable the setting just in case the Eclipse behavior changes in the future.

General Debugging Techniques

The general debugging techniques are the same in Java or Android programming. You can set breakpoints in your code by double-clicking the left-margin near the code line, or by choosing "Run" and "Toggle Breakpoint" from the top menu. You can see to the right we have set a breakpoint at the **setContentView()** line.

```java
Main.java

    package teencoder.androidprogramming;

⊕ import android.os.Bundle;

    public class Main extends Activity {

        @Override
        protected void onCreate(Bundle savedInstanceState)
        {
            super.onCreate(savedInstanceState);
            setContentView(R.layout.main);
        }
```

To run your application in the debugger, simply click on the "bug" icon at the top of the screen. At that point, Eclipse may ask you if you want to switch to the "Debug" perspective, just like in regular Java debugging. Once you choose to switch perspectives, you will see the Debug Perspective appear in Eclipse. Eclipse will load the application onto the emulator and then attach the debugger to the application. This could take a few seconds, so you may see a pop-up message in the emulator stating that the debugger is starting.

This message should only appear for a few seconds before the emulator starts your program. Be patient! If you click on the "Force Close" button, you will have to start your program all over again. Once this message disappears, your application will be running in debug mode. As soon as a breakpoint is hit, the program will pause and display the Debug perspective screen.

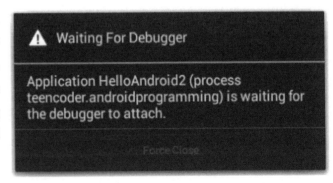

⚠ Waiting For Debugger

Application HelloAndroid2 (process teencoder.androidprogramming) is waiting for the debugger to attach.

Force Close

The Debug perspective should look familiar! It's the same basic layout used for normal Java programs. The size and location of each window can be changed, so your screen may not look exactly like the screen below.

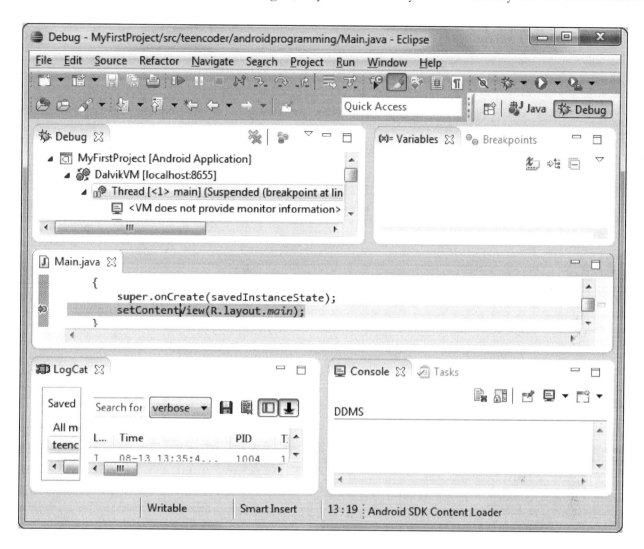

There are a few changes for Android, however. The Console window at the bottom of the screen is no longer the output window for your program. Instead, the Console window is a great place to view updates about the status of the emulator. This is an especially useful tool to use while the emulator is booting up. Here, you can follow the process as the program is compiled, installed, and run on the emulator.

The LogCat panel shows log messages generated by the Andoird system or your program. We'll show you later in this chapter how to create your own log messages.

In addition, you will notice the "Disconnect" button in the toolbar. When you find an error, this button will allow you to "disconnect" the debugger from the emulator. You can then go back to your code and make the necessary changes to your program.

Other than these two changes, the inner workings of the debugger are the same. You can step-through your program, view variables, and set additional breakpoints, just like a normal Java program.

Lesson Two: Dalvik Debug Monitoring Server (DDMS)

In addition to the basic debugger, Android includes another important programming tool: the "Dalvik Debug Monitoring Server", or DDMS for short. The DDMS gives you more information and control over aspects of your program that are specific to the emulator. This tool will allow you to monitor and interact with the emulator as its running.

 **What is a "Dalvik"?** While it might sound like some sort of alien robot arch-nemesis, Dalvik is actually the name of the Java Virtual Machine that runs Android applications. The Dalvik VM is optimized for high performance on small devices.

The DDMS Perspective

When your application is running in the emulator, you can interact with it by opening the DDMS perspective. To open the perspective, you can choose the DDMS button from the top-right corner of the screen or choose "Window → Open Perspective → Other → DDMS" from the Eclipse menu. Here's a screen shot:

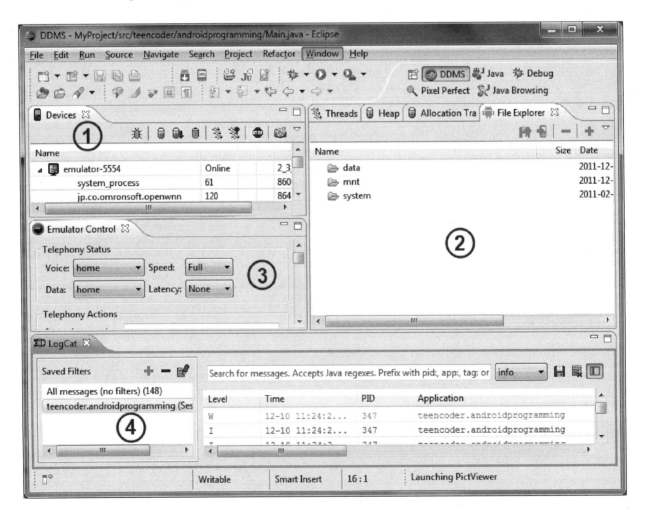

Let's take a look at the DDMS perspective section-by-section. The first section labeled with the circled "1" is the Devices frame. Here, you will be able to see any of the emulators that are currently running on your computer. If you have connected an actual Android device to your computer, you will also see that device listed in this frame. Under the emulator name, you will find a listing of all the running programs or processes

on the emulator. These programs are listed by their package name, so we can find our program by looking for the "teencoder.androidprogramming" listing. Notice that our program has a picture of a bug next to it. This shows that a debugger is attached to the program in the emulator.

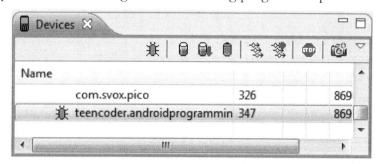

In the second section (2) of the DDMS perspective, you will see a number of tabs including one called "File Explorer". This is a very useful tool when your application is creating or using local files on the device. We described how to use the File Explorer in the previous chapter when learning about the Android file system. This area contains many other tabs to let you view threads, memory, and other internal details. It also contains an "Emulator Control" tab described below. Any of these tabs can be dragged into a separate "pane" in the DDMS display; it's very flexible. Your own display may not have exactly the same panes as our screen shot, but the content is there somewhere!

The third section (3) in the DDMS perspective is the "Emulator Control" section. We pulled this from the tabbed area into its own panel for easier viewing. The emulator is a powerful tool, but it is not a real device! If your application needs to respond to real-device events, like incoming phone calls and messages, this section is a lifesaver. Here, you can "send" messages to the device, simulate incoming phone calls, set GPS coordinates and even set the emulator's current data connection state, like "roaming", "searching" or "denied". This is an invaluable testing tool for programs that need incoming hardware events. Note that if you are debugging your application on a real device connected to your computer, the Emulator Control section will not work. It will only work on the emulator that is running on the computer.

The final section (4) in the DDMS is the LogCat window. This section is perhaps one of the most useful debugging parts of the entire DDMS! Here, you will see all kinds of messages about the current state of the emulator and your application. This information is especially helpful when you are debugging runtime errors. When an error occurs, the LogCat utility will log information about the problem in the viewer.

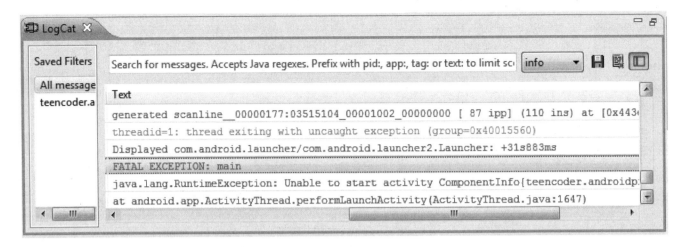

With this information, you should be able to better pinpoint and solve the problem in your code. In the example above, we can see that the application suffered a "Fatal Exception" while launching the main activity

Creating Your Own LogCat Messages

In addition to reading messages from the emulator, you can create and display your own debugging messages in the LogCat viewer. This is basically the same as using **System.out.println()** in a normal Java program to trace your program's progress to the console. Since you don't have access to the console in Android programs, using the built-in Android Log utility is especially handy when trying to display progress or troubleshooting information while your program is running.

To generate your own LogCat message, you must first import the **android.util.Log** class:

```
import android.util.Log;
```

Now you can insert a message with simple static calls on the **Log** object, like this:

```
Log.e("My Tag", "My Message");    // log a message at error level
Log.w("My Tag", "My Message");    // log a message at warning level
Log.i("My Tag", "My Message");    // log a message at info level
Log.d("My Tag", "My Message");    // log a message at debug level
Log.v("My Tag", "My Message");    // log a message at verbose level
```

The **e()**, **w()**, **i()**, **d()**, and **v()** method names are somewhat cryptic, but they're really just abbreviations for "error", "warning", "info", "debug", and "verbose". Programmers who write large applications are used to writing many log messages, and they're always looking to save a few keystrokes by shortening frequently-used function names. However the Android developers may have gone a bit overboard in this case by using just a single letter! You can choose the log level that matches the importance of your message.

The first parameter in each method is the "tag" for the message. The LogCat viewer can receive a multitude of messages while running an application. If you only want to view the messages that your code is sending, you can filter the messages and only show items with a certain tag value. This often helps to eliminate the clutter in the viewer and speeds up your debugging efforts.

Here's an example debug log message that lets us know we've reached a certain point in a program.

```
String userName = "Bob";
Log.d("MyApp", "userName has been set!");
```

Now when your program runs these lines of code, you will see the following output in the LogCat viewer:

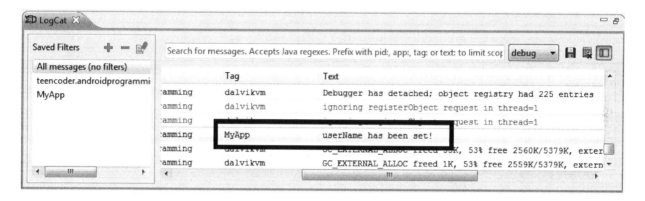

If you only want to view messages with your tag, you can click on the green plus sign ![plus] next to "Saved Filters" on the left side of the viewer. This will bring up the LogCat Message Filter Settings dialog:

Here, you can simply give your filter a name (any descriptive name is fine), and the set the "Log Tag" that you want to view. In our case, we used our "MyApp" tag in our log statements, so we set the log tag to "MyApp" in this filter. Click "OK" when finished.

Now when you click on the "MyApp" filter in the Saved Filters list on the left, the right-hand viewer pane will only show you log messages

Logcat Message Filter Settings

Filter logcat messages by the source's tag, pid or minimum log level. Empty fields will match all messages.

Filter Name:	My Application
by Log Tag:	MyApp
by Log Message:	
by PID:	
by Application Name:	
by Log Level:	verbose ▼

| OK | Cancel |

containing that tag. This is a great way to de-clutter the LogCat viewer and focus on your code's messages.

Lesson Three: Emulator Limitations

The Android emulator in the Eclipse software is very powerful. It does, however, have some notable limitations when it comes to debugging applications.

The first limitation is that calls and messages to the device can only be *simulated* on the emulator. This means that you can make it appear as though a call is coming in, but you cannot use your computer's microphone and speakers to fully implement the phone call. In addition, you cannot create real out-going messages and phone calls from the emulator. You can simulate messages between emulators, but if your application needs to place real calls or send messages, you will need to test that functionality on an actual Android device.

Another limitation is that Android devices come in many different hardware versions. Each device manufacturer may have slightly different implementations of the basic Android functionality. The emulator can simulate different screen sizes and resolutions, but it cannot emulate every single device on the market. If you are creating applications for Google Play, you may need to test your program on actual devices before you release it to the public.

The emulator does not support any USB, Bluetooth or headphone functionality. If your application uses either of these hardware accessories, you will need to test them on an actual device.

It is also difficult to emulate the multi-touch functionality of an Android device. If you have used one of these devices, you are aware that you can use two fingers to zoom in or out of pictures and websites. Since most computer screens do not support multi-touch, this is very difficult to test outside of an actual device.

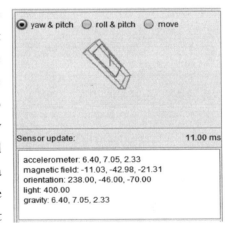

If you are creating games for Android, you may be interested in the *accelerometer* functionality on the device. This is the hardware piece that allows you to tell if the device is being tilted, turned or rotated by the user. Many game programmers use this data to allow a user to move objects around in a game program. Unfortunately, it is difficult to emulate accelerometer data. In fact, the basic emulator will not allow you to simulate this behavior at all. Instead, you will need to download and configure a separate tool called the "Sensor Simulator". This is a Google tool that will allow you to simulate all of the movements of the device. If you want more information on this tool, you can research it here: http://code.google.com/p/openintents/wiki/SensorSimulator.

Finally, it's important to remember that everything on the emulator is simulated information. While this is a useful tool for testing and debugging, nothing beats the real-world testing on an actual Android device! The Student Menu contains links to documents describing how to download your program to a real device later in the course, just in case you happen to have an Android device yourself and want to show off to your friends.

Activity: Note-able Bugs

In this activity, you will practice your debugging skills on a program that we have created for you. The program is a simple Note editor that should allow you to create, edit, save and load a single note in memory. Unfortunately, the program has a few serious errors! Your job will be to find and fix these errors using your debugging skills.

Your activity requirements and instructions are found in the "Chapter08_Activity.pdf" document located in your "TeenCoder/Android Programming/Activity Docs" folder. You can access this document through your Student Menu or by directly clicking on it from Windows Explorer (Windows) or Finder (Mac OS).

Complete this activity now and ensure your program meets the requirements before continuing!

Chapter Nine: Displaying Images

So far we have shown you how to create many different types of Android controls. In this chapter, we will learn how to spice up our applications with image resources.

Lesson One: Adding Image Resources

Resources are components bundled with your program that are not part of your source code. You have already seen how to create layout and string resources in XML files underneath your projects's "res" directory. Your image resources will also go in folders underneath the "res" folder.

The Drawable Folders

Your Eclipse Package Explorer window shows you all of the files and folders in your project. Underneath your "res" directory you will notice four "drawable" folders. In Android, a *drawable* is any resource that can be drawn onto the screen. You will use these folders to manage image "drawable" resources. So why do we need more than one drawable directory? The answer lies in the sheer number and variety of different Android devices that are available on the market today.

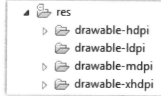

Your application may run on a device that is only 2 inches square or it may run on a tablet that is 10 inches or more in diagonal size. The Android OS will categorize the "size" of each screen as "small", "normal", large", or "extra large". In addition, devices may have different resolutions or screen densities. This is the measure of how many *pixels per inch* that a device can display. A low-density screen has fewer pixels per inch and does not have as clear a picture as that of a high-density screen. The screen density is also grouped by Android into "ldpi" (low density), "mdpi" (medium density), "hdpi" (high density), and "xhdpi" (extra-high density).

The following table shows the approximate physical size, density, and minimum width/height in "dp" of the "small", "normal", "large", and "extra large" device screen sizes. These values are *approximate* because new devices are released all the time, and the Android OS will make the decision internally what mode best matches a particular device.

Size	Density	Physical Size	Pixels Per Inch	Min Width (dp)	Min Height (dp)
Small	**ldpi**	2 – 4 inches	100 – 130	426	320
Normal	**mdpi**	3 – 5 inches	130 – 180	470	320
Large	**hdpi**	4 – 7 inches	180 – 260	640	480
Extra Large	**xhdpi**	7 – 10+ inches	260+	960	720

These different sizes and screen resolutions make designing an Android application a little bit trickier than a normal computer program! How do you use images that look good on small, low-density devices as well as larger, high-density devices? The answer is to create multiple images, one for each density.

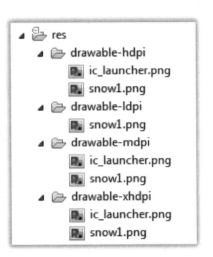

You will notice four folders underneath "res\drawable" called "drawable-ldpi", "drawable-mdpi", "drawable-hdpi", and "drawable-xhdpi". These folders hold different density images to match target screens.

If you plan on supporting all four device screen densities, then you should provide different versions of each image that you want to use in your application. Each image should have the same name, but should be placed into the correct folder in the "/res" directory. In the example to the right, we have added a "snow1.png" image go each of the drawable folders. While this may seem like a lot of extra work in the beginning, making an application look great on any device is well worth the effort.

How do you actually create images with different densities? You can use image editing software that allows you to save the same file in different "pixels per inch" formats. There is no one accepted standard pixels-per-inch value for each density category, but good target densities are 120 ppi (ldpi), 160 ppi (mdpi), 240 ppi (hdpi), and 320 dpi (xhdpi). If you don't have different versions of your image, you can create a "res\drawable" folder without any density suffix. Or you can just place a single image in any one of the existing "drawable" folders such as "res\drawable-mdpi". Android will find whatever images are available and do the best it can to display them on each device.

If you do have different versions of each image, how do you figure out which image to display on the screen? Actually, you don't have to! Android will do the work for you. Once you have added your images to the correct folders, the Android system will choose which image looks the best on the current device.

Image Formats

Image files come in many different formats such as GIF, BMP, JPG, PNG, or TIFF. Android supports three of these formats. The preferred image format is a *Portable Network Graphics* or PNG file. Most image files will use *data compression* to squeeze a large amount of image into a smaller file size. A PNG image uses *lossless* data compression, which means it does not lose any image quality when the data is compressed. The result is a high-quality picture in a small image size. PNG images also support *transparency*, which is important when overlapping graphics on the screen.

You can also use JPEG or JPG files (short for *Joint Photographic Experts Group*), which are typically smaller in size than PNG files. JPG files do not support transparency, however, which limits their usefulness, especially in games. In addition, JPGs use a "lossy" data compression, so your image may lose some of the fine details or appear a bit blurry. JPG files are supported, but not widely used by Android applications.

The final image type that Android supports is the GIF or *Graphics Interchange Format* files. This is an older type of image that does support transparency, lossless data compression, and even animation. However GIF images can only contain 256 different colors and are therefore strongly discouraged on the Android device.

Image Resources

Just like any other resource, you will want to refer to an image in one of the "drawable" folders by an ID in your Java code and your XML files. Once an image is placed into any drawable folder and the program is compiled, you can use the standard "R" resource prefix followed by "drawable" and then the image name (without extension). Do not include the density, such as "hdpi"; just use the common filename that you placed in one or more drawable folders. This example refers to an image named "snow1.png":

```
R.drawable.snow1
```

The exact same ID refers to all of the versions of "snow1" that you have placed in any drawable folder.

In your XML layout files, you can refer to an image with the format "@drawable/<image filename>". Our same "snow1" picture would have this XML name:

```
"@drawable/snow1"
```

We'll talk about how to access and display these image resources in the next lesson.

Lesson Two: The ImageView Control

In the last lesson, you learned how to add image resources to your project. Now you'll discover how to display images on the screen using an **ImageView** control from the **android.widget** package. Let's say that we want to show a "drawable" image resource called "snowflake.png". The XML layout to create an **ImageView** control and display an image looks like this:

```
<ImageView
    android:id="@+id/myImageView"
    android:layout_width="wrap_content"
    android:layout_height="wrap_content"
    android:src="@drawable/snowflake" />
```

In addition to the standard id, width, and height properties, we are adding one new property: "android:src". This attribute selects the image to display by using the unique ID value. Remember for images stored in the drawable resource folders, the XML ID format is "@drawable/<image filename>".

Notice that we did not specify in which drawable directory our image is located. Hopefully, we have added a snowflake image in each of the supported densities. But if there is only one image, the Android will find it.

Scaling and Cropping with ImageView

If we want more control over how the image is displayed in the control, we can use another attribute value called "android:scaleType". This attribute will control how the image is resized or adjusted to fit the size of the **ImageView** control. The scale type attribute can be set in the XML layout or in your Java code.

Java ImageView.ScaleType	XML Value	Description
MATRIX	"matrix"	Allows you to apply a 3D matrix of transforms for skewing, stretching, and rotating.
FIT_XY	"fitXY"	This value will scale the image to fit the height and width of the control. This will often distort the look of the image.
FIT_START	"fitStart"	Scales the image to fit entirely inside the available area while maintain the same aspect ratio (no distortion). Image will be aligned on the top and left edge of the display area.
FIT_CENTER	"fitCenter"	Scales the image to fit entirely inside the center of the available area while maintain the same aspect ratio (no distortion).
FIT_END	"fitEnd"	Scales the image to fit entirely inside the available area while maintain the same aspect ratio (no distortion). Image will be aligned on the bottom and right edge of the display area.

CENTER	"center"	Centers the image in the display area without any scaling
CENTER_CROP	"centerCrop"	Centers the image and scales it up without distortion to fill the entire area. Some parts may be cropped (cut) if they do not fit.
CENTER_INSIDE	"centerInside"	Centers the image and scales it up without distortion such that the largest dimension is completely filled.

For example, here we have modified our <ImageView> with a width of "fill_parent" so the image will cover the entire width of the screen. Then we specified a "scaleType" of "centerCrop" to scale the image to fill the entire area, cropping one side or another as needed. You can see the snowflake was scaled up without distortion to cover the horizontal area completely, but some of the top and bottom were cut off.

```
<ImageView
    android:id= "@+id/myImageView"
    android:layout_width="fill_parent"
    android:layout_height="wrap_content"
    android:src="@drawable/snowflake"
    android:scaleType="centerCrop"/>
```

Programmatically Managing the ImageView

You can also set the scale type attribute or manage other **ImageView** properties at runtime inside your Java code. Be sure to import the **android.widget.*** package and, of course, use the trusty **findViewById()** method to get a reference to the **ImageView** object by resource name.

Here we call **setScaleType()** on the **ImageView** and pass in the **ImageView.ScaleType. CENTER_INSIDE** value to scale and center the snowflake inside the area without cropping.

```
ImageView iv = (ImageView)findViewById(R.id.myImageView);
iv.setScaleType(ImageView.ScaleType.CENTER_INSIDE);
```

You can also change the image source at runtime as well by calling **setImageResource()** with a different ID:

```
iv.setImageResource(R.drawable.snow1);
```

Notice as you type "R.drawable." into your Eclipse IDE, you will see a handy pop-up list of all the available images in the drawable directories. That's just Eclipse trying to make your life easier!

TeenCoder™: Android Programming

Lesson Three: Horizontally Scrolling Images

The **ImageView** control is great when you have only one image to display on the screen. But what if you want the user to choose from a list of images to show? One possible way to let the user see a list of images is through a **HorizontalScrollView** control.

The **HorizontalScrollView** control in the **android.widget** package is a view that will display a horizontal scrolling list of items. The user can move through the items in the list by "flinging" the control left or right on the screen. The currently selected item is always the one located in the center of the list on the screen. You can create a simple **HorizontalScrollView** control in your program with the following XML layout:

```
<HorizontalScrollView
    android:layout_width="match_parent"
    android:layout_height="wrap_content">
    <LinearLayout
        android:id="@+id/myPhotos"
        android:layout_width="wrap_content"
        android:layout_height="150dp"
        android:orientation="horizontal"/>
</HorizontalScrollView>
```

Notice that we have used two different controls in this example. We start with the **HorizontalScrollView** control itself, setting it to stretch across the entire screen width and using just enough height to display the items. Inside the **HorizontalScrollView** we add another control: a **LinearLayout** with an id of "myPhotos". We will add our images to this layout element from within our code. To prevent the scrolling view from taking up too much of the screen, we will limit the height of the layout to 150dp units.

In order to add images to the scrolling view, we need to create an **ImageView** for each image. It takes a few lines of code to make each **ImageView**, so we'll write a handy function called **createImageView()**.

```
View createImageView(int resourceID)
{
    ImageView iv = new ImageView(getApplicationContext());
    iv.setPadding(5,5,5,5);
    iv.setImageResource(resourceID);
    iv.setLayoutParams(new LayoutParams(180, 150));
    iv.setScaleType(ImageView.ScaleType.FIT_XY);
    return iv;
}
```

Our function will take a single integer input which represents the resource ID for the image (eg: **R.id.snow1**). The function will return the completed **ImageView** control. Inside the function, we create the new **ImageView** control, using our application's context. Then we set a padding value of 5 units. This will provide a small border between the different images in the scrolling view. Next, we load the image resource ID into the **ImageView** control using the **setImageResource**() method.

We will also use a simple method called **setLayoutParams**() to set the size of our **ImageView** control. The parameter to this method is a **new LayoutParams** object, which we create with the desired width and height sizes. We want to make sure our images will fit within our **HorizontalScrollView**, which has a height of 150dp, so we will use a height that is no larger than 150, and a width that makes sense for our image. Finally, we will set the scale type of our image to "ScaleType.FIT_XY". This will automatically scale the image down to the size of our small **ImageView** controls.

Now that we can easily create an **ImageView** from a resource ID, we need to call **addView**() on the **LinearLayout** to insert an image into the **HorizontalScrollView**. You can do this anywhere such as **onCreate**() that makes sense in your code.

```
protected void onCreate(Bundle savedInstanceState)
{
    super.onCreate(savedInstanceState);
    setContentView(R.layout.main);

    LinearLayout myPhotos = (LinearLayout)findViewById(R.id.myPhotos);
    myPhotos.addView(createImageView(R.drawable.snow1));
    myPhotos.addView(createImageView(R.drawable.snow2));
    myPhotos.addView(createImageView(R.drawable.snow3));
}
```

We first get a handle to the **myPhotos LinearLayout** element. Then we load our images into the layout by calling the **LinearLayout**'s **addView**() method and passing in the **ImageView** produced by our own **createImageView**() method.

Notice that **HorizontalScrollView** images by themselves are often too small to be really useful. It's common to add a full **ImageView** control underneath in order to display a larger image. Android supports similar controls for displaying vertically scrolling images (**ScrollView**) and a 2-dimensional grid of images (**GridView**). Refer to your online Android documentation for more details.

153

TeenCoder™: Android Programming

Detecting Image Clicks

Let's learn how to detect a click on one of the images in the **HorizontalScrollView**. First, since we want to display a larger image when the user clicks on a thumbnail, we will add an **ImageView** control to our XML screen layout:

```
<ImageView
    android:id="@+id/myImageView"
    android:layout_width="wrap_content"
    android:layout_height="wrap_content"
    android:scaleType="fitCenter" />
```

Notice that we did not add the "android:src" attribute. We will assign the image ID for the larger **ImageView** each time the user clicks on a smaller **ImageView** in the **HorizontalScrollView**.

The **ImageView** control will send click events to a **View.OnClickListener** interface that has been assigned to the object. The **OnClickListener** interface defines just one method, **onClick()**, that will be called in response to user click events. So we are going to use a familiar pattern where our **Main** activity implements the **View.OnClickListener** interface and the **onClick()** method.

```
import android.widget.*;
import android.view.View;

public class Main extends Activity implements View.OnClickListener
{
    public void onClick(View v)
    {
        int resourceId = (Integer)v.getTag();
        ImageView iv2 = (ImageView)findViewById(R.id.myImageView);
        iv2.setImageResource(resourceId);
    }
}
```

Within our **onClick()** method we need to figure out which image resource was clicked and call **setImageResource()** on the larger **ImageView** with that resource ID. That way the same image will appear in the larger view. Unfortunately, getting the image resource ID is harder than you would expect! The **View** parameter to the **onClick()** method is the **ImageView** control that was clicked, however there is no way to directly pull the resource ID out of the **ImageView** object. You can call **setImageResource()** to load an image by ID, but there is no corresponding **getImageResource()** function to retrieve the ID.

154

We are therefore going to store an extra piece of data called a "tag" on each **ImageView** in our horizontal scroll bar. All **View** objects will let you store an object and retrieve it later. So we are going to store the resource ID as a tag when the **ImageView** is created and then pull the tag from the **View** inside **onClick()**.

In this case our tag will be an **Integer** object, and you can see it's easy to pull the tag from the **View**:

```
int resourceId = (Integer)v.getTag();
```

We next need to modify our **createImageView()** function to take two additional steps for each image we add to the **HorizontalScrollView**:

```
View createImageView(int resourceID)
{
    ImageView iv = new ImageView(getApplicationContext());
    iv.setPadding(5,5,5,5);
    iv.setImageResource(resourceID);
    iv.setLayoutParams(new LayoutParams(180, 150));
    iv.setTag(resourceID);
    iv.setOnClickListener(this);

    return iv;
}
```

First we call **setTag()** to store the resource ID integer on the control as a tag. Then we call **setOnClickListener()** to tell the control that the main activity (**this**) has the **onClick()** callback function to run each time the user clicks on the **ImageView**.

We are finally done! Let's summarize the steps involved with detecting and processing image clicks.

- Implement the **View.OnClickListener** interface in the activity
- Create the **onClick()** callback function on the activity to handle click events
  - Obtain the resource ID tag from the **View** with **getTag()**
  - Update the larger **ImageView** with the resource ID to change the displayed image
- When creating the smaller **ImageView** controls
  - Add the resource ID to the **ImageView** as a tag with **setTag()**
  - Call **setOnClickListener()** on the **ImageView**, passing in a reference to the activity

You could use other approaches with different coding techniques. You'll learn about "anonymous" inner classes in the next chapter, and that method could simplify these steps to some degree.

Let's run our program and try it out! When we click on an image in the list, it appears in the larger **ImageView** control on the bottom of the screen.

Lesson Four: Launcher Icons, Button Images, and Activity Backgrounds

Images can be used several additional ways inside an Android application. In this lesson, you'll learn how to configure application icons, button images, and backgrounds for your activity screen.

Launcher Icons

Every program has a *launcher icon*. This is image identifies your program in the application launcher on the device. When you create a new project, you receive a default icon of a little Android. While this is a cute image, it's not very descriptive of your application. If you are writing a program for Google Play, you should make a more creative image that better describes or "brands" your program. What should your icon look like? It's your decision, although you should follow some common rules:

- Don't include the name of your application in the image. The application launcher will write the name of your program under the icon automatically.
- Make sure your icon is crisp and colorful so that it stands out on any background.
- Don't make your icon needlessly complicated. Regardless of the screen density, the icon will be relatively small on the device. Tiny details on a small image never turn out very well.
- Take your time when creating this icon. It is the first impression for your application. Make it count!

The Android team has come up with many other tips and tricks for creating great launcher icons. You can check out http://developer.android.com/design/style/iconography.html or search online for "android launcher icon design". Once you settle on a design for your application icon, you will need to create three or four versions: one for each of the screen densities that you are targeting. Here are the overall sizes for the different densities:

- Low Density (ldpi) – 36 pixels x 36 pixels
- Medium Density (mdpi) – 48 pixels x 48 pixels
- High Density (hdpi) – 72 pixels x 72 pixels
- Tablets (xhdpi) – 96 pixels x 96 pixels

Each image should be added to the corresponding drawable directory in your project. By default, the launcher icon image is called "ic_launcher.png", but you can select a different name in the "AndroidManifest.xml" file. To change the name, open the XML and find the <Application> tag. You can change this attribute to any other valid drawable resource in your project:

```
android:icon="@drawable/ic_launcher"
```

How do you test your new launch icons in the emulator? Once you load your application into the emulator, you can exit it with the back arrow key. Then click on the application grid at the bottom to see a list of all installed applications and launch icons, including your own.

The ImageButton Control

ImageButtons are like regular buttons that allow you to display an image on the button instead of text. This can give your buttons a snazzy style or give button-like functionality to an image.

To create an **ImageButton** in your XML layout file, add the following code:

```
<ImageButton
    android:id="@+id/MyImageButton"
    android:layout_width="wrap_content"
    android:layout_height="wrap_content"
    android:src="@drawable/snowflake" />
```

Notice that this definition is very similar to the plain **Button** control. The only real difference is the addition of the "android:src" attribute, which points to a drawable image in your project. In addition to one static image selected in the layout, you can also choose to use different images on the button, depending on the state of the button. For example, you can have one image for the normal button, another image which shows that the button has focus and yet another to show that the button is being pressed down on the screen.

To add multiple button images, you will need to create a selector XML file in one of your "drawable" folders. The XML file should contain a <selector> root element and one or more child <item> elements. Each <item> can contain a "state" attribute such as "android:state_pressed" or "android:state_focused" and a corresponding "android:drawable" attribute with the drawable ID.

```
<?xml version="1.0" encoding="utf-8"?>
<selector xmlns:android="http://schemas.android.com/apk/res/android">
    <item android:state_pressed="true"
          android:drawable="@drawable/button_pressed" />
    <item android:state_focused="true"
          android:drawable="@drawable/button_focused" />
    <item android:drawable="@drawable/button_normal" />
</selector>
```

Put the <item> element for the normal button (without any special state attributes) last in the file, so it will be the default image if none of the <item> states above it matches the current button condition. Then save your XML file with any valid filename such as "button_selector.xml".

Once this file is saved in a project, you can use it as your **ImageButton**'s "android:src" attribute in the activity's XML layout file:

```
android:src="@drawable/button_selector"
```

The **ImageButton** will then use the images listed in the selector XML to choose the correct picture to display depending on the current state of the ImageButton. Our snowflakes now have normal (left), focused (middle), and clicked (right) images.

Activity Backgrounds

You can also use an image as the background of a layout. This might be useful if you are creating a game program or if you just want to add a little extra style to your application. To select an image resource as the background of a layout, add the "android:background" attribute to your layout element. For example, here we have added an image called "bg.png" as the background of a **LinearLayout** that covers the entire screen:

```
<LinearLayout
    ...
    android:background="@drawable/bg"
    ...
</LinearLayout>
```

You will then see the image appear behind any other controls or views on the screen.

Activity: Photo Album

In this activity, you will write a Photo Album application that will use a **HorizontalScrollView** and an **ImageView** control to display a list of images and display a larger version of the selected image.

Your activity requirements and instructions are found in the "Chapter09_Activity.pdf" document located in your "TeenCoder/Android Programming/Activity Docs" folder. You can access this document through your Student Menu or by directly clicking on it from Windows Explorer (Windows) or Finder (Mac OS).

Complete this activity now and ensure your program meets the requirements before continuing!

Chapter Ten: Dialogs

Android allows you to ask simple questions, display alerts and gather date/time inputs as pop-up *dialogs*. These dialogs will pause the underlying activity screen while the user completes the quick input sequence. You will learn in this chapter how to use these dialogs in your own application.

Lesson One: Anonymous Inner Classes

Before we talk about Android dialogs, let's take a small detour and learn about another feature of the Java programming language that will come in handy! Normally you code every class in a different "*.java" source file. The classes are not directly tied together except perhaps by inheritance or interface (**extends** or **implements**), and can only call the **public** (or **protected** if inherited) methods on other classes. However, it is possible to create a class *within* another class with a special arrangement called an *inner* or *nested* class.

Inner Classes

When one class is defined inside another class, the interior class is called an *inner class* or *nested class*.

```
public class OuterClass          // This is the outer class
{
    public class InnerClass()    // This is the inner class
    {

    }
}
```

You would usually define an inner class in situations where you want to break apart sections of code into their own classes, but it does not make any sense for the inner class to exist outside of some parent class. The **SharedPreferences** and **SharedPreferences.Editor** classes are a good example of this concept. You can only get the **Editor** from within an instance of the **SharedPreferences** object, and the functions the **Editor** carries out are tightly tied to the **SharedPreferences**.

You can declare the inner class as **public**, **private**, or **protected** just like any other member. Inner classes always have complete access to all of the parent class variables and functions, even they are **private**!

```
public class OuterClass
{
    private int a;          // private member variable of outer class
    private void b() {}     // private member function of outer class


    public class InnerClass()
    {
        void c()  // member function of inner class
        {
            int x = a;  // we can access the outer class variables from here
            b();        // we can call outer class member functions from here
        }
    }
}
```

Inner classes are commonly used in Java graphical programming (both Java Swing and Android) because so many graphical controls require you to implement an interface or create a subclass in order to receive callbacks. If the **OuterClass** in our example above contained many different controls, it may not be convenient to implement multiple interfaces on the main class, and you cannot extend the main class from more than one base class. This is where inner classes come to the rescue!

It's common practice to define an inner class just to handle a graphical object. For example, if a **Button** required an object to implement the **OnClickListener** interface, we could do that with an inner class.

```
public class MyActivity extends Activity
{
    public void onCreate(Bundle savedInstanceState)
    {
        Button mybutton = findViewById(R.id.myButton);
        myButton.setOnClickListener(new MyButtonListener());
    }
    class MyButtonListener implements OnClickListener     // inner class
    {
        public void onClick(View v) // Implement the onClick event
        {
            // Our button click is handled here!
        }
    }
}
```

In the code above, we have separated our **OnClickListener** into an inner class and tucked it inside our **Activity** class definition. We then create a new instance of the **MyButtonListener** inner class and pass it directly into the **setOnClickListener()** method. Now that particular instance of **MyButtonListener** will be used to handle the clicks from that one button. The **onClick()** event handler function can still use any member function or variable on the outer class, which is very convenient!

Anonymous Inner Classes

What would happen to our **MyButtonListener** inner class example if the parent **Activity** had more than one button? You could create a new instance of the inner class for each button, but then inside the **OnClick()** method you would still have to figure out which button was clicked by examining the input **View**.

Fortunately, you can use another kind of inner class to write a different version of handling code for each control. These dedicated inner classes, called *anonymous* inner classes, actually have no class name and are defined "on the spot" as you need them. Instead of calling "**new**" on a class name you define, you can call "**new**" on an existing interface or class name. Then define a class immediately afterwards in curly braces. As a result, you can create a different implementation for every single button or other control that needs you to implement an interface or create a subclass! The syntax will look a bit strange, so let's examine it carefully.

```
Button myButton = (Button) findViewById(R.id.myButton);


// add a click listener to the button
myButton.setOnClickListener(
    new OnClickListener() // anonymous inner class implements OnClickListener
    {                           // beginning curly brace for class
        public void onClick(View v)    // implement required interface method
        {
            // do whatever you want when myButton is clicked;
        }
    }                           // ending curly brace for class
);                              // end of call to setOnClickListener()
```

The parts in bold above show how we created a new anonymous inner class based on the **OnClickListener** interface. The resulting object implements **OnClickListener** and we pass that new object reference directly into the **setOnClickListener()** method. We placed the entire anonymous class definition inside the function parenthesis – complete with the overridden **onClick()** method. Inside the **onClick()** method we know that the **R.id.myButton** control is responsible for generating the event, because that is the only control that knows anything at all about the anonymous inner class!

When creating a new regular object, we use the **new** keyword followed by the object name.

```
new MyButtonListener()          // this class is not anonymous
```

Since we do not name an anonymous inner class, we don't call **new** on a class name. Instead, we call **new** on the interface name itself, followed immediately by the anonymous class definition:

```
new OnClickListener() { /* implementation */ }   // this class is anonymous
```

This does not mean we have created an instance of **OnClickListener** (you can't create interfaces directly), but rather that we have created a new instance of an anonymous class which implements the **OnClickListener** interface.

Limitations of Anonymous Inner Classes

Anonymous inner classes are a great shorthand method of creating quick classes in Java. You can keep the handling code for a control near the other logic you use to set up the control. However, these classes do have some limitations. First, an anonymous inner class is not intended to be a re-usable object and they can only extend or implement one class or interface. In addition, you cannot define a constructor because the constructor name should be the same as the class name, and anonymous inner classes have no name! Anonymous inner classes cannot be **static** and they cannot declare any **static** members in most cases. This limitation is also due to the fact that it is hard to access a static class that has no name.

Anonymous Inner Classes in Android

So far we have always shown examples where interfaces such as **OnClickListener** are implemented by the main **Activity**. Going forward we will start using anonymous inner classes where convenient to handle specific controls. The syntax may take a bit of getting used to. But you will see our code can be cleaner and clearer when event-handling code is defined immediately for a specific control instead of handled by a named class somewhere else. You will also frequently see anonymous inner classes in online Java Swing and Android tutorial documentation, so it's a good idea to become comfortable with the approach!

Lesson Two: Alert Dialogs

The **android.app.AlertDialog** is very commonly used by Android applications. This dialog will allow you to create a pop-up with a message for the user and then a series of action buttons at the bottom of the pop-up. You can choose to add up to three buttons to the dialog. Usually an alert dialog contains two buttons: a positive button, like a "Yes" or "OK" and a negative button, like a "No" or "Cancel". The user can choose one of the buttons in response to the alert dialog's message.

The look and feel of all dialogs will depend on the theme you have chosen in your manifest file. The image on the left shows a default "@style/AppTheme" while the image on the right shows the "@android:style/Theme.Light" theme

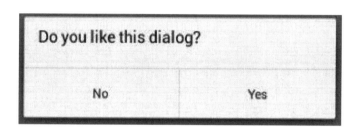

Unfortunately creating an **AlertDialog** is not as straightforward as you would think. The steps involved are:

1. Import the **android.app.*** and other packages to get easy access to most of the dialog-related classes
2. Define an inner class to represent your dialog
   a. The class should extend the **android.app.DialogFragment** class
   b. The class should override the **onCreateDialog**() method to produce the specific sort of dialog you want to display
   c. The class should implement a callback interface to receive the user's button clicks
3. From within your main code, create a new instance of your inner class and display it when needed
4. Android will dim your activity screen and display the dialog. When the user clicks one of the buttons, the button-handling code you defined when building the dialog will get executed.

Let's study each step in more detail!

Importing Packages

We will be using a variety of classes and interfaces to handle dialogs. You can import them all individually, or just place the following **import** statements at the top of your code, along with other Android-related imports:

```
import android.app.*;
import android.content.DialogInterface;
import android.widget.*;
```

Defining an Inner Class

Your main **Activity** class can conveniently handle each dialog you want to display by defining an inner or nested class for each dialog. This class will take care of creating the dialog interface, responding to user selections, and managing the pop-up display with the rest of the operating system.

The inner class must be declared as **static** and extend the **android.app.DialogFragment** base class.

```
public class Main extends Activity
{
    public static class MyAlertDialog extends DialogFragment
    {
        public Dialog onCreateDialog(Bundle savedInstanceState)
        {
            // your dialog creation code goes here
        }
    }
}
```

In this example we have declared a **MyAlertDialog** inner class within our **Main** activity. The class is **static**, which is a bit unusual for inner classes, but this is required by the Android dialog system. The class extends **DialogFragment**, the base class that will take care of interacting with the Android OS. We also overrode the **onCreateDialog()** method, which is the function Android will call when we need to produce a new **Dialog** object for display. Since **MyAlertDialog** is an inner class of **Main**, it will have full access to all of **Main's** protected and private functions and variables.

Using AlertDialog.Builder

Your inner class **onCreateDialog()** function will be called by Android when it is time to produce a **Dialog** object. **Dialog** is the base class for all types of pop-ups, including the **AlertDialog**. In order to create an instance of the **AlertDialog** class, you will use another class called **AlertDialog.Builder**. You should not attempt to just create a "**new AlertDialog()**" directly.

The first step is to create an instance of the **Builder** class so we can get to work. Create a **new AlertDialog.Builder** object, calling **getActivity()** to get a reference to the parent activity to pass into the constructor as the **Context** parameter.

```
public Dialog onCreateDialog(Bundle savedInstanceState)
{
    AlertDialog.Builder builder = new AlertDialog.Builder(getActivity());
```

Now we can use the **builder** reference to set the properties of the **AlertDialog** we want to create, including the display message, buttons, and other behavior.

The **AlertDialog** can display a message at the top. You can set the message text with the **builder**.setMessage() method. You can use any **String** value, although you should keep the message short as there is limited space on most devices.

```
builder.setMessage("Do you like this dialog?");
```

Next, you can set whether or not the user will be able to cancel the dialog window by clicking on the "Back" arrow button on their device. This is useful when you want to make sure the user responds to the alert before continuing with the application. Call the **setCancelable()** method with **true** to allow the user to cancel, or **false** to prevent the user from canceling.

```
builder.setCancelable(false);  // prevent the user from canceling alert
```

The final properties to set are the buttons for the dialog. You can choose up to three buttons. They are generally classified as "positive", "neutral", and "negative". You define the button text and underlying code completely, so the actual functions don't necessarily have to align with those three categories. Generally most programmers will use something like "OK" or "Yes" for the positive button and "Cancel" or "No" for the negative button. The neutral button is rarer but works just like the others.

You can also skip buttons altogether if you do not need any user input in the dialog window. If this is the case, make sure the user can cancel the dialog by using the back button!

Where are my buttons?

AlertDialog Buttons and Event Handler Functions

We have arrived at the hardest part about using dialogs. How do you define the buttons and, more importantly, define a function that will execute when a button is clicked? You're going to get a chance to put your new knowledge of *anonymous inner classes* to good use. Most Android and Java programmers prefer to use anonymous inner classes to define the event-handling function "on the spot" instead of implementing an interface elsewhere and then trying to figure out which dialog and button click was responsible for the event.

The **Builder** class has three methods to configure the three buttons:

```
setPositiveButton(<text id or string>, DialogInterface.OnClickListener listener)
setNegativeButton(<text id or string>, DialogInterface.OnClickListener listener)
setNeutralButton (<text id or string>, DialogInterface.OnClickListener listener)
```

The first parameter in each case is a resource text id or a literal string such as "OK" or "Cancel". The second parameter is a reference to an object that has implemented the **DialogInterface.OnClickListener** interface from the **android.content** package. This interface has one easy method:

```
void onClick(DialogInterface dialog, int which)
```

The first parameter to the callback is a reference to the dialog that created the event. The second is a representation of the button that was clicked such as **DialogInterface.BUTTON_POSITIVE**. If we were not using an anonymous inner class to implement the interface, you would use these parameters to figure out which button had been clicked. However we are going to implement the interface on the spot right now, so we are guaranteed that only this particular button can possibly call our listener function. You won't have to examine the **onClick()** function parameters at all!

To implement a listener function anonymously, replace the "listener" parameter in the **setPositiveButton()** with a full class definition starting with the new keyword, the interface name, curly braces to define the class and a definition of the **onClick()** method within the curly braces. The bolded code below shows an example.

```
builder.setPositiveButton("Yes",
        new DialogInterface.OnClickListener()       // anonymous inner class
        {
            public void onClick(DialogInterface dialog, int id)
            {
                // the positive button was clicked!
            }
        }
);
```

It's easy to get lost among the curly braces and opening and closing function parenthesis, so we have carefully spaced things out for clarity. The first line "**new DialogInterface.OnClickListener()** defines our anonymous class and the interface it implements. Next comes the opening curly brace for the class, and the closing curly brace is aligned underneath. Inside the class curly braces is a regular function definition to implement the **onClick()** method. Finally, on the last line we still need to close our call to **setPositiveButton()** with ending parenthesis and a semicolon. Whew!

What can you do inside your **onClick()** method? Anything you like! The anonymous inner class is effectively part of your parent **Activity**, so you can directly access any class member variables, functions, etc. We have one small hurdle because our inner class was declared a **static**, while our parent Activity class is non-static. That means we need to get a non-static reference to our parent activity before we can start working with the parent class member functions and data. Fortunately we can make one quick call to **getActivity()** and cast the result to match our parent activity class.

In the example below the **onClick**() function for the positive button will simply update another **TextView** on the screen to display a response to the positive button press.

```
public void onClick(DialogInterface dialog, int id)
{
    // the positive button was clicked!
    Main myActivity = (Main)getActivity();
    TextView myView = (TextView)myActivity.findViewById(R.id.textView1);
    myView.setText("I agree!");
}
```

To set up negative or neutral buttons on your **AlertDialog**, simply call **setNegativeButton**() or **setNeutralButton**() in the same manner, defining your **onClick**() handler on the spot.

The final step in our **onCreateDialog**() method is to return our completed **AlertDialog** back to the Android system. Call the **builder**.create() method, which will produce an instance of **AlertDialog** with all of the message attributes, buttons, listener functions, and other properties we specified earlier. Then return that object from the **onCreateDialog**() method:

```
return builder.create();
```

We've covered quite a bit of ground; let's put together all of the source code to define an **AlertDialog** with a single button.

```
package teencoder.androidprogramming;

import android.app.*;
import android.content.DialogInterface;
import android.os.Bundle;
import android.view.View;
import android.widget.*;

public class Main extends Activity
{
    public static class MyAlertDialog extends DialogFragment
    {
        public Dialog onCreateDialog(Bundle savedInstanceState)
        {
            // create our AlertDialog.Builder object
            AlertDialog.Builder builder = new AlertDialog.Builder(getActivity());
```

```
                // set the dialog message and cancelable status
                builder.setMessage("Do you think Dialogs are cool?");
                builder.setCancelable(false);

                // create one positive "Yes" button that will update a TextView
                builder.setPositiveButton("Yes",
                    new DialogInterface.OnClickListener()    // anonymous inner class
                    {
                        public void onClick(DialogInterface dialog, int id)
                        {
                            // the positive button was clicked!
                            Main myActivity = (Main)getActivity();
                            TextView myView = (TextView)findViewById(R.id.textView1);
                            myView.setText("I agree!");
                        }
                    }
                );   // end of call to setPositiveButton()

                return builder.create();

        } // end of onCreateDialog() method
    } // end of MyAlertDialog definition
}   // end of Main class
```

OK, we know how to define a dialog and how it will react to user inputs. But how do we actually show it?

Displaying a Dialog

The decision to display a dialog will usually come from somewhere in your activity code, perhaps in response to a user's button click. The two specific steps needed to show our **MyAlertDialog** are shown below.

```
DialogFragment newFragment = new MyAlertDialog();
newFragment.show(getFragmentManager(), "myDialog");
```

First, we create a new instance of the **MyAlertDialog** inner class and store the result in a **DialogFragment** reference. Then we call the **show()** method on the reference, passing in two parameters. The first parameter is simply **getFragmentManager()**, which obtains a reference to the **FragmentManager** used by the operating system to handle the dialogs. The second parameter is a string which can contain any name you like for your dialog. We won't use this string name for anything ourselves, though it is possible to search for running dialogs by specific names.

If our activity is using a **Button** to launch the dialog, the example below shows how the activity's **onCreate()** method can set up the **Button** with an anonymous inner **onClickListener()** class. When the button is clicked we will launch our **MyAlertDialog**!

```
protected void onCreate(Bundle savedInstanceState)
{
        super.onCreate(savedInstanceState);
        setContentView(R.layout.main);

        Button b = (Button)findViewById(R.id.button1);
        b.setOnClickListener(new OnClickListener()
            {
                public void onClick(View arg0)
                {
                   DialogFragment newFragment = new MyAlertDialog();
                   newFragment.show(getFragmentManager(), "dialog");
                }
            } // end of anonymous inner class
        ); // end of setOnClickListener() call
}
```

When the user clicks on the activity button the results, of course, are well worth it!

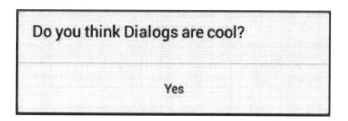

In your own application you can use all three buttons (positive, negative, and neutral) and make as many inner class versions of **DialogFragment** as you need. There are also a variety of coding approaches to making dialogs with **DialogFragment**. Our examples are simple and work well, but you can find other techniques in the online Android documentation. For instance, you can create a dedicated layout XML file and show a highly customized dialog interface with more than a simple message and set of buttons. We have only scratched the surface of dialogs and **DialogFragment** features!

One final important note: the DialogFragment object is new as of Android 3.0 (API version 11). Therefore, when creating new Android projects in Eclipse, it's especially important to change the default "Minimum Required SDK" to Android 3.0.

Minimum Required SDK: API 11: Android 3.0 (Honeycomb)

Lesson Three: AlertDialog Lists

A standard **AlertDialog** will show a message and some buttons, but you can also create a dialog that displays a list of items to the user. Let's re-work our **MyAlertDialog** example from the last lesson to show a list if items.

The first step is to create an array of **Strings** that will be used in your list. Make this array a member of your inner class so you can access it from your listener function.

What's your favorite pet?
Dog
Cat
Horse

```java
public static class MyAlertDialog extends DialogFragment
{
        String[] pets = {"Dog", "Cat", "Horse"}; // data array for alert list
```

Now, when creating your dialog, instead of calling one of the button functions like **setPositiveButton()**, you call the **Builder.setItems()** method instead. It works exactly the same way as **setPositiveButton()**, but accepts an array of strings instead of a single string. You should also avoid calling **setMessage()** to display text; instead use **setTitle()** if you want to display a title above your list.

```java
builder.setTitle("What's your favorite pet?");
builder.setItems(pets,
    new DialogInterface.OnClickListener()   // anonymous inner class
    {
        public void onClick(DialogInterface dialog, int id)
        {
          // the id contains the index into the input array
          String pet = pets[id];

          Main myActivity = (Main)getActivity();
          TextView myView = (TextView)myActivity.findViewById(R.id.textView1);
          myView.setText("I like my " + pet);
        }
    }
);
```

We have created the click listener as an anonymous inner class just as we did with the buttons. In this case you will actually use the "**id**" parameter in **onClick()** though! When the user clicks on one of the items, the alert list will close and the **id** will contain the zero-based index into the input data array. You can then get that value from the array and do something useful with it. In the example above our input data array was **pets**, so we were able to get the selected pet within the **onClick()** method using **pets[id]**.

AlertDialog Radio Button Lists

You can tweak your alert list slightly to show radio buttons on each line item. This allows you to select one of them by default when you create the dialog.

To create a list of radio buttons, just use the **setSingleChoiceItems**() method instead of **setItems**(). This method takes three parameters: the array of items, the index number of the default selection, and a click listener for the list. A default index of "-1" will not set any radio button by default.

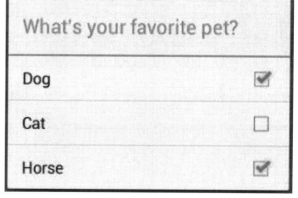

```
builder.setTitle("What's your favorite pet?");
builder.setSingleChoiceItems(pets, 0,
    new DialogInterface.OnClickListener()    // anonymous inner class
    {
        public void onClick(DialogInterface dialog, int id)
        {
            // the id contains the index into the input array
            String pet = pets[id];

            Main myActivity = (Main)getActivity();
            TextView myView = (TextView)myActivity.findViewById(R.id.textView1);
            myView.setText("I like my " + pet);
        }
    }
);
```

In this example we called **setSingleChoiceItems**() and added the default index parameter "0" right after the data array. Otherwise the code is identical.

Finally, we'll also mention that the alert list can use checkboxes instead of radio buttons. You'll get a callback each time the user clicks on a particular checkbox. The dialog does not close automatically on the first click; the user will close it when done with the back button.

To learn more, please refer to the Android documentation for the **AlertBuilder setMultiChoiceItems**() function at http://developer.android.com/reference/android/app/AlertDialog.Builder.html or search online for the keywords "Android AlertBuilder".

Lesson Four: Date and Time Dialogs

It's very common to ask the user to enter a date or time value. Two built-in dialogs allow you to get this information easily using a standard pop-up screen.

The DatePickerDialog

The **android.app.DatePickerDialog** will let the user enter a month, day, and year value. The look and feel of the dialog will depend on the theme you have chosen in your manifest file. The image on the left shows a default "@style/AppTheme" while the image on the right shows the "@android:style/Theme.Light" theme.

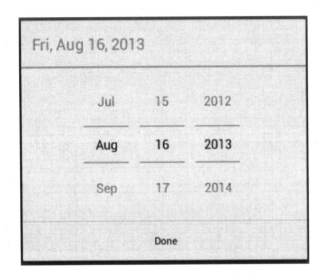

You can use the same code pattern as the **AlertDialog** to create and use the **DatePickerDialog**. Begin by creating an inner class that extends **DialogFragment**, overrides **onCreateDialog()**, and implements the **DatePickerDialog.OnDateSetListener** interface to handle the user button clicks.

```java
public static class MyDatePicker extends DialogFragment
                            implements DatePickerDialog.OnDateSetListener
{
    public Dialog onCreateDialog(Bundle savedInstanceState)
    {
        // Use the current date as the default date in the picker
        Calendar c = Calendar.getInstance();
        int year = c.get(Calendar.YEAR);
        int month = c.get(Calendar.MONTH);
        int day = c.get(Calendar.DAY_OF_MONTH);

        // Create a new instance of DatePickerDialog and return it
        return new DatePickerDialog(getActivity(), this, year, month, day);
    }
}
```

As expected, the Android system will call your **onCreateDialog()** method when it's time to create a new **Dialog** object. Within **onCreateDialog()** we need to figure out the year, month, and day values to use as the initial date setting, which we do with a **java.util.Calendar** object. Then, we can create a **DatePickerDialog** with the **new** keyword. The constructor takes five parameters:

```
DatePickerDialog(Context context, DatePickerDialog.OnDateSetListener callBack,
                 int year, int monthOfYear, int dayOfMonth)
```

The first value is the **Context** for the dialog, which we provide by calling **getActivity()** to return the current **Activity** reference. The second parameter is the "**this**" reference to the inner class which implements the **OnDateSetListener** interface to receive the user clicks (we'll talk more about this in a minute). The last three parameters are the initial integer values for the dialog's year, month and day. The month value is a zero-based value for the month. This means that month 0 is "January", month 1 is "February" and so on. This is a little different than we are used to seeing, so pay attention to the value that you set for this parameter! The final day parameter is a standard 1 through 31 representing the day of the month.

Next we need to implement the **onDateSet()** method in our **MyDatePicker** class to satisfy the **OnDateSetListener** interface. This method will be called when the user clicks the "Done" button, and it gives us an opportunity to read the user's chosen date from the dialog.

```
void onDateSet(DatePicker view, int year, int monthOfYear, int dayOfMonth)
{
    Main myActivity = (Main)getActivity();
    TextView myView = (TextView)myActivity.findViewById(R.id.textView1);
    myView.setText(year + "/" + monthOfYear + "/" + dayOfMonth);
}
} // end of MyDatePicker
```

Can you spot an error in the code above? The **monthOfYear** parameter is also zero-based, and we did not account for that when formatting the resulting value for the **TextView**. If the user selects February 5th, 2012 our resulting text value is **2012/1/5**, which shows January! We need to add one to the month value in order to display the month correctly.

```
myView.setText(year +"/"+ Integer.toString(monthOfYear + 1) +"/"+ dayOfMonth);
```

Now the right date is shown: **2012/2/5**.

We could have chosen to implement the **OnDateSetListener** interface as an anonymous inner class defined directly in the constructor parameters for the **DatePickerDialog** when it is created inside **onCreateDialog()**. However, since the **DatePickerDialog** only has one button, it's easy to implement the interface as a separate method on the inner class.

The TimePickerDialog

Android also has a built-in dialog for picking a time of day. The **android.app.TimePickerDialog** will allow the user to choose an hour and minute. You can use a version that shows the 12-hour format with AM/PM option or the 24-hour time. In 24-hour time, all afternoon hours have 12 added to them. Both of these examples show 10:39 PM. On the 24-hour version on the right side, the hours are 10 + 12 = 22.

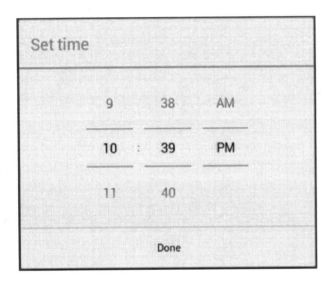 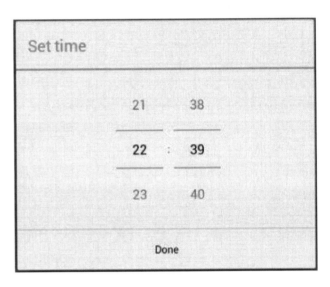

Creating and using this dialog is almost identical to creating and using the **TimePickerDialog**. Begin by creating an inner class that extends **DialogFragment**, overrides **onCreateDialog()**, and implements the **TimePickerDialog.OnTimeSetListener** interface to handle the user button clicks.

Your code inside the **onCreateDialog()** method will first figure out some values to use for the initial time setting, again using the **Calendar** object. You can then create the **TimePickerDialog** in a familiar manner. The constructor takes five parameters: the context reference, a reference to **OnTimeSetListener** interface, the initial hours (always 0-23 in 24-hour format), the initial minutes (0-59), and a **boolean** flag that controls the display format.

```
TimePickerDialog(Context context, TimePickerDialog.OnTimeSetListener callBack,
                 int hourOfDay, int minute, boolean is24HourView)
```

If you set **is24HourView** to **false**, you will see the AM/PM display. You can use the 24-hour display by setting this flag to **true**. The following example **MyTimePicker** class extends **DialogFragment**, implements **OnTimeSetListener**, and overrides the **onCreateDialog()** method.

```
public static class MyTimePicker extends DialogFragment
                                    implements TimePickerDialog.OnTimeSetListener
{
    public Dialog onCreateDialog(Bundle savedInstanceState)
    {
        // Use the current time as the default values for the picker
        Calendar c = Calendar.getInstance();
        int hour = c.get(Calendar.HOUR_OF_DAY);
        int minute = c.get(Calendar.MINUTE);


        // Create a new instance of TimePickerDialog and return it
        return new TimePickerDialog(getActivity(), this, hour, minute, false);
    }
```

We used the **Calendar** object to get the current hour and minute, and built the **TimePickerDialog()** with a reference the **Activity** for context, the "**this**" reference for the listener interface, the current hour and minute, and "**false**" for the boolean flag to get an AM/PM display.

Once again it's convenient to implement the callback interface on the **MyTimePicker** inner class. The **onTimeSet()** interface method will be called when the user clicks the "Done" button.

```
    public void onTimeSet(TimePicker view, int hourOfDay, int minute)
    {
        Main myActivity = (Main)getActivity();
        TextView myView = (TextView)myActivity.findViewById(R.id.button1);
        myView.setText(hourOfDay + ":" + minute);
    }
}
```

In this example we get the hour and minute from the callback and build an "hour : minute" string to display in a **TextView**. The value you will receive for the **hourOfDay** parameter in the callback will always be in 24-hour time. So if the user selects 3:45 PM in the dialog, you will get an **hourOfDay** equal to 15.

What about the Cancel Button?

Readers who are familiar with older versions of Android OS may remember that the date and time picker dialogs used to have both a "Set" and a "Cancel" button. But the current Android picker dialogs only have a single "Done" button. If you want to add a "Cancel" button on your own, how would you do it? The secret is that both **DatePickerDialog** and **TimePickerDialog** are subclasses of **AlertDialog**, and the "Done" button is really just the "positive" button. This means you can manually add a second "negative" button on your own when building the dialog inside **onCreateDialog()**.

The code below creates a new **TimePickerDialog** and, instead of returning immediately, saves the reference so we can call **setButton()** on it. Notice we have provided the "Cancel" text for the negative button, but you can change the text to something else if you want.

```
public Dialog onCreateDialog(Bundle savedInstanceState)
{
    // Use the current time as the default values for the picker
    Calendar c = Calendar.getInstance();
    int hour = c.get(Calendar.HOUR_OF_DAY);
    int minute = c.get(Calendar.MINUTE);


    TimePickerDialog d = new TimePickerDialog(getActivity(),
                                    this, hour, minute,false);


    d.setButton(DialogInterface.BUTTON_NEGATIVE, "Cancel",
        new DialogInterface.OnClickListener()
        {
            public void onClick(DialogInterface dialog, int which)
            {
                dialog.cancel();
            }
        }
    );
    return d;      // return the dialog now that we're done with it

}
```

The **setButton()** function lets you establish a positive, negative, or neutral button with the first parameter. The second parameter contains the display text ("Cancel"), and the third parameter is a reference to the **OnClickListener** interface that will be called if the button is clicked. We have implemented the **onClick()** method in an anonymous inner class right away. The only thing we do inside **onClick()** is call the **cancel()** method on the **dialog** in order to safely close it.

You can use exactly the same approach to add a "Cancel" button to the **DatePickerDialog**.

Our examples for both date and time pickers show you how to receive the parameters in the callback interface functions and then do something with the data. While we simply echoed the data back to the screen in a **TextView**, your program will likely do something more important with those values!

Creating Time and Date Picker Dialogs

To create and display a new time or date dialog, you will run exactly the same code from within your main activity that we showed earlier for **AlertDialogs**.

```
DialogFragment newFragment = new MyDatePicker();
newFragment.show(getFragmentManager(), "myDateDialog");


DialogFragment newFragment = new MyTimePicker();
newFragment.show(getFragmentManager(), "myTimeDialog");
```

Just create a new instance of your inner class that extends the **DialogFragment**, and then call **show()** to display the dialog.

Activity: Reminder Alarm

In this activity, you will create an application that sets a one-time alarm on the device. You will use a **DatePickerDialog** and **TimePickerDialog** to help the user choose the date and time for the alarm. You will also use an **AlertDialog** to have the user confirm the alarm before it is set on the device.

Your activity requirements and instructions are found in the "Chapter10_Activity.pdf" document located in your "TeenCoder/Android Programming/Activity Docs" folder. You can access this document through your Student Menu or by directly clicking on it from Windows Explorer (Windows) or Finder (Mac OS).

Complete this activity now and ensure your program meets the requirements before continuing!

Chapter Eleven: Menus and Notifications

In this chapter you are going to learn about some advanced ways to send notification messages to the user. You'll also add application menus and context menus to give users different ways to control your program.

Lesson One: Implicit Intents

An *implicit* **Intent** is used to ask the Android system to perform a service, without telling it exactly what application or class to use for the service. For example, you might tell Android that you want to view an image on the device. The Android system will search the device for applications that can view images and will present the user with the resulting list of applications. If there is only one application that can handle images, Android will simply start that application and tell it to load your image file.

This means that you are telling Android to show the image in best way for either the device or the user. This is a very powerful capability, since your application doesn't have to know anything about the image viewer. Your application just "waves the picture around" until another application grabs and shows it to the user.

So how do you create an implicit **Intent** in your application? To do this, you will typically need one to two pieces of information: the action that you want to perform, and (optionally) the data that you are passing along. Android has a series of pre-configured actions that you can use to call other applications.

One of the most common implicit **Intent** actions is the "View" action. This action is used to start the most appropriate viewer for the data you provide. This data can be anything from a text note to a website address. You create the "View" **Intent** with your data and the Android system will do the rest.

You will use a slightly different constructor to create an implicit **Intent**.

```
Intent(String action, Uri uri)
```

The first parameter, **action**, simply defines what you want the **Intent** to do. There are many pre-defined actions on the **Intent** class such as **Intent.ACTION_VIEW** or **Intent.ACTION_DIAL**. But what is the second "Uri" parameter? **URI** is short for "Uniform Resource Indicator", which is a fancy term for a **String** that contains some special formatting.

Using Uniform Resource Indicators

You are probably very familiar with one type of URI, which is a website URL like "http://www.HomeschoolProgramming.com". The first part of the string "http:" defines the sort of resource that is then described by the remaining data. You can build URI strings to define other things like telephone numbers and email actions! Here are some examples:

- mailto:John.Doe@example.com
- tel:1-866-555-1212
- http://www.HomeschoolProgramming.com
- file://myFile.txt
- content://contacts/people/5

While you can guess what the first four URIs represent, what does "content:" mean? In the Android world a "Content Provider" is an application that manages some sort of structured data. So in the example above we are routing the URI to the "Contacts" application, and adding in some extra parameters "/people/5" that makes sense to that application.

The **Uri** class is part of the **android.net** package, so import that package at the top of your source file:

```
import android.net.*;
```

Now, to create a **Uri** object from a given string, call the static **parse**() method on the **Uri** class like this:

```
Uri uri = Uri.parse("http://www.HomeschoolProgramming.com");
```

Then you can create your **Intent** with an action and the **Uri**, and call **startActivity**() to raise the request!

```
Intent viewIntent = new Intent(Intent.ACTION_VIEW,uri);
startActivity(viewIntent);
```

You can launch your implicit **Intent** from any convenient spot in your code, such as the **onClick()** handler function for a button on your **Activity**. If you follow this example, you'll see that the built-in Android web browser launch and navigate to the website we specified in the **Uri**.

Let's look at some other implicit **Intent** examples. The next piece of code will open the Contacts application and display information about the people in your contacts list.

```
Uri uri = Uri.parse("content://contacts/people");
startActivity(new Intent(Intent.ACTION_VIEW,uri));
```

You can also use the **Intent.ACTION_DIAL** action to launch the phone dialer application on the device. If you use just the action by itself with no **Uri**, then the phone dialer application will appear.

```
startActivity(new Intent(Intent.ACTION_DIAL));
```

If you add a **Uri** with a phone number, then the phone number will be pre-populated into the dialer window.

```
Uri uri = Uri.parse("tel:1-866-555-1212");
startActivity(new Intent(Intent.ACTION_DIAL,uri));
```

There are many more types of **Intent** actions defined such as **ACTION_CALL**, **ACTION_EDIT**, and **ACTION_WEB_SEARCH**. You can refer to the Android **Intent** documentation for a complete list.

Catching Exceptions with Try/Catch

If you try to launch an **Intent** with a **Uri** containing invalid data, or with an action that your application does not have permission to use, the **startActivity()** method may throw an exception that can crash your program. If you receive a pop-up message like the one shown to the right, then your application has generated runtime exception.

It is possible to cleanly "catch" these exceptions and handle them within your code so your program does not crash. We discussed this important concept in Chapter Seven, so you may want to review that material now.

In this example, we have attempted to actually place a phone call using the **ACTION_CALL** action. Since we are running in the emulator, our application does not have permission (or the hardware) to actually place a phone call. Therefore the call to **startActivity()** will raise an **Exception** that we will catch.

```
Uri uri = Uri.parse("tel:1-866-555-1212");
try
{
    startActivity(new Intent(Intent.ACTION_CALL,uri));
}
catch(Exception e)
{
    String errorMessage = e.getMessage();  // "Permission Denial..."
}
```

In a real program the code in your **catch** block should take whatever corrective action is necessary when an error occurs.

Listening for Implicit Intents

You can register your own activity to listen for implicit **Intents**. Maybe you have created a fantastic new image editor or you've created a brilliant text editor for reading notes. In this case, you want your activity to be on Android's list of possibilities when the user attempts to edit an image or read a note.

To register for **Intents**, you will need to add an <intent-filter> element to your "AndroidManifest.xml" file. The filter will go within an <activity> element, and that will tell the Android system the activity is capable of responding to certain events.

If you look in "AndroidMainfest.xml" for "MyFirstProject" or any other simple Android project, you can see there is already one <intent-filter> in place. This one tells Android which activity should be launched when the user starts the application – in this case **Main**.

```
<activity
    android:name=".Main"
    android:label="@string/app_name" >
    <intent-filter>
        <action android:name="android.intent.action.MAIN" />
        <category android:name="android.intent.category.LAUNCHER" />
    </intent-filter>
</activity>
```

Let's register our **Main** activity to receive "View" and "Edit" **Intents** that may be raised for image data types. This will place our activity on a list of available applications when a user attempts to view or edit an image on their device. To do this, we'll add this new <intent-filter> for the **Main** activity right after the closing tag for the existing <intent-filter>:

```
<intent-filter>
    <action android:name="android.intent.action.VIEW"/>
    <action android:name="android.intent.action.EDIT"/>
    <category android:name="android.intent.category.DEFAULT"/>
    <data android:mimeType="image/*" />
</intent-filter>
```

This <intent-filter> has three types of information. One or more "action" elements hold the names of the action that that your activity will be listening for. The "category" element contains additional information about your activity. In most cases, you can just use the "DEFAULT" category in this tag. The final piece of information in our intent-filter is the "mimeType" or data type that our activity will handle. In our case, we are listening for all types of images. If we wanted to listen for one particular type of image, such as JPEG, we could use **android:mimeType="image/jpeg"** instead. For a listing of other data types available, please refer to the Android **Intent** online documentation.

Now that you have registered to receive implicit **Intents**, what happens when some other application raises one that you can handle? Your activity will be created and go through the start-up sequence beginning with the **onCreate**() method. Inside **onCreate**() you can call the **getIntent**() method to get a reference to the **Intent** that started the activity.

```
Intent intent = getIntent();
```

The **Intent** will contain a string describing the action or reason why the activity was launched. For our example **Main** activity, we have actually registered for these three actions: MAIN (in the first <intent-filter>) and VIEW and EDIT (in the second <intent-filter>).

The **Intent** object contains pre-defined static **String** members matching the possible actions in your "AndroidManifest.xml" file. For example, "android.intent.action.MAIN" from the manifest XML has a matching **Intent.ACTION_MAIN** string member. Similarly, "android.intent.action.VIEW" has a matching **Intent.ACTION_VIEW** member, and so on.

If your activity can be started by different kinds of **Intents**, then you will want to check the action in the **Intent** to see what the user is trying to do. You can get the action using the **Intent**'s **getAction()** method.

```
String action = intent.getAction();
```

Then, compare the action to the enumerated action strings on the **Intent** class to see why your activity was launched. Here's an example for our **Main** activity that checks for each of the three actions we support:

```
Intent intent = getIntent();
String action = intent.getAction();
if (action.equals(Intent.ACTION_MAIN))
{
    // we were launched by user starting our application
}
else if (action.equals(Intent.ACTION_VIEW))
{
    // we were launched by an implicit VIEW Intent
}
else if (action.equals(Intent.ACTION_EDIT))
{
    // we were launched by an implicit EDIT Intent
}
```

Based on the action, the **Intent** may contain some extra information you need to retrieve, such as the **Uri** or any extra data attached by the calling application with **putExtra()**. You can easily retrieve those pieces of information from the **Intent** using **getData()** for the **Uri** or **getExtras()** for the **Bundle** of name-value pairs.

```
Uri uri    = intent.getData();   // get the Uri from the Intent
Bundle bun = intent.getExtras(); // get the name-value Bundle from the Intent
```

At this point, you can work with the information you received like any other data in your application.

Pending Intents

There is one last type of **Intent** used in Android programs: the *pending* **Intent**. A **PendingIntent** is a lot like an implicit **Intent**. The difference is that a **PendingIntent** will allow the receiving activity to run with your application's permissions instead of its own permissions. This is a very powerful tool, since so much of your Android functionality is limited by the permissions registered to your application.

Let's say you create an **Intent** that will require the receiving activity to connect to the Internet. If your application has registered for permission to connect to the network, you can use a **PendingIntent** to communicate with the receiving activity. This will allow the receiving activity to also use your network permission to open a network connection. Since you are allowing another application to use your permissions as its own, make sure you trust the other application! We'll put **PendingIntents** to use in the next lesson.

Lesson Two: User Notifications

Imagine that your program needs to notify the user that something has happened. Perhaps you received a message, or the device has reached certain target GPS coordinates, or your program has successfully completed some task. Android provides at least two different ways to send notifications to users.

Toast Notifications

The first notification method that we will learn is also the simplest: the **Toast** message. If you can picture a piece of bread getting popped up by a toaster, you'll understand where the **Toast** message gets its name! An Android **Toast** will display a pop-up message on the screen for a short period of time. This is very similar to the concept of a message box in C# or Java programming. **Toast** messages do not have any buttons and will disappear automatically after a short time.

This is a Toast message!

Toast messages can display any text and can be set to show for as long as you like. Typically, however, **Toast** messages are short and brief; this ensures that the user's experience isn't interrupted by long-winded messages that require some user action to clear. Since the messages will disappear automatically, the user can miss them altogether if they are not looking at the device! Therefore you should only use **Toast** messages for informational updates and not critical user messages.

Creating a **Toast** message is very simple. Toast is part of the **android.widget** package, so import that package at the top of your source file. Then, you can use the static **Toast.makeText()** method to create a new **Toast** object initialized with your message and display duration.

```
static Toast makeText(Context context, <string or resource id>, int duration)
```

You can use your activity's "**this**" reference for the first **Context** parameter, as usual.   You can also call **getApplicationContext**() if you are somewhere (like an anonymous inner class) that itself is not an activity. The second parameter can be a **String** or a string resource id. The third parameter is the length of time the message should be displayed. You can use either **Toast.LENGTH_SHORT** or **Toast.LENGTH_LONG** for the duration. Here is an example:

```
Toast myToast = Toast.makeText(getApplicationContext(),
                        "This is a Toast message!", Toast.LENGTH_SHORT);
```

Here, we have declared and initialized a **Toast** variable called "myToast". Our message will show the text "This is a Toast message!" and will appear on the screen briefly. You can choose to show the message for longer by specifying **Toast.LENGTH_LONG** instead, although **Toast.LENGTH_SHORT** is often enough time for the user to see and understand your message.

By default, the **Toast** message will appear towards the bottom of the **Activity** screen. If you want to change this location, you can set the message "gravity" with the **Toast.setGravity**() method:

```
void setGravity(int gravity, int xOffset, int yOffset)
```

The first parameter should be one of these enumerated values from the **android.View.Gravity** class:

Value	Description
android.view.Gravity.BOTTOM	Puts the message on the bottom-center area of the screen.
android.view.Gravity.CENTER	Puts the message in the center of the screen
android.view.Gravity.LEFT	Puts the message on the left-center area of the screen
android.view.Gravity.RIGHT	Puts the message on the right-center area of the screen
android.view.Gravity.TOP	Puts the message on the top-center area of the screen

The **xOffset** and **yOffset** parameters will "push" the message *away* from its normal position in the X or Y directions. So if you choose **Gravity.LEFT**, for instance, then a positive **xOffset** would push the message display a number of pixels to the right. You can make your **Toast** message appear just about anywhere you like on the screen by using some combination of gravity and X or Y offset values. Here we have aligned our **myToast** message exactly in the center of the screen:

```
myToast.setGravity(android.view.Gravity.CENTER, 0, 0);
```

Finally, to show the **Toast** message on the screen, you simply call the **show**() method on your **Toast** object:

```
myToast.show();
```

That's it! Now you can quickly and easily display any short text to the user.

Let's put all of the methods together in a complete example. Here we are going to display a "Look at me!" message on the right-center side of the screen, inset to the left by 50 pixels.

```
Toast myToast = Toast.makeText(this,
                "Look at me!",
                Toast.LENGTH_SHORT);
myToast.setGravity(Gravity.RIGHT, 50, 0);
myToast.show();
```

A **Toast** notification is a very simple way to inform the user of some event. However, it does have its drawbacks. Toast is only on the screen for a few seconds and then disappears forever. If the user is looking away from their device, there is a chance they will miss the message altogether. This is why **Toast** is great for informative messages, but not critical messages. If you need the user to know some important information, you'll want to use another notification method such as an **AlertDialog**.

Status Bar Notifications

All of the dialogs and messages we have discussed so far require your activity to be running on the screen. But what if your activity is running in the background and needs to get the user's attention? Each Android device has a *status bar* at the top of the screen. The status bar can display icons when there are important messages available. This is where you will see if you have a voicemail waiting or have received a text message. When the user swipes the status bar down, they can view more information about the message. Clicking on the message can actually launch one of your program's activity screens! All messages placed on this status bar are *persistent*, which means they will remain in the status area until the user clears them out.

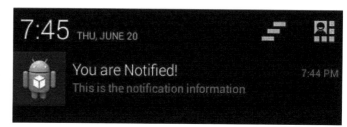

In the example above we have created a message on the status bar that consists of our launcher icon and a "Notify!" message. When the user swipes down the notification, they will see a longer message and the option to clear the event. Clicking on the message can take the user to a dedicated activity in our program.

Normally your program would only raise a notification when running in the background, because there is no other way to get the user's attention. But for testing purposes you can always raise a notification from any convenient spot in your main activity screen (such as **onCreate**() or in response to a button click). So how does your program create a notification? There are a few steps involved.

1. Create an implicit **android.content.Intent** object that sets the **Activity** to be run when the user clicks on the notification details area.
2. Create an **android.app.PendingIntent** object that will wrap your first **Intent** and give your future activity the same permissions as your main program.
3. Create an **android.app.Notification** object and configure it with the **PendingIntent** and other notification details
4. Get the system's **android.app.NotificationManager** and use it to actually place the **Notification** in the status bar

You will want to import these classes at the top of your source file to make your coding easier:

```
import android.app.Notification;
import android.app.NotificationManager;
import android.app.PendingIntent;
import android.content.Context;
import android.content.Intent;
```

Of course if you get tired of importing individual classes, you can import entire packages:

```
import android.app.*;
import android.content.*;
```

Now, let's get started! Recall that an implicit **Intent** is one that your application can raise that will target an activity outside the current program. Normally a notification should launch a dedicated **Activity** to handle the message for the user. For now let's skip that since creating a new **Activity** is a bit of work. The intent we create can be completely empty so that no **Activity** gets triggered when the user clicks on the message:

```
Intent implicitIntent = new Intent();
```

The next step is to create a **PendingIntent** around your implicit **Intent**. This will allow the status bar to take actions with the permissions already granted to your program. To create a **PendingIntent** you can use the static **getActivity**() method on the **PendingIntent** class.

```
static PendingIntent getActivity(Context context, int requestCode,
                                 Intent intent, int flags)
```

The first familiar parameter is the **Context**, which can be your launching Activity's "**this**" reference. You can also call **getApplicationContext()** to get a **Context** reference. The second parameter, **requestCode**, is not currently used so you can set it to zero. The third parameter is just the implicit **Intent** we already created. The final **flags** parameter for now can also be set to zero. When we are ready to launch a new activity later we'll set this flag to **Intent.FLAG_ACTIVITY_NEW_TASK**. Let's use the **getActivity()** method now:

```
PendingIntent pendIntent = PendingIntent.getActivity(getApplicationContext(),
                                        0, implicitIntent, 0);
```

Next we need to turn our attention to creating the **Notification** itself. The **Notification** contains an image for the status bar, a message to display, and other details. Android applications will typically use their launcher icon as the image in the status bar. This allows the users to easily tell which application is sending the notification.

We will use a **Notification.Builder** class to create a new **Notification** for our application. We can create a builder with the new keyword and pass in the main activity or application context to the constructor.

```
Notification.Builder builder = new Notification.Builder(
                                        getApplicationContext());
builder.setSmallIcon(R.drawable.ic_launcher) ;
builder.setTicker("Notify!");
builder.setContentTitle("You are Notified!");
builder.setContentText("This is the notification information");
builder.setContentIntent(pendIntent);
builder.setAutoCancel(true);

Notification notify = builder.build();
```

We are adding quite a bit of information to our notification. Let's take a look at the code line-by-line. The first line creates the **Notification.Builder** object. The next line uses the builder **setTicker()** method to set the "ticker" text, which is the text that appears in the status bar at the top of the screen when the notification is first displayed. This is typically just a short description of the notification. The **setSmallIcon()** method will set the icon that appears in the status bar with the notification. You can set a different icon for the larger image displayed with the message description with the **setLargeIcon()** method.

The **setContentTitle()** and **setContentText()** methods will set the title and text that is displayed when the user swipes to display the full notification and description. The **setContentIntent()** method will add the pending intent to our **Notification**. You can choose to have the notification auto-cleared when the user clicks on it by calling **setAutoCancel(true)**. Finally, we call the **build()** method, which will build the **Notification** object with the information we entered. Now our status notification is all ready to go! We just have to pass it to the Android system.

To raise a **Notification** to the Android system we first need to get a reference to the **NotificationManager**, which is a system service in charge of all notifications. You can call the **getSystemService()** method from your activity to get a reference to the **NotificationManager** like this:

```
NotificationManager nm = (NotificationManager)getSystemService(
                                     Context.NOTIFICATION_SERVICE);
```

Finally, we now have an implicit and pending **Intent**, a **Notification** object, and the **NotificationManager**. To send the notification to the Android system, call the **notify()** method on the **NotificationManager**:

```
nm.notify(0, notify);
```

This method takes two parameters: an integer ID for the status message and the **Notification** object. The ID value is used to identify the different status bar notifications that your application generates. If you are sending more than one **Notification** within your application, you must have a unique ID number for each message. In our case, we just used a value of 0, since this is our only message.

Here is a complete example that puts all the steps together! For testing, you can run these steps in your activity's **onCreate()** method or in response to a button click.

```
Intent implicitIntent = new Intent();


PendingIntent pendIntent = PendingIntent.getActivity(getApplicationContext(),
                                     0, implicitIntent, 0);


Notification.Builder builder = new Notification.Builder(
                                     getApplicationContext());
builder.setSmallIcon(R.drawable.ic_launcher) ;
builder.setTicker("Notify!");
builder.setContentTitle("You are Notified!");
builder.setContentText("This is the notification information");
builder.setContentIntent(pendIntent);
builder.setAutoCancel(true);


Notification notify = builder.build();


NotificationManager nm = (NotificationManager)getSystemService(
                                     Context.NOTIFICATION_SERVICE);

nm.notify(0, notify);
```

When you run the above code example, you will see the **Notification** appear on the status bar. Swiping down on the icon will reveal the full notification title and description. Clicking on the description right now will do nothing since we passed an empty **Intent** in the notification. The notification should be automatically cleared when you click on the description.

If you choose not to set the auto-cancel feature, then the user can manually dismiss the notification with a "Clear" button, depending on their Android UI.

Handling Notifications with an Activity

In most cases you don't just want the user to read a brief notification message; you want them to take some action in your program. When the user clicks on the detailed message you can have the notification launch a particular **Activity** in your program.

To create a new **Activity** to handle the notification, follow the standard steps:

1. Create a new Java class that inherits from **Activity**
2. Create your layout XML to design the **Activity** screen.
3. Add your new **Activity** to the "AndroidManifest.xml" file
4. Create your implicit **Intent** based on this new activity class instead of using an empty **Intent**.

You are familiar with the first three steps already. For demonstration we have created a new **NotifyActivity**, a "notify_activity.xml" layout, and modified the "AndroidManifest.xml".

The "NotifyActivity.java" source code contains just the minimum **onCreate()** override to select the layout.

```
public class NotifyActivity extends Activity
{
    public void onCreate(Bundle savedInstanceState)
    {
        super.onCreate(savedInstanceState);
        setContentView(R.layout.notify_activity);
    }
}
```

The "notify_activity.xml" simply contains one **TextView** to let us know the **Activity** was launched successfully.

```xml
<?xml version="1.0" encoding="utf-8"?>
<LinearLayout xmlns:android="http://schemas.android.com/apk/res/android"
    android:layout_width="match_parent"
    android:layout_height="match_parent"
    android:orientation="vertical" >


    <TextView
        android:id="@+id/textView1"
        android:layout_width="wrap_content"
        android:layout_height="wrap_content"
        android:text="Let's handle this notification!"
        android:textAppearance="?android:attr/textAppearanceMedium" />


</LinearLayout>
```

Finally, we added an <activity> element to the "AndroidManifest.xml". Notice the format is slightly different. Instead of adding <intent-filter> elements, we have used a few special attributes "**android:launchMode**", "**android:taskAffinity**", and "**android:excludeFromRecents**".

```xml
<activity android:name=".NotifyActivity"
    android:label="@string/app_name"
    android:launchMode="singleTask"
    android:taskAffinity=""
    android:excludeFromRecents="true">
</activity>
```

What's going on here? Simply put, when your activity is launched from the status bar, it is not part of your normal application flow. It's more like a little standalone application that does a specific task. When you exit the activity with the back arrow, you want the user to return to whatever they were doing previously.

Now, we simply modify the original code so the implicit **Intent** will launch the **NotifyActivity** class:

```java
Intent implicitIntent = new Intent(getApplicationContext(),
                            NotifyActivity.class);
```

That's it! When the user clicks on your message detail area (on left), the **NotifyActivity** will be launched.

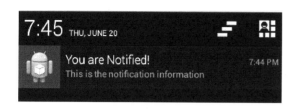 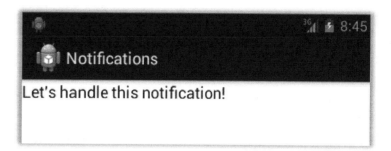

There are many advanced things you can do with notifications. You can make them play a sound, flash some lights, or vibrate the device. Starting with the Jelly Bean version of Android, you can even add buttons to your notifications! For a discussion of these advanced techniques, you can refer to the Android documentation at http://developer.android.com/guide/topics/ui/notifiers/notifications.html, or search online for "Android notifications".

Activity #1: Reminder Alarm Notification

In this activity, you will change your Reminder Alarm application to send a status bar **Notification** instead of a simple pop-up message. The title of the **Notification** will be the user-defined alarm name and the description will be the user-defined alarm description.

Your activity requirements and instructions are found in the "Chapter11_Activity1.pdf" document located in your "TeenCoder/Android Programming/Activity Docs" folder. You can access this document through your Student Menu or by directly clicking on it from Windows Explorer (Windows) or Finder (Mac OS).

Complete this activity now and ensure your program meets the requirements before continuing!

Lesson Three: The Action Bar

Most applications on Mac OS or Windows desktop computers have some type of menu hanging out at the top of the application. This menu offers the user quick-access to functionality like file saving or printing.

Android applications also may need to include this type of quick-access menu. All Android devices prior to OS version 3.0 (pre-tablet) included a "menu" button. When the user presses this button, the application will display a menu with additional options at the bottom of the screen. When the user is finished with the menu, it disappears from the screen.

The menu system worked well while Android devices were relatively small. However, as devices became larger and more popular, users began to request access to menu buttons on a more permanent basis. For this reason, on newer Android devices using OS 3.0 or greater, the menu button is gone, replaced by an

ActionBar. The **ActionBar** is similar to the option menu, except it will appear at the top of the screen and will be visible throughout the life of the activity.

The action bar may contain the application name and launcher icon in the top left for identification, and combinations of other icons and text to the right representing actions the user can take. In the example above, the Messaging app allows users to create a new message or launch a search from the action bar. The specific actions listed can change from screen to screen as the user navigates through your application.

ActionBar Icons

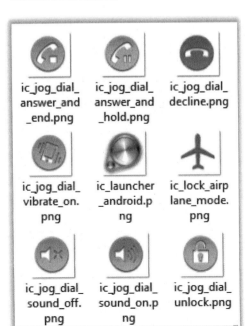

You can choose to have as many buttons in your **ActionBar** as you need. However, since screen space is at a premium, use as few as possible. Most of the menus in Android include some sort of graphical icon. In fact, it's often considered poor design to present a non-graphical menu to the user.

You can choose to create your own **ActionBar** icons, or use the pre-designed graphics that come with the Android SDK. You can find the standard **ActionBar** icons in the following directory on your computer: "/android-sdk/platforms/android-17/data/res/". Here, you will see "drawable" folders that contain images in different screen densities and even folders that contain landscape-specific graphics.

The ActionBar icons in the SDK drawable directories start with "ic_menu" at the beginning of the filename. If you want to use an icon from the SDK directory, you should copy the icon files from the SDK drawable directories to your own project just in case the names or icons change in a future SDK. Once copied, you can then refer to the menu icons in your code with the "R.drawable." syntax.

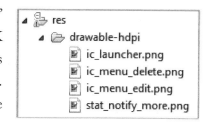

For our upcoming example, we are going to add "Delete" and "Edit" buttons to our action bar, so we'll go ahead and copy the "ic_menu_delete" and "ic_menu_edit" images into our own drawable folder.

Creating the Action Bar XML

Action bars are considered "menus" in Android programming. To define a menu, you will need to add another XML file to your project. To do this, bring up the Android XML Wizard by selecting "File → New → Android XML File" from the Eclipse menu.

Select the "Menu" Resource Type from the top combo box and then type in an XML file name. The Root Element should only offer the "Menu" option. Click the "Finish" button when done.

Your new XML file will appear under your "res/menu" folder.

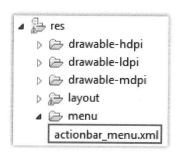

When you double-click on the new XML file under your menu folder, Eclipse will display two tabs in the middle of the screen. The first is a graphical "Layout" tab that lets you manage the XML file with a graphical UI (similar to the main screen layout Graphical Designer). The second tab lets you see and edit the underlying XML directly.

If you click on the XML tab you'll see the default menu XML doesn't have much in it. The root element is called "menu", which tells the Android system that this is a menu layout file.

```xml
<?xml version="1.0" encoding="utf-8"?>
<menu xmlns:android="http://schemas.android.com/apk/res/android" >




</menu>
```

We can add one or more <item> elements representing choices on the **ActionBar** menu. You may include as many "item" elements as your application requires (although remember that less is more). Each "item" includes an ID that will be used in our program to identify which item was chosen by the user, and a title that may appear near the icon on the ActionBar button.

Below we have added two **ActionBar** items with titles "Delete" and "Edit". We have given them unique IDs and also specified the icons we copied into our project "res/drawable" folders using the "@drawable" syntax. In addition, the property "showAsAction" indicates that if there is enough room on the action bar, the title will be shown as well as the icon.

```xml
<item android:id="@+id/actionDelete"
      android:title="Delete"
      android:icon="@drawable/ic_menu_delete"
      android:showAsAction="ifRoom|withText"/>

<item android:id="@+id/actionEdit"
      android:title="Edit"
      android:icon="@drawable/ic_menu_edit"
      android:showAsAction="ifRoom|withText"/>
```

Displaying the ActionBar

Now that we have our XML layout, we can display the **ActionBar** on the screen. When the application starts, the **onCreateOptionsMenu()** method is called on our **Activity**. The Ecilpse new project wizard will automatically create this method for you, but you can create it on your own if needed. To manually add this override to an activity, first import the **android.view.*** package at the top of your source code:

```java
import android.view.*;
```

Now, create the **onCreateOptionsMenu()** method in your **Activity** as shown below.

```
public boolean onCreateOptionsMenu(Menu menu)
{
    // get the MenuInflater object from the Android system
    MenuInflater mi = getMenuInflater();

    // "inflate" the menu using our actinobar_menu layout XML
    mi.inflate(R.menu.actionbar_menu, menu);

    return true;   // all done!
}
```

Inside this method we use a class called **MenuInflater**. This object's job is to take our XML layout and convert it into a graphical **ActionBar** at the top of the screen. We first get a reference to the Android system's **MenuInflator** with the **getMenuInflater()** method. Then we simply call the **inflate()** method on it, passing in the unique ID of our layout (**R.menu.actionbar_menu**) and the menu object we received as a parameter to the method.

So far so good! When we run our application, we will see our two-item **ActionBar** at the top of the screen. Of course, we actually want those items to do something, so let's figure that out next.

Responding to ActionBar Buttons

At this point, the user can click on the **ActionBar** buttons, but they won't do anything. To fix this, we need to override another method in our **Activity** named **onOptionsItemSelected()**.

```
public boolean onOptionsItemSelected(MenuItem item)
{
    if (item.getItemId() == R.id.actionDelete)
    {
        // the Delete button was clicked
    }
    else if (item.getItemId() == R.id.actionEdit)
    {
        // the Edit button was clicked
    }
    return super.onOptionsItemSelected(item);
}
```

The **onOptionsItemSelected()** function will be called when the user clicks on an item icon in the **ActionBar**. The **MenuItem** parameter contains the unique ID of the **ActionBar** item that was clicked, and that ID should match one of the defined "R.id" values we placed in our <item> elements inside the XML layout. So we simply call **getItemId()** on the **MenuItem** and comparing that integer value to each of our known **ActionBar** item IDs until we find a match. Then we can take whatever action is required by our application for that button. **ActionBars** are pretty easy, right?

Activity #2: Reminder Alarm Menu

Up until now, our Reminder Alarm application will allow us to set new alarms, but it did not let us edit or delete existing alarms or see a list of the alarms we have already created. In this activity, we will add those features!

Your activity requirements and instructions are found in the "Chapter11_Activity2.pdf" document located in your "TeenCoder/Android Programming/Activity Docs" folder. You can access this document through your Student Menu or by directly clicking on it from Windows Explorer (Windows) or Finder (Mac OS).

Complete this activity now and ensure your program meets the requirements before continuing!

Lesson Four: Context Menus

An **ActionBar** will allow you to take actions regarding the entire activity screen. But what if you wanted to edit or delete a particular item on the screen? In this case a *context* menu is a great addition to your design.

A context menu is a list of options or actions that are specific to one particular control on the screen. Let's think about the picture gallery application we demonstrated in Chapter Nine. When the user selects a picture from the gallery, a larger image appears on the bottom part of the screen.

You may want to share or delete that particular image. These options are specific to the image you are viewing, not the activity as a whole. In this case, a context menu is a very useful tool.

In Windows and on the Mac, a context menu often appears when you press the right-button on the mouse. Since there is no way to press a right-button on an Android device, the engineers came up with the idea of a "long-press". A long-press occurs whenever the user presses and holds their finger on the screen for more than a few seconds. This event is used to show a context menu for the item under the user's finger. When

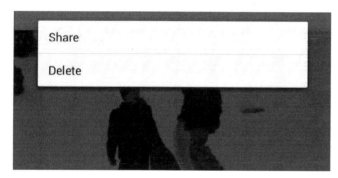

the context menu appears the rest of the screen will darken in the background. The user can select one of the context menu options or just hit the back arrow key to cancel.

On the emulator you can generate a long-press by simply clicking and holding down the left mouse button on a control.

The steps needed to create a context menu are nearly identical to creating an ActionBar. The only major difference is that you never add an icon to the context menu; they are text-only.

Creating the Context Menu XML

A context menu requires an XML layout file just like the options menu. You create the XML exactly the same way, using the "File → New → Android XML File" wizard from the Eclipse menu.

Choose the "Menu" Resource Type and add a valid XML file name to the File field. Then click "Finish" when done.

Your context menu XML layout should contain nearly the same <item> elements as the **ActionBar**. The only difference is that you are only setting an ID and title, but not an icon! In the example below we have added two menu options: "Share" and "Delete". We will be able to refer to their unique IDs in our code by **R.id.menuShare** and **R.id.menuDelete**. You can add as many menu items as you need to the layout. Just keep in mind the limited space that you have to work with on the screen.

```xml
<?xml version="1.0" encoding="utf-8"?>
<menu xmlns:android="http://schemas.android.com/apk/res/android" >

    <item   android:id="@+id/menuShare"
            android:title="Share" />

    <item   android:id="@+id/menuDelete"
            android:title="Delete" />
</menu>
```

Displaying the Menu

Now that we have our menu XML layout file, we need to display it whenever the user long-presses a specific control on the screen. The first step in this process is to get a reference to the control and then register the control for a context menu. Your activity's **onCreate()** method is a handy place to do this. In our example the main center image in the picture gallery has an ID of **R.id.imageView1**. So we get a reference to that **ImageView** object and then call **registerForContetxtMenu()**, passing in that reference.

```java
ImageView iv = (ImageView)findViewById(R.id.imageView1);
registerForContextMenu(iv);
```

Now the Android system will call the **onCreateContextMenu()** method whenever the user long-presses on this control. We next need to override this method in our **Activity** class. Be sure to import the **android.view.*** and **android.view.ContextMenu.*** packages to get all the classes you need for this method!

```
public void onCreateContextMenu(ContextMenu menu, View v,
                                ContextMenuInfo menuInfo)
{
    super.onCreateContextMenu(menu, v, menuInfo);
    MenuInflater inflater = getMenuInflater();
    inflater.inflate(R.menu.my_image_context, menu);
}
```

Inside this method, first call the base class version of **onCreateContextMenu**() and pass in the parameters we received. The rest is identical to the option menu; simply get a reference to the **MenuInflater** and call **inflate**() with the ID of our context menu XML layout file. Now when the user long-presses the **ImageView** control, our context menu will appear.

Responding to Menu Buttons

At this point, the user can click on our context menu buttons, but they won't do anything. To fix this, we need to override another method in our **Activity**: the **onContextItemSelected**() method.

```
public boolean onContextItemSelected(MenuItem item)
{
    if (item.getItemId() == R.id.menuShare)
    {
        Toast myToast = Toast.makeText(this,"Share Clicked",Toast.LENGTH_SHORT);
        myToast.show();
    }
    else if (item.getItemId() == R.id.menuDelete)
    {
        Toast myToast = Toast.makeText(this,"Delete Clicked",Toast.LENGTH_SHORT);
        myToast.show();
    }
    return true;
}
```

The **MenuItem** parameter contains the unique ID of the context menu entry that was selected. So just compare that ID to the ID of each menu item until you get a match, and then take whatever action is necessary for that menu item. In the example above we just display a little **Toast** message to verify that we understand which menu item was clicked.

203

Activity #3: Reminder Alarm Context Menu

Our Reminder Alarm program is almost complete! The only thing left to do is give the user a way to delete an existing alarm from the system. We will do that by creating a context menu for the **AlarmList** activity.

Your activity requirements and instructions are found in the "Chapter11_Activity3.pdf" document located in your "TeenCoder/Android Programming/Activity Docs" folder. You can access this document through your Student Menu or by directly clicking on it from Windows Explorer (Windows) or Finder (Mac OS).

Complete this activity now and ensure your program meets the requirements before continuing!

Chapter Twelve: Messaging and Networking

If you have used a smartphone in the last few years, you're probably familiar with the concept of *messaging*. Many people can't live without the messaging capabilities of their phone! In this chapter you will learn how to send and receive messages in your application. We'll also explore some simple networking concepts to allow your application to fetch online data from the Internet.

Lesson One: SMS Messages

SMS stands for "Short Message System" and is a way for smart phone users to send text messages back and forth on the cellular network. This is a great way to communicate small memos or pieces of information from one person to another. Just about every cell phone on the market today includes this functionality. You can take advantage of this popular messaging system in your applications to send chat messages during a game, send status updates in an application or even location updates for a tracking application. You can also, of course, just send text messages to another phone for a person to read.

Handling SMS Messages in the Emulator

You do not need a real Android device (or multiple devices) to test SMS functionality in your program. You can actually run more than one copy of the Android emulator and the same time and then send messages back and forth between the emulators.

To launch one or more emulators manually, select "Window → AVD Manager" from your Eclipse menu. Then click on the AVD emulator you have already configured and click the "Start" button. You can start as many extra emulators as you need from the same virtual device definition.

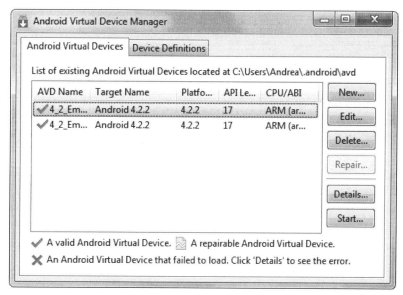

Once you have two emulators up and running, you will need to figure out the "phone number" for each emulator. The number is located in the top-left corner of the title bar at the top of the emulator:

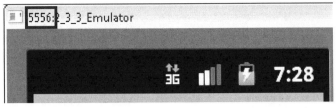

The emulator shown to the right has the phone number "5556". Any SMS messages sent to this number will appear as a new message in this emulator. You can use the built-in Android "Messaging" application to practice sending messages between two emulators.

From the first emulator's home screen, click on the applications grid at the bottom. Then find the "Messaging" icon and open that application. If

necessary, click on "New Message" on the ActionBar to bring up the composition screen. Then enter the phone number of the second emulator in the "To" address. Enter your message in the details area and click "Send".

The next three images show what it looks like when the second emulator receives a message. The first screen on the left shows the message notification arriving at the status bar.

The second image shows the expanded notification when you "swipe" down on the status bar.

The third screen shows the message in the Android messaging application.

Now that you know how messaging works on the emulator, let's learn how to create messages programmatically in an Android application.

There are two ways of handling SMS messages in Android: you can use implicit **Intents** to send messages through the standard SMS application, or you can write code to send the messages straight from your application. We'll take a look at the simplest method using implicit **Intents** first.

Sending SMS Messages with Intents

The easiest way to send messages is to use the existing SMS messaging application on the device. You can just hand off your message to this application using an implicit **Intent**. The first step is to create a new **Intent** with the action **android.content.Intent.ACTION_VIEW**.

```
Intent smsIntent = new Intent(android.content.Intent.ACTION_VIEW);
```

Now we can add the message information using **Intent** "extras". The first extra is the "address", or phone number where we are sending our message:

```
smsIntent.putExtra("address", "5556");
```

You can even enter multiple phone numbers by separating them with semi-colons:

```
smsIntent.putExtra("address", "5554; 5556");
```

Then we set the "sms_body" of the message with another extra:

```
smsIntent.putExtra("sms_body", "Hello again!");
```

Next we will need to tell Android what type of **Intent** we are creating. When you are sending an SMS message, you will use the type "vnd.android-dir/mms-sms":

```
smsIntent.setType("vnd.android-dir/mms-sms");
```

Finally, we launch the messaging application by calling **startActivity()** with the implicit **Intent**. This will bring up the device's SMS message application, with the address and body already entered on the screen.

```
startActivity(smsIntent);
```

All you have to do is click the "Send" button and your message is off to the recipient!

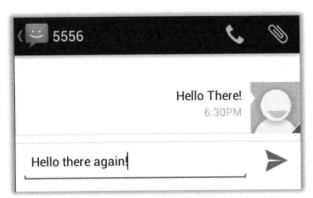
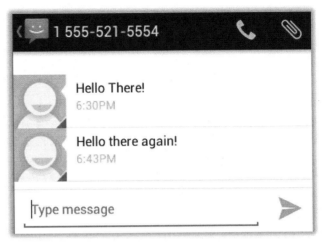

Using the built-in messaging application with an implicit **Intent** method is very simple. You leave all the extra user interface and messaging work to the Android application and don't need to "re-create the wheel" in your own program.

Lesson Two: Sending SMS Messages from an Application

In the last lesson, we learned how to use the built-in SMS Messaging application with **Intents** from our application. This is a quick and simple way to include messaging in your application, but it does have its drawbacks. When you use the built-in messaging, the user is thrown into another application in order to send the message. They must then navigate back to your application when they are finished sending the message. If you want a more seamless look, you can send and receive SMS messages straight from your application!

Sending SMS Messages from an Application

The first step in sending SMS messages from your application is to register the correct permission in the "AndroidManifest.xml" file. You can add this line near the top, above your <application> element:

```
<uses-permission android:name="android.permission.SEND_SMS"/>
```

Now we are ready to add some messaging code to our application. Most of the built-in Android classes relating to messaging are in the **android.telephony** package, so you will want to import that package at the top of your source file.

```
import android.telephony.*;
```

The Android **SmsManager** class is used to send or receive SMS messages in your application. You should not create a new instance of this class. Instead you will get a reference to the system's instance using the static class method **getDefault**():

```
SmsManager sms = SmsManager.getDefault();
```

Now you can send a message with a single line of code, providing you know the phone number (or address) and the message text. The **SmsManager.sendTextMessage**() function is all you need:

```
void sendTextMessage(String destination, String serviceCenter, String text,
                PendingIntent sentIntent, PendingIntent deliveryIntent)
```

The first parameter is simply the target phone number such as "5556". You can set the **serviceCenter** parameter equal to **null**. The third **text** parameter contains the body of the message. The fourth and fifth parameters are used to let our application know when the message is sent and when it is delivered. These parameters are optional, so you can just leave them as **null** for now. We'll learn how to track messages in a minute. Here's a quick example using just the target phone number and a text message:

```
sms.sendTextMessage("5556", null, "I can do this myself!", null, null);
```

The target device will then receive your text message.

Tracking Message Delivery

A message is "sent" when it leaves the original device, and is "delivered" when it reaches the target device. Your application can be notified by Android when your message is sent and delivered. These notifications use **PendingIntents**, similar to the way a **Notification** on the status bar can launch one of your activities. If you want notification for one or both events, you'll create a **PendingIntent** for the fourth and/or fifth parameters in the **SmsManager.sendTextMessage**() method.

The official Android online documentation does not contain much detail about exactly how to receive status updates. Fortunately a number of Android enthusiasts have figured out how things work and posted their findings online! So if you can't find the information you are looking for in the Android documentation, don't be afraid to look elsewhere!

The overall process for receiving message "sent" notifications is as follows:

1. Create a **PendingIntent** that contains an implicit **Intent**. The implicit **Intent** will have an action you specify such as "SMS_SENT".
2. Define an object that extends the **BroadcastReceiver** class and implements the **onReceive()** method. This is the method we want Android to call when an **Intent** is raised with our action.
3. Register your **BroadcastReceiver** object with the Android system by calling **registerReceiver()** from your **Activity**. Use a filter that will only call our function when the specific action such as "SMS_SENT" is contained in an implicit **Intent**.
4. Use the **PendingIntent** from step 1 in your call to **SmsManager.sendTextMessage()**. The Android system will then know to raise the implicit **Intent** you created when the message is sent.
5. When your **Activity** closes, un-register the **BroadcastReceiver** object to avoid memory leaks.

This is a little bit complicated, so let's go through each step carefully.

First, in order to create a **PendingIntent** containing an implicit **Intent** that can be broadcast to applications when an event happens, you will use the static **PendingIntent.getBroadcast()** method like this:

```
PendingIntent msgSentIntent = PendingIntent.getBroadcast(this, 0,
                                  new Intent("MY_SMS_SENT"), 0);
```

This method takes four parameters. The first is just the current context or the "**this**" reference to our **Activity**. You can call **getApplicationContext()** instead if you don't have a handy activity reference. The second parameter is an integer request code, which is not currently used by the Android system. We will just set this parameter to zero. The third parameter is a new implicit **Intent** that will be broadcast to all applications when the message is sent. We want to give the intent some unique action string that we can detect later! We're using "MY_SMS_SENT". The final parameter can contain additional flags for advanced operations that we won't worry about now, so just leave that value as zero. Save the resulting **PendingIntent** object because we'll use it later in **SmsManager.sendTextMessage()**.

The next two steps involve defining a subclass of the **BroadcastReceiver** object and registering that object with the Android system. We want our receiver to be called when an implicit **Intent** is broadcast containing our unique action string "MY_SMS_SENT". It's most convenient to implement the **BroadcastReceiver** object as an anonymous inner class; however we also need to keep track of that object so we can un-register it when the **Activity** closes.

The two objects we need for this task, **BroadcastReceiver** and **IntentFilter**, are in the **android.content** package. So you can import those two classes individually or the entire **android.content.*** package:

```
import android.content.BroadcastReceiver;
import android.content.IntentFilter;
```

Next, declare a **BroadcastReceiver** member variable in your **Activity**. Later you will set this member variable equal to the anonymous inner class you create and register with the Android system. Keeping track of the object reference will allow us to un-register it later.

```
public class Main extends Activity
{
    BroadcastReceiver mySentReceiver = null;
```

Now when you're ready to start listening for messages (such as in your **onCreate**() method), you will need to call the **registerReceiver**() method with two parameters: a **BroadcastReceiver** object and an **IntentFilter**.

```
registerReceiver(BroadcastReceiver receiver, IntentFilter filter)
```

For the first parameter we'll define an anonymous inner class that inherits from **BroadcastReceiver** and implements the **onReceive**() method. The **BroadcastReceiver.onReceive**() method will be called whenever an implicit **Intent** is broadcast that matches the action string defined in the **IntentFilter**.

Below we show how to build an anonymous inner class version of **BroadcastReceiver** and assign the object to our **mySentReceiver** class member variable.

```
mySentReceiver =
    new BroadcastReceiver()        // anonymous inner class
    {
        public void onReceive(Context context, Intent intent)
        {
            if (getResultCode() == Activity.RESULT_OK) // if message sent ok
            {
                Toast t = Toast.makeText(context, "Message Sent!",
                                                Toast.LENGTH_LONG);
                t.show();
            }
            else  // else some send error occurred
            {
                Toast t = Toast.makeText(context,"Message Error!",
                                                Toast.LENGTH_LONG);
                t.show();
            }
        }
    };
```

This code may look involved, but it's actually very simple. We first create our new **BroadcastReceiver** object and then override the only method we care about: the **onReceive**() method. Inside this method, we call **getResultCode**(), which will give us a status code for the sent message. If this code is **Activity.RESULT_OK**, then the message was sent from the device without any problems. Any other code means some error occurred and the message was not sent! We're just popping up a little **Toast** message to confirm whether or not the message was sent.

Android discourages you from doing anything fancy from within the onReceive() method! You shouldn't display dialogs requiring user feedback, launch other messages, or attempt to use system services that might need to call you back later.

Now that we've created and saved our **BroadcastReceiver** it's time to register the object with an **IntentFilter**. You can simply create an **IntentFilter** with the **new** keyword, passing in our unique action string to the constructor.

```
registerReceiver(mySentReceiver, new IntentFilter("MY_SMS_SENT"));
```

Next, update your call to **SmsManager.sendTextMessage**() to include our new **PendingIntent** as the fourth parameter.

```
sms.sendTextMessage("5556",null,"I can do this myself too!",msgSentIntent, null);
```

Now we'll receive a **Toast** message when the message is sent!

Message Sent!

You need to take one last step to avoid memory leaks when your application exits: un-register the **BroadcastReceiver** when your **Activity** is destroyed. So let's override the **Activity.onDestroy**() method and safely clean up:

```
public void onDestroy()
{
    super.onDestroy();  // always call the base class version
    if (mySentReceiver!= null)     // just to be safe
    {
        unregisterReceiver(mySentReceiver);  // unregister BroadcastReceiver
    }
}
```

Now that we know how to receive a message "sent" event, we can follow identical steps to receive a message "delivered" event. This event will fire when the sending device receives confirmation that the target device got the message. You are going to follow the same five steps, creating a **PendingIntent** with a unique action string. Then register an implementation of **BroadcastReceiver** to handle the callback when an implicit **Intent** is broadcast with our unique action string. Don't forget to de-register the receiver in the activity's **onDestroy**() method.

If you are monitoring both the sent and delivered events at the same time, then you will need to declare a second **BroadcastReceiver** variable at the class level and remember to un-register both of them in your **onDestory**() method. We will use **mySentReceiver** and **myDeliveryReceiver** in our examples.

Unfortunately the emulator does not support the "delivered" notification when an SMS message reaches another emulator, so you won't be able to test this without a real Android device. But here is a complete example for future reference:

```
// Delivery notification only works on a real device - NOT ON EMULATOR!!!
PendingIntent msgDeliveredIntent = PendingIntent.getBroadcast(this, 0,
                                new Intent("MY_SMS_DELIVERED"), 0);
myDeliveryReceiver =
    new BroadcastReceiver()    // anonymous inner class
    {
        public void onReceive(Context context, Intent intent)
        {
            if (getResultCode() == Activity.RESULT_OK)
            {
                Toast t = Toast.makeText(context, "Msg Delivered!",
                                            Toast.LENGTH_LONG);
                t.show();
            }
            else
            {
                Toast t = Toast.makeText(context,"Msg Error!",
                                            Toast.LENGTH_LONG);
                t.show();
            }
        }
    };
registerReceiver(myDeliveryReceiver, new IntentFilter("MY_SMS_DELIVERED"));

// send the text message, specifying our PendingIntent for delivery callback
SmsManager sms = SmsManager.getDefault();
sms.sendTextMessage("5556", null, "I can do this myself!",
            null, msgDeliveredIntent);
```

Again, notice that we are only checking the "RESULT_OK" result code message. You can check for more result codes to get more specific information on any errors that occurred. The unique action string in this example is "MY_SMS_DELIVERED".

Receiving SMS Messages in an Application

Now that our application can send SMS messages, we may want to receive them as well! Fortunately the procedure for catching general SMS messages from other applications or devices is very similar to monitoring our own SMS message "sent" status events. We are going to use the familiar **BroadcastReceiver** object and simply implement the **onReceive**() method differently with a special **IntentFilter**. To summarize the steps:

1. Define an object that extends the **BroadcastReceiver** class and implements the **onReceive**() method. This is the method we want Android to call when an **Intent** is raised with an SMS message.
2. Register your **BroadcastReceiver** object with the Android system by calling **registerReceiver**() from your **Activity**. Use a filter that will only call our function when an SMS message is received.
3. When your **Activity** closes, un-register the **BroadcastReceiver** object to avoid memory leaks.

Also, very importantly, your application must define permission to receive SMS messages in your "AndroidManifest.xml" file. Otherwise your application will not receive any inbound SMS events at all!

```
<uses-permission android:name= "android.permission.RECEIVE_SMS" />
```

Of course we'll keep track of the **BroadcastReceiver** object at the class level with a member variable:

```
public class Main extends Activity
{
    BroadcastReceiver mySmsReceiver = null;
```

Now, for our **BroadcastReceiver** class we'll need to do a bit more work inside the **onReceive**() method.

```
public void onReceive(Context context, Intent intent)
```

The **Intent** will contain a **Bundle** object holding all of the information about the message(s) received.

The **Bundle** object is part of the **android.os** package, and we'll be using the **android.telephony. SmsMessage** class also. So let's first import those classes at the top of our source code:

```
import android.os.Bundle;
import android.telephony.SmsMessage;
```

Now, let's get started on our anonymous inner class extension of **BroadcastReceiver**! The first thing we'll do inside the **onReceive()** method is get the **Bundle** of information from the **Intent**.

```
mySmsReceiver =
    new BroadcastReceiver()    // anonymous inner class
    {
        public void onReceive(Context context, Intent intent)
        {
            Bundle bundle = intent.getExtras();
            if (bundle == null)
                return; // error - no Bundle present
```

There can actually be more than one SMS message contained in the **Bundle**; the device might get several at about the same time and we want to make sure we process them all. Each message is stored in a binary **PDU** (**P**rotocol **D**escription **U**nit) format that we'll need to convert to a nicer **SmsMessage** object.

The **Bundle** contains information as a series of name-value pairs. The name is a **String** key and the value can be one of the basic data types, an **Object**, or an array of information. The SMS message data is stored in an **Object** array under the key "pdus". There will be one entry in the array for each message received, and that entry is actually an array of bytes.

Let's continue our **onReceive()** example. Next we get the array of **Object** values from the bundle with the "pdus" key. Again for safety always check the return value for **null** before trying to use it!

```
Object[] pdus = (Object[]) bundle.get("pdus");
if (pdus == null)
    return; // error - no PDU values present
```

Now that we have safely received an array of messages, let's iterate over each message and process it.

```
for (int i=0; i<pdus.length; i++)  // for each message
{
    // convert from PDU to SmsMessage
    SmsMessage message = SmsMessage.createFromPdu(
                                        (byte[]) pdus[i]);

    // get from address and message text
    String from = message.getOriginatingAddress();
    String text = message.getMessageBody().toString();
```

Above we have cast each value in the array to a **byte[]** array. We then pass that **byte** array into the **SmsMessage.createFromPdu()** method to create a handy **SmsMessage** from the binary PDU. Once we have a **SmsMessage** then we can retrieve the message's sender with the **getOriginatingAddress()** method and the message's text with the **getMessageBody()** method.

Finally, what are we going to do with the data? To finish this example we'll just build a little **Toast** message that lets the user know what messages were received.

```
                            // format a nice display string and show with a Toast
                            String display = from + " sent you: " + text;
                            Toast t = Toast.makeText(context,display,Toast.LENGTH_LONG);
                            t.show();
                }
            }
        };
```

Once you have created your **BroadcastReceiver**, you need to register it with the Android system using a filter that will make the callback whenever an SMS message is received. To register your receiver, you will create an **IntentFilter** with the action "android.provider.Telephony.SMS_RECEIVED" like this:

```
    registerReceiver(mySmsReceiver,
                new IntentFilter("android.provider.Telephony.SMS_RECEIVED"));
```

Now, how do we test our new SMS message receiver? You can actually send a fake SMS message to your emulator from the DDMS perspective in Eclipse! Select the "DDMS" button on the top-right of the Eclipse IDE, or if you can't find it select "Window → Open Perspective → DDMS" from the Eclipse menu.

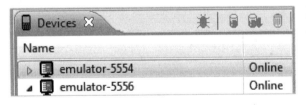

If you have more than one emulator running, select the one you are running your program on in the "Devices" window.

Next find the "Emulator Control" window and type in the "Incoming number" which can be any fake phone#, select the "SMS" radio button, and type in some message text. When you're ready hit the "Send" button.

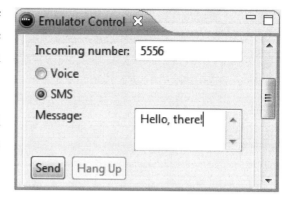

If you can see your emulator screen at the same time, you'll see a descriptive **Toast** message pop up with the message sender and contents!

5556 sent you: Hello, there!

 When registered to receive SMS messages, your application will get *all* of the messages sent to the device! You may have to look at the message data and decide if the message is something you want to process or ignore.

Don't forget to un-register your receiver in the activity's **onDestroy**() method.

```
public void onDestroy()
{
    super.onDestroy();
    if (mySmsReceiver != null)
    {
        unregisterReceiver(mySmsReceiver);
    }
}
```

Lesson Three: Using HTTP Networking

The Android SDK contains built-in features to allow an application to use networking features such as accessing files and resources on the Internet. In this lesson, we'll show how to make an HTTP connection and download data from the Internet inside your application.

HTTP and URLs

There are two main concepts that you need to understand in order to perform basic networking: HTTP and URLs. You've probably seen "http" many times as you type your favorite websites into a web browser.

HTTP stands for **H**yper**T**ext **T**ransfer **P**rotocol and is a standard for downloading web pages and files on the Internet. This protocol defines how web servers and browsers should request and receive files. The actual file downloaded can be in any recognized format such as HTML, an image, XML, or plain text.

In order to use the HTTP protocol, you will need to specify a unique address for a file or resource on the Internet. The unique address for a particular resource is called a URL, or **U**niform **R**esource **L**ocator. You probably use URLs every day as you surf the Internet. Here is an example URL:

```
http://www.HomeschoolProgramming.com
```

The URL has two main components: a protocol identifier and a resource name. In the example above, the protocol identifier is "http" and the resource name is "www.HomeschoolProgramming.com". There are many other types of protocols a URL can contain, including "ftp", "https" and "file", but for this course, we will stick with the common "http" protocol.

Using the Built-In Browser

The simplest way to surf the web on an Android device is using the built-in Web Browser application. You can create an implicit **Intent** from your code that will be handled by the built-in browser. The **Intent** should contain the URL address that you want to reach. The URL is actually stored in a similarly-named object called a URI (**U**niform **R**esource **I**dentifier). What's the difference between URL and URI? Not much! A URL is just a more specific version of a URI that tells you exactly how to access a resource.

To create a **Uri** object, use the static **Uri.parse**() method on a string containing the URL you want to reach.

```
Uri myURI = Uri.parse("http://www.homeschoolprogramming.com");
```

Now we can create an implicit **Intent** with the "ACTION_VIEW" type and our URI object:

```
Intent uriIntent = new Intent(Intent.ACTION_VIEW, myURI );
```

Finally, we simply raise the implicit **Intent** to the Android system where it will launch the built-in web browser. Implicit intents are raised by calling the **startActivity()** method with the intent:

```
startActivity(uriIntent);
```

This is a very quick and simple way to show a website from your application. Just like using the built-in SMS

Messenger, this approach will cause users to actually leave your application to go to another one. The user will then have to return to your application when finished.

Your program does not need any special Android permission since we're actually using another application to access the Intenet. If you want more control over the HTTP connection, or you want to send or receive data within your own application, you will need to write the HTTP-handling code yourself.

Using HTTP from an Android Application

In order to make a network connection from our own application, there are a number of steps to take.

1. Register for permissions in your "AndroidManifest.xml" file
2. Check the network status to make sure your device is connected to the Internet
3. Establish an HTTP connection to fetch a specific URL resource

Android Network Permissions

In order to create an Android program that accesses the Internet, you will need to register for one or more permissions in your "AndroidManifest.xml" file. The main permission is the "INTERNET" permission, which will allow you to communicate through the network to the Internet.

```
<uses-permission android:name="android.permission.INTERNET"/>
```

In addition, if you want to check the network state of the device before attempting any network functionality, you will need to register for the "ACCESS_NETWORK_STATE" permission as well.

```
<uses-permission android:name="android.permission.ACCESS_NETWORK_STATE"/>
```

In our code, we will use a number of classes from the standard Java Class Library and the **android.net** package. You should import the **java.net**, **java.io**, and **android.net** packages at the top of any source file that accesses the network. These packages will provide all of the classes and objects that we will need to make our HTTP connections. We'll also use a few items from **android.content**, so import that also!

```
import java.net.*;
import java.io.*;
import android.net.*;
import android.content.*;
```

Checking Network State

It's usually a good idea to check the device's current network state before you attempt to make any network connections in your program. Android devices will move around with their owner, which means that they can be in or out of network service at any time. Checking the network state first will save you some troubleshooting later in the program.

Since we want to check the network state frequently, it's a good idea to write a function we can call whenever our program needs to make a network connection. This saves a lot of repeated code in our application. We'll name our function **isNetworkAvailable()** and want it to return a boolean **true** if the device is connected.

```
public boolean isNetworkAvailable()
{
}
```

Now, how do we check the network status inside this function? The first thing to do is get a reference to the Android system's **ConnectivityManager** object. To get this object, we call the **getSystemService()** method and specify the **Context.CONNECTIVITY_SERVICE**, casting the result to a **ConnectivityManager**.

```
ConnectivityManager cm = (ConnectivityManager)
                    getSystemService(Context.CONNECTIVITY_SERVICE);
```

Now we can use the **ConnectivityManager** to get a **NetworkInfo** object containing the network status:

```
NetworkInfo networkInfo = cm.getActiveNetworkInfo();
```

For safety, check to make sure the **NetworkInfo** object is not **null** and then call the **isConnected()** method to see if the network is currently connected. If **isConnected()** returns **true**, then our method also will return **true** to show we can access the network. Otherwise, we will return **false**, to show the network is not available. Here is the full **isNetworkAvailable()** method:

```
public boolean isNetworkAvailable()
{
    // get a reference to the ConnectivityManager
    ConnectivityManager cm = (ConnectivityManager)
            getSystemService(Context.CONNECTIVITY_SERVICE);

    // get the current NetworkInfo object
    NetworkInfo networkInfo = cm.getActiveNetworkInfo();

    // if we have a valid NetworkInfo and we are connected
    if (networkInfo != null && networkInfo.isConnected())
    {
        return true;    // yes this device is connected
    }
    return false; // not connected for some reason
}
```

Note that a device can go in and out of network coverage at any time. This means even if your **isNetworkAvailable()** method returns **true**, by the time you make a network connection you might no longer be in coverage! So calling **isNetworkAvailable()** is a good first step to avoid wasting time, but you need to still be prepared to handle connectivity errors in the rest of your code.

Networking and the Android User Interface

By default, Andorid will not allow you to make network calls within the main program flow that controls your user interface and responds to user events. This restriction is in place because network calls can take many seconds to complete, and your user interface would be effectively frozen while waiting for the call to finish. You will receive an exception (**NetworkOnMainThreadException**) if you attempt to do this normally.

It is *best practice* to perform your network operations as a background task, allowing the user to continue working with a responsive UI in the meanwhile. However, creating and managing these background tasks (also called "threads") is a somewhat advanced topic beyond the scope of this course. So we are going to override the default Android behavior and allow network calls in our main user interface program flow.

First, add an **import** to the **android.os.StrictMode** class at the top of your source file. Then, inside your activity's **onCreate()** method, add the following two lines of code:

```
StrictMode.ThreadPolicy policy = new StrictMode.ThreadPolicy.Builder().
                                                permitAll().build();
StrictMode.setThreadPolicy(policy);
```

We won't go into detail about these lines of code, but typing them in exactly as-is within your **onCreate**() method will change the default restriction. Now we can make our network connections within the main user interface flow, including listener callbacks to button clicks, etc. Please remember that in a commercial-quality application, you should not take this shortcut! Instead you will want to use something called an **AsyncTask** to handle the networking in the background. Refer to your online Android documentation for more details.

Making an HTTP Connection

To make an HTTP connection with our program, we will use a **java.net** class called **HttpURLConnection**. This is a general-purpose, simple HTTP client that works for most networking requirements. This class is currently recommended by the Android development team.

Before we make a connection, we must create a **URL** that represents the location that we wish to access.

```
URL url = new URL("http://www.HomeschoolProgramming.com");
```

The **URL** constructor takes a single **String** representing your target address. Make sure that you include the "http://" protocol at the beginning since this is an important part of the **URL**.

Now we can use the **URL** object's **openConnection**() method to create a **HttpURLConnection**:

```
HttpURLConnection httpConn = (HttpURLConnection)url.openConnection();
```

Now we have the ability to make the Internet connection, but we haven't actually completed the connection yet! Before we complete the connection, we can set up any additional information that may be needed for our connection. In our case, we will set our request method to "GET", which means we are expecting to get back some information from our target URL location.

```
httpConn.setRequestMethod("GET");
```

Now we can finalize our connection by calling the **connect**() method:

```
httpConn.connect();
```

At this point, the Android system will attempt to connect to our URL address and prepare to download the target resource. In order to verify that this connection worked properly, we will get the response code that was returned by the web server:

```
int response = httpConn.getResponseCode();
if (response == HttpURLConnection.HTTP_OK)  // if successful
```

If the connection was successful, we will get an "HTTP_OK" response. We can then start retrieving the data from the connection. Pulling data from the server is done through an **InputStream**, very similar to the way we learned to read and write file data in Chapter Seven. You may want to review the concepts in that chapter.

Downloading Text Data

You can get an **InputStream** by calling **getInputStream()** on the HTTP connection object. Then, for text files, you can wrap the **InputStream** in an **InputStreamReader** and **BufferedReader** object so we can easily read lines of text. Remember that you can call **readLine()** on the **BufferedReader** until **null** is received. When finished you should **close()** your **BufferedReader** and **disconnect()** your **HttpURLConnection**.

One last thing: networking operations will throw exceptions when errors happen. So you must wrap all of the risky network code with a **try/catch** block in order to catch these exceptions. Eclipse will let you know if you have failed to add a **try/catch** around any function that throws an exception.

In the example below we are reading the returned text data line-by-line, building up a larger string. When finished, we put the entire string into an **EditView** control so we can see what we received.

```
try
{
    if (isNetworkAvailable())  // only try this if network is available
    {
        // make URL and open the HttpUrlConnection
        URL url = new URL("http://www.HomeschoolProgramming.com");
        HttpURLConnection httpConn = (HttpURLConnection)url.openConnection();
        httpConn.setRequestMethod("GET");

        // connect to the web server and get response code
        httpConn.connect();
        int response = httpConn.getResponseCode();
        if (response == HttpURLConnection.HTTP_OK)
        {
            // get InputStream and wrap in handy readers
            InputStream in = httpConn.getInputStream();
            InputStreamReader isr = new InputStreamReader(in);
            BufferedReader br = new BufferedReader(isr);

            String line = "";
            String file = "";
```

```java
            // read lines of text until nothing left on stream
            do
            {
                line = br.readLine();
                if (line != null)
                    file += line;  // add line to larger string
            }
            while (line != null);
            br.close();        // always close your input stream!

            // put whatever we received in a multi-line EditText
            EditText et = (EditText)findViewById(R.id.editText1);
            et.setText(file);
        }
        httpConn.disconnect();  // always disconnect when finished!
    }
}
catch(Exception e)
{
    // handle errors here
    Toast t = Toast.makeText(getApplicationContext(),
                        e.toString(),Toast.LENGTH_LONG);
    t.show();
}
```

Whew! After all that code, what do we get? That looks pretty strange! What you are looking at is the HTML file that gets returned by the web server when you go to our home page. It doesn't make much sense without a full web browser to parse the HTML and display the graphical web page.

Networking

Hello world!

```
<!DOCTYPE html PUBLIC "-//W3C//DTD XHTML 1.0
Transitional//EN" "http://www.w3.org/TR/xhtml1/
DTD/xhtml1-transitional.dtd"><html xmlns="http://
www.w3.org/1999/xhtml"><head><meta http-
equiv="Content-Type" content="text/html;
charset=UTF-8" /><title>Computer programming for
kids and teens!</title><meta name="description"
```

Your program can still usefully download other types of text files such as XML or plain text. You can then get information out of the text files for processing by your application.

Downloading Binary Data

Instead of text files, you can also use the **InputStream** to pull in binary data. If your URL points to a particular image such as http://www.homeschoolprogramming.com/images/teencoder_android.png, then you need to translate the binary data into an image format we can use on the device. To work with binary image data, import the following two classes at the top of your source file:

```
import android.graphics.Bitmap;
import android.graphics.BitmapFactory;
```

The **Bitmap** class will hold the image data. The **BitmapFactory** can create a **Bitmap** from a binary stream. In the example below, we use the **BitmapFactory.decodeStream()** method to translate the **InputStream** into a bitmap image.

```
InputStream in = httpConn.getInputStream();
Bitmap imageBmp = BitmapFactory.decodeStream(in);
```

Then we can place the downloaded image into an **ImageView** control by calling **setImageBitmap()**:

```
ImageView iv = (ImageView)findViewById(R.id.imageView1);
iv.setImageBitmap(imageBmp);
```

If we use the URL "http://www.homeschoolprogramming.com/images/teencoder_android.png", we'll pull the TeenCoder logo from our website.

No matter what you do with the **InputStream** data, remember to close the stream when you are finished with it. This will release the memory it uses back to the Android system.

```
in.close();
```

Finally, once we are done with our HTTP connection, we will need to call **disconnect()** in order to free up system resources:

```
httpConn.disconnect();
```

That's all it takes to make a simple HTTP connection and download data to your Android application. Using this method, you can pull text, images, XML files, etc. from the Internet right into your program.

Activity: Weather Application

In this activity, we will use a network connection to get current weather data from an online weather source!

Your activity requirements and instructions are found in the "Chapter12_Activity.pdf" document located in your "TeenCoder/Android Programming/Activity Docs" folder. You can access this document through your Student Menu or by directly clicking on it from Windows Explorer (Windows) or Finder (Mac OS).

Complete this activity now and ensure your program meets the requirements before continuing!

Chapter Thirteen: Creating Home App Widgets

An Android *app widget* is a small graphical extension of your program that can be placed on the user's home screen. In this chapter you will learn how to create, configure, and update app widgets.

Lesson One: Creating App Widgets

In the ever-changing and highly-competitive world of mobile applications, usability is extremely important. You can create an *app widget* that an Android user may choose to place on their home screen. This widget will give the user easy access your program and allow them to see information at-a-glance. Your widget can automatically update the displayed information at specific intervals.

You have already used widgets in the emulator home screen, but probably didn't realize it! You can see examples of a Digital Clock widget, Google Search widget, and the Music widget in the image to the left. The Google widget will allow you to enter search keywords and launch the built-in web browser application with the results. The Music widget gives you quick access to your favorite songs.

Application *shortcuts* are small, static icons that launch your full program. But app *widgets* can be larger and display interactive data – a small part of your program runs directly on the home screen.

Adding and Removing Widget from the Home Screen

Users can add or remove any available widget from the home screen. You have this ability both in the emulator and on a real Android device. To add a widget, open the Apps screen and choose the "Widgets" tab at the top.

Here you will see a list of available widgets that are installed on the system. Click and hold on the widget you want and it will appear on the home screen. For example,

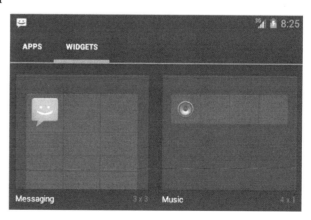

select the Music widget and you will see a digital music player on the home screen. To remove a widget from the home screen, simply long-press on the widget until a Remove button appears in the ActionBar. Drag the widget to the Remove button... and presto it's gone!

App Widget Dimensions

An Android device's home screen is divided into blocks, or cells. A small handheld phone may have a 4 x 4 cell grid while a larger tablet may have 8 x 7 cells or more. One cell can hold an application shortcut or an app widget. The size of these cells may vary from device to device, but the accepted rule of thumb is that each cell is around 74 device-independent pixels in width and height.

In the example to the left we have added three app widgets and four application shortcuts to the home screen. Now the home screen 4 x 4 cell grid is completely full! We have added the rectangular grid outline so you can see the cells. Notice that the app widgets actually spread over more than one cell. The Google search and Android help widgets each take one cell row and four cell columns in the grid. The analog clock takes a 2 x 2 group of cells. Application shortcuts always take just one cell.

You can design your app widget to take any number of cells. Just remember that smaller is better. Users will be less likely to add a huge app widget to their home screen that won't leave any room for other applications.

To read more on recommended design techniques for app widgets, take a look at the Android documentation located at http://developer.android.com/guide/practices/ui_guidelines/widget_design.html or search online for "Android app widget design".

The AppWidget Project

To create an app widget, you'll first need an Android project. We are going to use a project cleverly called "AppWidget" as the basis for our app widget example. Of course, you can create your own Android project and name it whatever you like. You're a "pro" at creating new Android projects by now, so we'll assume you can handle this step on your own. You can also add an app widget to any existing Android project.

Widget Provider XML

To create an App Widget for your Android application, you will first need to create an app widget provider

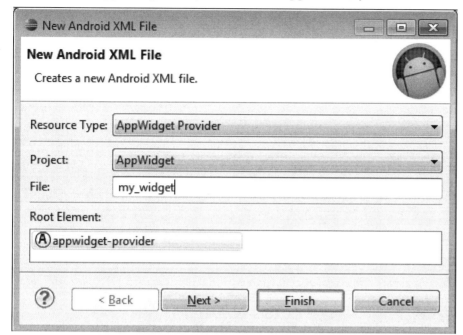

XML file. This file will contain the basic information about your widget's size, update interval, and layout.

We'll use the "New Android XML File" wizard again, so select "File → New → Android XML File" from the Eclipse menu. Pick your project in the "Project" combo box and select "AppWidget Provider" in the "Resource Type" box at the top. Then enter a valid XML file name and click "Finish".

Your new XML file will appear under "res/xml". Like other Android XML files you have the option of managing the file through a graphical editor or by directly editing the underlying XML.

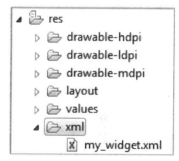

The default XML doesn't contain much information:

```xml
<?xml version="1.0" encoding="utf-8"?>
<appwidget-provider xmlns:android="http://schemas.android.com/apk/res/android" >

</appwidget-provider>
```

We'll quickly want to add some attributes to define the widget's size, update period, and layout:

```xml
<?xml version="1.0" encoding="utf-8"?>
<appwidget-provider xmlns:android="http://schemas.android.com/apk/res/android"
    android:updatePeriodMillis="0"
    android:minHeight="40dp"
    android:minWidth="110dp"
    android:initialLayout="@layout/my_widget_layout">
</appwidget-provider>
```

The **android:updatePeriodMillis** attribute sets the amount of time (in milliseconds) between updates for our widget. Each app widget can ask the Android system to call the widget's **onUpdate**() method periodically. This will allow you to keep your widget's information fresh and updated. If the device is asleep when the update is due, the system will wake up the device and update the widget.

The smallest update interval is 30 minutes. Wait… why are we setting an update period in milliseconds if the minimum interval is 30 minutes or 1,800,000 milliseconds? Clearly the Android development team made a design change at some point and we are left with an attribute value that has a resolution much higher than it needs to be! Because widget updates will wake up a sleeping device, you are really discouraged from updating too frequently. Some widgets may update only once a day (or 86,400,000 milliseconds). If your widget does not need updates at all, just put a value of zero in the **updatePeriodMillis** attribute.

The **android:minWidth** and **android:minHeight** attributes declare the default number of device-independent pixels that our widget will use horizontally and vertically on the home screen. To figure out these sizes, you first need to decide how many cells you will need across and down for the widget. Once you know these numbers, you can use this simple formula to estimate the device-independent pixel sizes.

```
dpUnits across or down = (number of cells * 70) - 30
```

We can then use the resulting number to set our widget's **minWidth** and **minHeight**. This is the minimum amount of space that we require to show our widget interface. A widget two cells wide and one cell high would have **minWidth** of (2 * 70) – 30 = 110dp and a **minHeight** of (1 * 70) – 30 = 40dp.

The final attribute, **android:initialLayout**, will select the XML layout file that contains the visual design of our app widget. You haven't created one yet, but in our example we're assuming the file name will be "my_widget_layout.xml". Making the widget XML layout is the next task!

App Widget Layout XML

You will use the same sort of XML layout file for your app widget as you do for a full **Activity**. To create a new XML layout file, select "File → New → Android XML File" from the Eclipse menu. Ensure the Resource Type is "Layout" and add your XML file name such as "my_widget_layout". Then select one of the layout types at the bottom that are supported by app widgets (see below) and click "Finish".

App widgets take up less space and have far less functionality than a regular activity. In fact, an app widget layout can only use one of these three layout types: **FrameLayout**, **LinearLayout**, or **RelativeLayout**. In addition, only a dozen or so controls are supported on an app widget display. The ones you are familiar with include **Button**, **ImageButton**, **ImageView**, and **TextView**. A full list of supported widget controls can be found in the Android documentation at http://developer.android.com/guide/topics/appwidgets/index.html or you can search online for "Android app widgets".

If we wanted to create an app widget showing the current day and time, our XML layout might contain a pair of **TextView** controls stacked vertically with a **LinearLayout**:

```xml
<?xml version="1.0" encoding="utf-8"?>
<LinearLayout xmlns:android="http://schemas.android.com/apk/res/android"
    android:layout_width="match_parent"
    android:layout_height="match_parent"
    android:orientation="vertical" >

    <TextView
        android:id="@+id/timeText"
        android:text="Time goes here!"
        android:layout_width="wrap_content"
        android:layout_height="wrap_content"/>
    <TextView
        android:id="@+id/dateText"
        android:text="Date goes here!"
        android:layout_width="wrap_content"
        android:layout_height="wrap_content"/>

</LinearLayout>
```

Remember that all of your controls defined in the layout need to fit within the width and height that you configured in the app widget provider XML file. Notice that we defined some default text for each control (e.g. "Time goes here!") just to get us started, but we'll of course want to update that text from our code later.

Once you save your layout XML file, make sure that the provider XML file (e.g. "my_widget.xml") links to the layout XML filename in the **android:initialLayout** attribute of the <appwidget-provider>:

```xml
android:initialLayout="@layout/my_widget_layout">
```

Unfortunately, if you build and run your program with just the widget provider XML and the layout XML, the Android system will not recognize your widget. So there is nothing to see yet.

Updating AndroidManifest.xml

You are going to create a Java class that Android will use to enable, disable, and update your app widget. In order to let the Android system know how to use your class, you need to modify the "AndroidManfiest.xml" file. Inside your <application> element (at the same level as any other <activity> elements), you will need to add a <receiver> element for each kind of app widget your application wants to define.

```
<application
        android:allowBackup="true"
        android:icon="@drawable/ic_launcher"
        android:label="@string/app_name"
        android:theme="@style/AppTheme">


    <receiver android:name=".MyDateWidget" >
        <intent-filter>
            <action android:name="android.appwidget.action.APPWIDGET_UPDATE" />
        </intent-filter>
        <meta-data android:name="android.appwidget.provider"
                    android:resource="@xml/my_widget" />
    </receiver>


</application>
```

The <receiver> element has only one attribute: "android:name". This value tells Android the name of our Java class that will handle the widget. We have not yet created that class, but we're going to call it **MyDateWidget**.

The <intent-filter> element registers our app widget to receive **APPWIDGET_UPDATE** events from the Android system. All communication to app widgets is done with **Intents**, so this <intent-filter> should look familiar to you. **Activity** screens also use <intent-filters> to define the **Intents** they can handle.

Finally, the <meta-data> element contains an important link to the widget's provider XML file we created earlier ("my_widget.xml"). That XML file sets the widget's width, height, update frequency, and layout.

In the next lesson you'll learn how to create your **MyDateWidget** class to allow your widget to be added to the home screen.

Lesson Two: Interacting with App Widgets

In the last lesson, we created the definition and layout for our app widget. Now we need to add the code that will allow the widget to be placed on the home screen, update the display, and respond to user clicks.

The AppWidgetProvider Class

In order for your app widget to work with an Android device, you need to create a special class that Android will call in order to enable, disable, or update the widget. We have already specified the name of the class, **MyDateWidget,** in the "AndroidManifest.xml" file above, so now it's time to create this class!

Your widget class will extend a built-in class called the **AppWidgetProvider**. An **AppWidgetProvider** is a kind of **BroadcastReceiver** that knows how to catch **Intents** intended just for your app widget. Since the **AppWidgetProvider** base class is doing all the hard work, all your derived class needs to do is override one or more methods to respond to the events you care about. As usual, you can create a new Java class by selecting "File → New → Class" from the Eclipse menu, or right-clicking on your project's source tree and selecting "New → Class". Give your class the name you specified in the "AndroidManifest.xml" – **MyDateWidget** in our example.

You will need to import the **android.appwidget.AppWidgetProvider** class at the top of your new file and make **MyDateWidget** extend that class. Here is a shiny new "MyDateWidget.java" source file:

```
package teencoder.androidprogramming;
import android.appwidget.AppWidgetProvider;


public class MyDateWidget extends AppWidgetProvider
{
}
```

Ok, we've done quite a bit of work – defined an app widget provider XML, a layout XML, modified the "AndroidManifest.xml", and created an **AppWidgetProvider** class. We haven't really added anything to **MyDateWidget** yet, but we can finally see the fruits of our labor!

In order to test an app widget in the emulator, you should just run your Android program in the emulator as normal. Each time you run the program, your entire project is actually re-installed into the emulator and registered with the Android system according to your "AndroidManifest.xml" file. So even if you exit your program immediately with the back arrow and go back to the Android home screen, your application is still installed and can be re-launched. Click on the application grid icon at the bottom to see all programs installed in the emulator, and in our case the "AppWidget" application is still present and ready to go.

Since we also listed an app widget (**MyDateWidget**) in the manifest file, we can now add the widget to the emulator's home screen. First, make sure you have enough room for a widget that will take one cell row and two cell columns. Then, simply go to your Apps, select "Widgets", and find our "AppWidget" in the list. Click and hold on the widget to add it to the home screen.

You can see our widget's layout covers two cell columns and one cell row. The actual widget display right now is pretty boring – it just contains the two **TextViews** and default text we added to the layout way back in Lesson One. In order to update our app widget controls with more interesting information we'll have to write some code in our **AppWidgetProvider** class.

Remember that the **AppWidgetProvider** base class will catch events such as enable, disable, and update. You can decide which of these events you want to process in your code and override the callback method defined for each event. There are six possible methods you can override.

Method	Description
`void onAppWidgetOptionsChanged(` `Context context,` `AppWidgetManager mgr,` `int appWidgetId, Bundle newOptions)`	This method is called when your widget layout has changed. Android may decide to change the size of your layout, and this method gives you a chance to complete any special processing during this event.
`void onDeleted (Context context,` `int[] appWidgetIds)`	This method is called when each instance of a widget is removed from the home screen. If this particular widget needs any sort of clean-up (removing files, etc.), this is your chance!
`void onDisabled(Context context)`	This method is called when the last copy of your widget is removed from the home screen.
`void onEnabled (Context context)`	This method is called when the first copy of your widget is added to the home screen.
`void onReceive (Context context,` `Intent intent)`	This method is called whenever any broadcast **Intent** is received by your widget. By default it is responsible for calling the other event methods in this table. You should not override **onReceive**() unless very specialized event processing is needed!
`void onUpdate (Context context,` `AppWidgetManager mgr,` `int[] appWidgetIds)`	This method is called by Android at the interval time that you defined in your app widget provider XML file. This is your chance to periodically update the widget's visual controls with new data.

Some of these method descriptions talk about more than one copy of the widget on the home screen. Is that possible? Yes! Users can repeatedly add as many copies of the same widget to the home screen as they like. This may seem odd, but consider a "weather" widget. A user might add one copy to view the weather in New York and another instance to view the weather in California.

The **onEnabled**() and **onDisabled**() methods are called when the very first widget instance is added and when the very last instance is removed from the home screen. If you need to do any one-time setup or clean-up for all copies of your widget, do so in those functions. You also get an **onDeleted**() callback each time an individual widget is removed from the screen.

Notice that the **onReceive**() is responsible for interpreting the incoming event and calling the other methods. If you override **onReceive**(), you must remember to call the other methods manually. If you do not, they will not run! Unless you are performing some advanced techniques, it's often best to not override this method. Instead, let the default **AppWidgetProvider onReceive**() implementation do its job.

Updating your Widgets

The most commonly overridden method in the **AppWidgetProvider** class is the **onUpdate**() method, which gives you a chance to periodically change the information shown in your widget view controls. You will only get one **onUpdate**() callback at each time interval, and you will need to update all copies of your widget on the screen at that time. To override **onUpdate**(), first add a few **import** statements to the top of your code:

```
import android.appwidget.AppWidgetManager;
import android.content.Context;
import android.widget.RemoteViews;
```

Then add the **onUpdate**() method within your **AppWidgetProvider** class definition:

```
public class MyDateWidget extends AppWidgetProvider
{
    public void onUpdate(Context context, AppWidgetManager appWidgetManager,
                    int[] appWidgetIds)
    {
        // update your widget view here!
    }
}
```

There are three parameters to the **onUpdate**()method. The first parameter is the **Context** in which the **AppWidgetProvider** is running. The second parameter is an **AppWidgetManager** object. This object is used to get information and status about installed app widgets. The final parameter is an array of integer IDs; there will be one unique ID for each copy of your widget that is on the home screen.

Don't forget, if you want your **onUpdate**() method to be called, you need to return to your app widget provider XML file and set the "android:updatePeriodMillis" attribute to 30 minutes (1800000 ms) or greater.

```
android:updatePeriodMillis="1800000"
```

Now, since your **onUpdate**() method is responsible for updating all copies of the app widget, you will want to loop over the **appWidgetIds** array, performing whatever processing is necessary for each widget, and ensuring that each widget's controls are updated.

What processing is necessary for our example date/time widget? We would like to get a pair of strings showing the current date and time, and then update the two **TextView** controls on our widget with that data. Here is the Java code that will get the current date and time and build these two strings:

```
java.util.Date now = new java.util.Date();  // get the current date and time

// create utility DateFormat objects that can build date/time strings
java.text.DateFormat dateFormat = java.text.DateFormat.getDateInstance();
java.text.DateFormat timeFormat = java.text.DateFormat.getTimeInstance();

// use the DateFormat objects to build date / time strings from current time
String currentDate = dateFormat.format(now);
String currentTime = timeFormat.format(now);
```

Now that we have the data we want to show in the **currentDate** and **currentTime** strings, what do we do with it? In a normal **Activity** we could use **findViewById**() to get the **TextView** control and then simply call **setText**() on the control. Unfortunately, with app widgets, it's not that easy.

Using RemoteViews

Widgets are run as part of the home screen application on an Android device. This poses a certain security concern, since the home screen application has nearly unlimited permissions on the device. If the Android system allowed all programs direct control of widgets on the home screen, they would be granted super access to the device. This could be potentially dangerous in the wrong hands! Instead, the developers at Android decided that applications will manage their widgets through a special class called **RemoteViews**. A **RemoteViews** allows an activity to manage app widget controls using only that application's permissions.

You can build a new **RemoteViews** object with the package name (e.g. "teencoder.androidprogramming") of the current context and the unique ID of the layout XML for your widget.

```
RemoteViews views = new RemoteViews(context.getPackageName(),
                                    R.layout.my_widget_layout);
```

The **context**.getPackageName() method will return the package name of the current context. The second parameter will tell the view which layout contains the definition of the widget controls. We are still using the "widget_layout.xml" we created in the previous lesson.

Now we can use the **RemoteViews** object to update the views on our widget. There are many "set" method on **RemoteViews**; below is a listing of the more common methods to update the controls we know about:

Method Name	Description
setTextViewText(int viewID, String text)	Sets the text value in a **TextView** control.
setImageViewBitmap(int viewID, Bitmap bitmap)	Sets the bitmap image in an **ImageView** control.
setViewVisibility(int viewID, int visibility);	Controls the visibility of the control on the screen (**View.VISIBLE**, **View.INVISIBLE**, or **View.GONE**)

There are many other methods that you can use from this class. See the Android documentation at http://developer.android.com/reference/android/widget/RemoteViews.html or search online for "Android RemoteViews" for more information.

Since we have a pair of **TextView** controls, we will use the **setTextViewText**() method:

```
views.setTextViewText(R.id.dateText, currentDate);
views.setTextViewText(R.id.timeText, currentTime);
```

The first parameter is the unique ID of the control from the layout, and the second parameter contains the string data we want to place into the control.

When done, we need to apply all of our **RemoteViews** changes to the widget. We will use the **AppWidgetManager** object that was passed into the **onUpdate**() method. This object has a method called **updateAppWidget**() that is responsible for (you guessed it!) updating the widget views on the screen.

```
appWidgetManager.updateAppWidget(appWidgetId, views);
```

The first parameter is the unique ID for the particular copy of the app widget we're updating. The second parameter is the **RemoteViews** that we have created with this app widget's updated information.

Since we want to update all copies of our date/time app widget with the same value, we'll create a **for**() loop to iterate over each control. Within the loop we'll update the **RemoteViews** and then call the **AppWidgetManager**.**updateAppWidget**() method to update the views. Let's review a complete example **onUpdate**() method that pulls together all of the code demonstrated so far.

```
public void onUpdate(Context context, AppWidgetManager appWidgetManager,
                        int[] appWidgetIds)
{
    java.util.Date now = new java.util.Date();

    java.text.DateFormat dateFormat = java.text.DateFormat.getDateInstance();
    java.text.DateFormat timeFormat = java.text.DateFormat.getTimeInstance();

    String currentDate = dateFormat.format(now);
    String currentTime = timeFormat.format(now);

    for (int i=0; i<appWidgetIds.length; i++)
    {
        int appWidgetId = appWidgetIds[i]; //get current widget
        RemoteViews views = new RemoteViews(context.getPackageName(),
                                        R.layout.my_widget_layout);

        views.setTextViewText(R.id.dateText, currentDate);
        views.setTextViewText(R.id.timeText, currentTime);

        appWidgetManager.updateAppWidget(appWidgetId, views);
    }
}
```

Notice our **for()** loop gets the unique widget ID from the input array and then passes that ID into the **updateAppWidget()** method call to update each widget on the screen. In many cases there will be only one copy of your widget running, and it wouldn't make any sense for a user to add more copies. But you can't predict what users will do, so it's important to write your code to handle all scenarios.

It's not very useful to show two date/time widgets on the screen, each displaying the same time. It would be better if the user could select a different timezone for each widget so they could see the time in New York and California, for example. In the next lesson we'll show you how to configure each widget.

The onUpdate() method is called when you first add the widget to the home screen. But, that first onUpdate() call will only contain the unique id for the newly added widget, not all widgets. So in our date/time widget example, you would see different timestamps on the widgets matching when they were added to the home page. Once the periodic (30 minute) update kicks in, one onUpdate() call should contain the full list of IDs for all copies and they would then display the same information.

Launching an Application Activity from a Widget

You may want to perform an action when the user clicks on your widget. For example, you may want to launch your main application activity screen. There are three basic steps to make this happen:

1. Create an **Intent** that will launch your **Activity** class
2. Create a **PendingIntent** around your launching **Intent** to maintain the same security permissions
3. Register the **PendingIntent** with the **RemoteViews** object so it will be launched when the user clicks on a view

All of these steps are completed within your **onUpdate**() method, where you have access to the **RemoteViews** and **AppWidgetManager** objects.

First, we can easily create an **Intent** that will launch our application's **Main** activity class (or some other activity if you prefer). This is the same type of **Intent** that we would use to switch from one **Activity** to another in a standard application.

```
Intent intent = new Intent(context, Main.class);
```

Since we are using a widget and not a regular application, we will need to wrap our **Intent** into a **PendingIntent**. This will ensure that our application's security permissions are used to launch the **Intent**. To create a **PendingIntent** around our activity **Intent**, use the static **PendingIntent.getActivity**() method.

```
PendingIntent pi = PendingIntent.getActivity(context, 0, intent, 0);
```

The parameters for **getActivity**() are the same as described in Chapter Eleven. Use the current context as the first parameter and the **Intent** as the third parameter. The second and fourth parameters can be left at zero.

Now we have created our **Intent** and **PendingIntent**, we need to tell the app widget to use them when the user clicks on a particular control in the widget view. You can actually create different intents for each control in your view if you like! But for our example we'll just use the same intent for both the date and time **TextView** controls. To attach a **PendingIntent** to a control, call the **setOnClickPendingIntent**() method on the **RemoteViews** object. Make sure you do this before calling the **updateAppWidget**() method.

```
views.setOnClickPendingIntent(R.id.dateText, pi);
views.setOnClickPendingIntent(R.id.timeText, pi);
```

Below we have enhanced the **for**() loop in our example **onUpdate**() method to add these pending intents through the remote views.

```
for (int i=0; i<appWidgetIds.length; i++)
{
    int appWidgetId = appWidgetIds[i]; //get current widget
    RemoteViews views = new RemoteViews(context.getPackageName(),
                                        R.layout.my_widget_layout);

    views.setTextViewText(R.id.dateText, currentDate);
    views.setTextViewText(R.id.timeText, currentTime);

    Intent intent = new Intent(context, Main.class);
    PendingIntent pi = PendingIntent.getActivity(context, 0, intent, 0);

    views.setOnClickPendingIntent(R.id.dateText, pi);
    views.setOnClickPendingIntent(R.id.timeText, pi);

    appWidgetManager.updateAppWidget(appWidgetId, views);
}
}
```

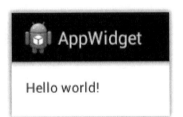

Now we can test out our user click-handling.   In the emulator, if we click on either the time or date fields, you will launch the **Main** activity for the "AppWidget" application. Admittedly there's not much happening over on our **Main** activity screen, but at least we were able to launch it successfully from our app widget!

Launching Built-in Services from a Widget

Instead of launching one of your own program activity screens, you can also choose to have your widget raise an implicit **Intent** for processing by one of the built-in Android applications. The procedure is exactly the same as launching your own activity; you just need to create a different **Intent** with an action and data that will be recognized by some other service.

For example, let's change our date/time widget to launch a web browser going to the official United States time website, http://time.gov. For this **Intent** we'll use **Intent.ACTION_VIEW** as the action and create a **Uri** object to hold our URL address. We still wrap it in a **PendingIntent** created from **getActivity()**.

```
Intent intent = new Intent(Intent.ACTION_VIEW,
                           android.net.Uri.parse("http://time.gov"));
PendingIntent pi = PendingIntent.getActivity(context, 0, intent, 0);
```

The rest of the procedure is exactly the same! Call **RemoteViews.setOnClickPendingIntent**() for each control you want to respond to the user click, and call the **AppWidgetManager.updateAppWidget**() method when finished. Now when the user clicks on our widget, we'll see the built-in web browser with the target URL instead of our own activity.

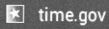

time.gov

Be careful in your onUpdate() method not to write code that will take a long time to complete! Android will give you 5-10 seconds for this method to return before deciding that your application is "unresponsive" and displaying an ugly error message to the user. There are advanced techniques you can use to perform your processing in the background if your widget updates will take a long time.

Activity #1: Weather App Widget

In this activity, we will expand our Weather Application from the last chapter to include an app widget that can be placed on the home screen. The widget will show an image and information about the current weather.

Your activity requirements and instructions are found in the "Chapter13_Activity1.pdf" document located in your "TeenCoder/Android Programming/Activity Docs" folder. You can access this document through your Student Menu or by directly clicking on it from Windows Explorer (Windows) or Finder (Mac OS).

Complete this activity now and ensure your program meets the requirements before continuing!

Lesson Three: Widget Configuration Activity

Many app widgets are fairly simple; they display data like the current time or receive user input to launch a specific task. But what if your widget could use some configuration? In our date/time widget, we may want to allow the user to select a different website to launch when they click on the widget. Android provides a way for you to show a one-time configuration screen when the widget is first added to the home screen.

To create this one-time configuration, you will need to add a new **Activity** to your project. This activity should be added just like any other regular application **Activity**. You will need to create an XML layout file, create a class that extends **android.app.Activity** class, and then add the **Activity** information to your project's "AndroidManifest.xml" file.

Configuration Layout

Let's go ahead and create a configuration activity that will allow the user to enter a different website for our date/time widget. The XML layout is created normally through "File → New → Android XML File" from the Eclipse menu. We'll pick "my_config_layout" as the XML filename and choose the default **LinearLayout** model.

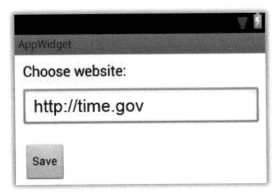

Our configuration screen will have three controls: a **TextView**, **EditText**, and **Button**. The text view will tell the user what to do ("Choose website:"). The initial text value of the **EditText** control is helpfully pre-populated with the default website "http://time.gov". The user can enter a new URL in the edit field and click the "Save" button when finished.

Since the configuration screen is based on a full-featured **Activity**, it is not limited to the controls supported by the widget layout. Instead, you are free to create the screen just like you would any regular **Activity** screen. Our example layout is very simple, but your own may be more complicated based on the configuration needs of your widget.

Configuration Activity Class

Once we have completed the XML layout file, we can turn our attention to the **Activity** class. Create this class just like you would any other activity and override the **onCreate**() method. Make sure to set the content view to your newly created XML layout for the configuration screen. In the example below we have created a class called **MyWidgetConfig** that will handle our widget's configuration.

```java
public class MyWidgetConfig extends Activity
{
    public void onCreate(Bundle savedInstanceState)
    {
        super.onCreate(savedInstanceState);
        setContentView(R.layout.my_config_layout);
```

This configuration activity screen will appear once each time you add a new copy of your widget to the home screen. The widget will not actually be added to the home screen until the activity closes though! When the activity closes you will need to communicate a status result to Android to show if the user successfully configured the widget. It's possible the user clicks the back arrow button and exits the configuration activity without doing anything. In this case we don't want Android to add the widget to the home screen at all.

Your **onCreate**() method needs to handle three tasks.

1. Get and save the unique ID of the widget that is being configured
2. Set a button-click listener (or similar method) to process the configuration when the user is done
3. Set the return code letting Android know if the configuration was successful

The unique ID of the widget being configured is stored in the **Intent** used to launch the **Activity**. You are familiar with how to get the **Bundle** of extras from the **Intent** and then retrieve values based on a string key. In this case the key name is **AppWidgetManager.EXTRA_APPWIDGET_ID** and the value is an integer. You should declare an **int** variable as a class member to store the result for when the user closes the activity.

```java
public class MyWidgetConfig extends Activity
{
    int widgetID;       // this member variable will hold the ID for this widget

    public void onCreate(Bundle savedInstanceState)
    {
        super.onCreate(savedInstanceState);
        setContentView(R.layout.my_config_layout);

        // Store widget ID for current widget in class member
        Bundle extras = getIntent().getExtras();
        widgetID = extras.getInt(AppWidgetManager.EXTRA_APPWIDGET_ID,
                            AppWidgetManager.INVALID_APPWIDGET_ID);
```

The **getInt**() method on the **Bundle** takes a second parameter which will be the default returned if the key name is not found in the bundle. We have specified **AppWidgetManager.INVALID_APPWIDGET_ID** which is a pre-defined constant just in case a real ID is not found. We can check this value to make sure that we have a valid widget to work with.

The second step inside **onCreate()** is to set a default return code to let Android know if the configuration was completed successfully.

```
    // by default cancel the widget installation if user hits back button
    setResult(RESULT_CANCELED);
```

This will set an initial value for the result to **RESULT_CANCELED**. If the user leaves the configuration screen without choosing the "Save" button, this is the value that the **Activity** will hold when it closes. Android will get this value to determine whether or not to add the widget to the home screen.

Finally, we need to define the function that will execute when the user clicks the "Save" button. We are going to create an anonymous inner class that implements the **OnClickListener** interface for the **Button** object.

```
    Button b = (Button)findViewById(R.id.button1);
    b.setOnClickListener(
        new View.OnClickListener()
        {
            public void onClick(View v)
            {
                // code to execute when the Save button is clicked goes here!
            }
        }
    );
```

In your **onClick()** function, you will need to complete these tasks:

- Gather the user's configuration input
- Configure the widget using the input
- Set an **Activity** result code indicating the configuration was successful
- Close the **Activity**

The exact code for the first two tasks will depend on what you need to configure. In our example we need to read the website URL from the edit field and then create the **Intent** and **PendingIntents** that will be used when the user clicks on one of the widget views. These intents are identical to what we already coded in the **onUpdate()** method, but now we are using the URL from the configuration screen instead of a fixed value.

It's easy enough to pull the current value from the edit field, as shown below.

```
EditText websiteText = (EditText)findViewById(R.id.editText1);
String strWebsite = websiteText.getText().toString();
```

Then we'll create the two intents just as before, using our user's **strWebsite** URL:

```
Intent intent = new Intent(Intent.ACTION_VIEW,
                           android.net.Uri.parse(strWebsite));
PendingIntent pi = PendingIntent.getActivity(getApplicationContext(), 0,
                                             intent, 0);
```

Setting the **PendingIntent** to launch when the user clicks on either of the two **TextView** controls is very similar to what you've done in the **onUpdate()** method. First we create a **RemoteViews** object using the package name retrieved from the **Context** and the layout of the widget. Then we call **setOnClickPendingIntent()** with the unique control ID for each field and the **PendingIntent** we created.

```
RemoteViews views = new RemoteViews(MyWidgetConfig.this.getPackageName(),
                                    R.layout.my_widget_layout);

views.setOnClickPendingIntent(R.id.dateText, pi);
views.setOnClickPendingIntent(R.id.timeText, pi);
```

We're almost done! Remember that once we've finished updating the **RemoteViews** we need to call **updateAppWidget()** on the **AppWidgetManager** using the unique ID for the widget.

```
AppWidgetManager widgetManager = AppWidgetManager.getInstance(
                                                  MyWidgetConfig.this);
widgetManager.updateAppWidget(widgetID, views);
```

Notice we're using **widgetID** which is the integer value we stored as a class member during **onCreate()**.

OK, we have finished configuring our widget; now we need to signal to Android that configuration was successful and close out the **Activity** screen. We will do this by calling **setResult()** with a **RESULT_OK** return code and an extra **Intent** containing the widget's unique ID. First we create the **Intent** and then store the ID as an "extra" with the same key name we used earlier to get the ID from the activity-starting **Intent**. Then we call **setResult()** with **RESULT_OK** and the new **Intent**:

```
Intent resultValue = new Intent();
resultValue.putExtra(AppWidgetManager.EXTRA_APPWIDGET_ID, widgetID);
setResult(RESULT_OK, resultValue);
```

Finally, we want to close the configuration **Activity** completely. By calling the **finish()** method the **Activity** will close and the user will return to the home screen.

```
finish();            // close the Activity
```

Adding the Configuration Activity to the Android Manifest

We have completed our **Activity** class for the widget configuration step. Now we can add our new **MyWidgetConfig** activity to the "AndroidManifest.xml file". This will look just like any other **Activity** that we have added to the manifest, with one exception. Our configuration **Activity** will need to register to receive the **APPWIDGET_CONFIGURE** broadcast events. This requires an <intent-filter> element:

```
<activity android:name=".MyWidgetConfig"
          android:label="@string/app_name">
    <intent-filter>
        <action android:name="android.appwidget.action.APPWIDGET_CONFIGURE"/>
    </intent-filter>
</activity>
```

Adding Configuration to Widget Definition

Finally, we will need to add a line to our app widget "provider" XML file to tell the Android system that we have a configuration class for this widget. If we do not add this information to the app widget definition, Android will not display our **MyWidgetConfig** screen.

The "android:configure" attribute should be added to the <appwidget-provider> element in the widget definition file. The value should specify the full name of the configuration class including the package name.

```
android:configure="teencoder.androidprogramming.MyWidgetConfig"
```

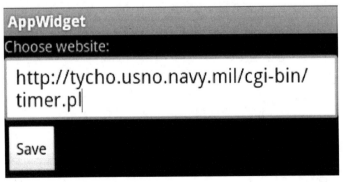

That's it! Now when you add your app widget to the home screen, you will see the **MyWidgetConfig** activity appear before the widget is installed. The user can select an alternate website to retrieve time information when the user clicks on the widget.

After successful configuration, when we click on one of the date/time fields the web browser will launch using the new URL.

**Time goes here!
Date goes here!**

Wait just a minute! What happened to our initial **onUpdate()** call to set the first time and date values? It looks like our app widget did not get a chance to initialize those values!

Unfortunately, when you are using a configuration activity for an app widget, the initial **onUpdate()** call is not received when the app widget is added to the home screen. It is the responsibility of the configuration activity itself to perform all initialization of the widget controls.

US Naval Observatory Master Clock Time

http://tycho.usno.navy....

Apr. 04, 14:29:10 UTC	Universal Time
Apr. 04, 10:29:10 AM EDT	Eastern Time
Apr. 04, 09:29:10 AM CDT	Central Time
Apr. 04, 08:29:10 AM MDT	Mountain Time
Apr. 04, 07:29:10 AM PDT	Pacific Time
Apr. 04, 06:29:10 AM AKDT	Alaska Time
Apr. 04, 04:29:10 AM HAST	Hawaii-Aleutian Time

US Naval Observatory

Completing the First Update with Configuration Activities

When the user clicks the "Save" button in our example configuration **Activity**, we are creating a **RemoteViews** object, updating some parts of the views, and then calling the **updateAppWidget()** method on the **AppWidgetManager** to save the results to the widget. This is a perfect opportunity to also update the text values in our controls or perform any other UI initialization of the widget.

You can cut-and-paste the UI initialization code from the **onUpdate()** method if it is short and simple enough, or you might consider creating a new class that holds the logic. Then you can use that same class from both the **onUpdate()** method in widget class and the initial configuration activity.

Activity #2: Weather App Widget Configuration

In this activity, we will expand our Weather Widget to include a configuration component. After all, the weather information is useless if you don't have a way to set the location!

Your activity requirements and instructions are found in the "Chapter13_Activity2.pdf" document located in your "TeenCoder/Android Programming/Activity Docs" folder. You can access this document through your Student Menu or by directly clicking on it from Windows Explorer (Windows) or Finder (Mac OS).

Complete this activity now and ensure your program meets the requirements before continuing!

Chapter Fourteen: Final Project

In this final chapter you will use your Android programming skills to create a brand new game! We are not teaching any new material, so we will introduce the game in the first lesson and then you will complete a series of hands-on activities to complete the final project. You are encouraged to be creative and make any adjustments you like as we go along.

Lesson One: Introducing "Maelstrom"

Our game is called "Maelstrom", which is another word for a large *whirlpool* that can suck down any objects that get too close. This whirlpool is located in the middle of an ocean where all sorts of sea creatures are in danger of getting pulled down! You can see from the screen shot to the right that there are five different creatures (shark, crab, turtle, whale, and fish) that follow a spiral pattern in the middle where the whirlpool awaits.

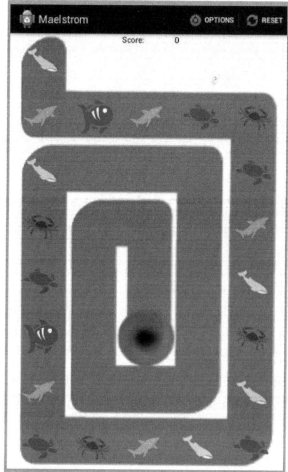

Game Play

The player's job is to keep creatures from getting to the center whirlpool spot. Once a creature enters the whirlpool the game is over! New creatures are coming in from the top-left corner of the screen. The player can remove creatures from the path by matching 3 or more of the same type next to each other along the spiral pattern. Each creature removed will add one to the player's score.

Matching can be accomplished by swapping any two creatures that are next to each other in the up/down/left/right positions, even across the spiral path boundaries. You cannot swap a creature into an empty space, however. When matched creatures are removed the rest will fall backwards along the path, moving further away from the whirlpool. Each time the player makes a swap move, however, a new creature will be added to the path. You can see the next incoming creature at the top-left corner (though that creature does not count for matching).

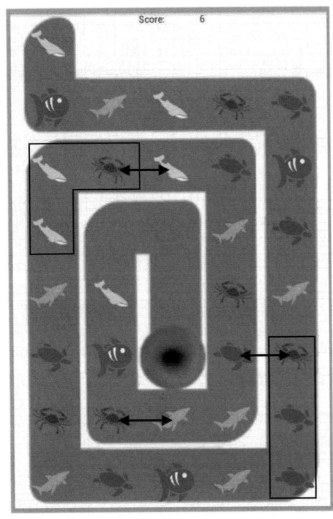

Let's examine some possible swap moves based on the example to the left. The player could swap a crab and whale as shown in the upper left and then three whales next to each other in the spiral pattern (outlined by the boxed area) would be removed. All creatures further along the spiral towards the whirlpool would fall back three spaces to fill the empty gaps.

The player could also swap a turtle and crab as shown on the lower right. This swap is across the spiral route boundaries but that's allowed! The resulting three turtles in a line along the route would be removed and all of the creatures further along the path would again fall back into the empty spaces.

A player can also make a swap move that does not result in a match. Sometimes there are no matches that can be made, but the player can look ahead and work towards making a match. The arrow in the bottom-left area shows a swap of a shark and crab without making a match.

Getting three creatures in a row or column that crosses the spiral does not count – matches can only be made along the spiral route and not across the bands! Should the player happen to make a swap that results in 4 or more of the same creature in a matched set, then all matched creatures will be removed.

Once you have completed the initial gameplay, we will add some options that allow the user to make the game easier or harder:

- The user will be allowed to select the number of different sea creatures (3, 4, or 5). The more types of creatures the harder it will be to make a match.
- The user will be allowed to enable a timer that will automatically add the next incoming creature after a few seconds if the player does not make a move.
- The user can adjust the number of seconds on the timer interval (between 2 and 10); a faster timer will make the game harder.

We'll also have an **ActionBar** menu that allows the user to access the settings screen or restart the game.

Activity One: Building the Activity Starter

We have provided an activity starter project that implements some of the game logic and other infrastructure for you. In this activity you will establish a functional "Maelstrom" project in your Eclipse workspace that builds and runs without any errors. We will also review each of the activity starter components and identify the pieces that you will be working on in the remaining steps.

Your activity requirements and instructions are found in the "Chapter14_Activity1.pdf" document located in your "TeenCoder/Android Programming/Activity Docs" folder. You can access this document through your Student Menu or by directly clicking on it from Windows Explorer (Windows) or Finder (Mac OS).

Complete this activity now and ensure your program meets the checkpoint requirements before continuing!

Activity Two: Starting the Game

In this activity you will complete some initial code in order to get the game started. When you are done, the initial sea creatures should be added to the spiral route when the program first runs.

Your activity requirements and instructions are found in the "Chapter14_Activity2.pdf" document located in your "TeenCoder\ Android Programming\Activity Docs" folder. You can access this document through your Student Menu or by directly clicking on it from Windows Explorer (Windows) or Finder (Mac OS).

Complete this activity now and ensure your program meets the checkpoint requirements before continuing!

Activity Three: Handling Player Clicks

In this activity you will begin working on the main game logic in the **onClick**() method. This method is responsible for letting the user select and de-select sea creatures and attempt to make swaps.

Your activity requirements and instructions are found in the "Chapter14_Activity3.pdf" document located in your "TeenCoder/Android Programming/Activity Docs" folder. You can access this document through your Student Menu or by directly clicking on it from Windows Explorer (Windows) or Finder (Mac OS).

Complete this activity now and ensure your program meets the checkpoint requirements before continuing!

Activity Four: Swapping Sea Creatures

In this activity you will finish the game logic to let the player swap sea creatures and remove matched sets from the game board. You'll also handle the "game over" condition and end up with a basic, playable game!

Your activity requirements and instructions are found in the "Chapter14_Activity4.pdf" document located in your "TeenCoder/Android Programming/Activity Docs" folder. You can access this document through your Student Menu or by directly clicking on it from Windows Explorer (Windows) or Finder (Mac OS).

Complete this activity now and ensure your program meets the checkpoint requirements before continuing!

Activity Five: Adding a Timer

In this activity you will make the game more challenging to play by adding a game timer. Each time the player makes a valid move, they will then have a few seconds to again make another move. If they do not, then the timer will automatically push a new sea creature onto the beginning of the path.

Your activity requirements and instructions are found in the "Chapter14_Activity5.pdf" document located in your "TeenCoder/Android Programming/Activity Docs" folder. You can access this document through your Student Menu or by directly clicking on it from Windows Explorer (Windows) or Finder (Mac OS).

Complete this activity now and ensure your program meets the checkpoint requirements before continuing!

Activity Six: The Action Bar

This activity will implement an **ActionBar** allowing the player to reset the game or launch a settings screen. On the settings screen the player will be able to adjust the number of different sea creatures, the timer interval, and enable or disable the timer entirely. That way a player can make the game challenging for their personal skill level.

Your activity requirements and instructions are found in the "Chapter14_Activity6.pdf" document located in your "TeenCoder/Android Programming/Activity Docs" folder. You can access this document through your Student Menu or by directly clicking on it from Windows Explorer (Windows) or Finder (Mac OS).

Complete this activity now and ensure your program meets final checkpoint requirements!

Activity Seven: Saving and Loading Preferences

In this last activity you will finish the game completely by handling the loading and saving of user preferences from the **Settings** screen. You will also load the current settings from the main **Game** in the **onStart**() method.

Your activity requirements and instructions are found in the "Chapter14_Activity7.pdf" document located in your "TeenCoder/Android Programming/Activity Docs" folder. You can access this document through your Student Menu or by directly clicking on it from Windows Explorer (Windows) or Finder (Mac OS).

Complete this activity now and ensure your program meets the final checkpoint requirements!

Wrap-up and Extra Credit

Great job! You have now finished your final project. If you want to continue adding new features to the game for extra credit, you might consider:

- Decrease the timer interval as the player reaches certain score levels. This way the difficulty will increase as the game-play lasts longer.
- Give the player a scoring bonus for matching more than 3 shapes at a time, or matching multiple sets of creatures on one move (requires **GameBoard** modification).
- Replace or improve the graphics (background and/or sea creatures) to make a completely different game theme such as space ships circling a black hole.

We hope you enjoyed learning about the Android programming environment and continue writing new Android programs on your own! Information about how to publish your Android programs to Google Play (the Android Market) can be found from your Student Menu.

What's Next?

Congratulations, you have finished the *TeenCoder™: Android Programming* course! If you are interested in writing useful Android programs for yourself or others, you now have a solid foundation for further study. Additional Android topics may be made available on our website.

You may also choose to pursue the C# programming language and learn how to write Windows-based games through our TeenCoder™ C# Series. The C# development environment gives you an easy drag-and-drop way to design Windows applications.

The KidCoder Visual Basic series covers graphical Windows and game programming in an easy-to-use language. The KidCoder Web Design series will teach you simple HTML, CSS, and JavaScript techniques so you can build your own websites.

We hope you have enjoyed this course produced by Homeschool Programming, Inc. We welcome student and teacher feedback on our website. You can also visit our website to request courses on other topics.

http://www.HomeschoolProgramming.com

Index